A Mind in Frame

A Mind in Frame

THE THEOLOGICAL THOUGHT
OF THOMAS TRAHERNE
(1637–1674)

by

Thomas Richard Sluberski

THE LINCOLN LIBRARY   The Lincoln Library Press
Cleveland, Ohio

Lincoln Library Press, Inc.
812 Huron Road E, Suite 401
Cleveland, OH 44115
(216) 781-9440
www.TheLincolnLibrary.com

ISBN-13: 978-0-912168-24-1
ISBN-10: 0-912168-24-2

The title of this book, *A Mind in Frame,* is taken from I *Century* 10; III *C* 3, 60; *Christian Ethicks* pp. 255-56 by Thomas Traherne.

Cover photo: Brasenose Library. Copyright © Tali Amitai-Tabib, used with permission, www.taliamitai.com

Printed in the United States of America
10 9 8 7 6 5 4 3 2 1

DEDICATION

Rather than even try to list all of the people, institutions, and events
to which I am indebted and grateful, *A MIND IN FRAME*
is dedicated to the ways genetics, nationality, family, friends,
education, opportunities and the pull of the future form our own
"frame of mind."

Table of Contents

Introductory Preface

This manuscript was completed some time ago and supposed to be submitted for publication shortly thereafter. It was never really forgotten, merely put aside for what I considered more pressing matters, but it has continually tugged at my subconscious like a child who wants the attention which is his due.

When I was doing the research, I had different interests, different goals, different attitudes. Back then I had wanted to write a systematic theology, later I also became interested in ethics, and I was always fascinated with the seventeenth century and particularly the Metaphysical poets. Fortuitously (or as Traherne might have put it, felicitously) I came across Thomas Traherne, a seventeenth century poet, theologian, and ethicist, who encompassed all of these interests of mine at the time, and this study of his work enabled me to immerse myself in the most important systematic theologies and works on ethics written up to and including the seventeenth century, as well as to read much of the poetry, literature, and literary criticism of the time, both European and American. It all seemed so perfect back then and seemed to lead to my doing further research in systematics, ethics, and literary criticism. As it was, I think I was able to indulge all these interests and to get them out of my system, preparing myself for so many more possibilities undreamed of back then.

Some of those directions were already apparent in the midst of getting my doctorate. Working for the Lutheran World Federation in Geneva, teaching at Valparaiso University and serving on the chapel staff in the volatile late 60s and early 70s beckoned me to a wider world than a professorship. The post at Concordia, Bronxville, introduced me to the world which was New York City. I got involved in film festivals and the art world, spent two summers at the Edward Albee Foundation in Montauk, and then, by surprise, fell in love with a parish in Hastings-on-Hudson. The college graciously allowed me to keep my full-time tenured post while shepherding a congregation for eleven eventful years. In 1987 I was appointed Executive Director of the American Lutheran Publicity Bureau while still maintaining my post as professor. And in 1992 the Lutheran

Church—Missouri Synod called me to be their first Russian Missions Consultant. What a glorious two and half years those were, teaching and preaching across eleven time zones from the Baltics to Vladivostok and lots of places in between, producing films there with one of the most important Russian film companies at the time and co-directing the world's first four-continent live television broadcast among so many other firsts.

All the while I had been taking student trips (and even ran a travel agency for a summer), but on what I thought would be my last trip in 2002 with forty-one students ("All the Best of Italy—Milan to Capri"), the travel company was so impressed, it offered me a free trip to anyplace in the world they had tours. I had been to almost all of them except, as I remember, Vietnam and Brazil. I chose Brazil and traveled there in June of 2002, an experience which radically altered again the direction of my life. I was forced to think back on what had made me happiest, where had I been most fulfilled, when had I done the most good—and the results were rather surprising: Russia first, the parish second, and teaching third; writing a systematics or an ethics or literary criticism were far down the list. Brazil not only matched but promised to exceed the revelation that Russia had been for me. To everyone's surprise (even my own), I resigned my tenured full professorship after thirty-one years at Concordia in January of 2004 and took a position with ULBRA (the Lutheran University of Brazil) in Canoas near Porto Alegre which has over 80,000 students on twenty campuses and a unique way of doing education.

But I have to bring closure to those other early expectations and aspirations. Publishing this is one way to show my thanks and gratitude to the people and institutions that enabled me to investigate widely and thoroughly systematics, ethics, and seventeenth century literature. I think Thomas Traherne might approve, not only of my exposition of his thought, but also with what I have done with my life. From one Tom to another he might well have said—a "felicitous" choice!

I am grateful for the opportunity to have done it then. And just as one would not alter a good baby picture or erase a luminescent early memory or forget a pleasurable experience, I have decided to leave this document very much as I left it in 1973 because, in general, it has not been superseded and can stand as it is.

However, in view of the plan of Boydell & Brewer Ltd. (Woodridge, UK, and Rochester, New York) to publish an eight-volume definitive edition of the works of Thomas Traherne beginning in the Spring of 2005 (too late to be included in this study), I am compelled to reevaluate this manuscript, revisit the research in the field, and add an appendix to the original bibliography. Most of the subsequent studies do not seem to contradict, but rather supplement and confirm some of my own findings.

And now I can move on. I have benefited from the experience, paid my dues, and expressed my gratitude.

Rio de Janeiro, Brazil
May 1, 2007

Preface

Thomas Traherne might possibly have called the writing of a dissertation an "Art" (one of the five intellectual virtues). As he describes it, "Art is that Habit, by which we are assisted in composing Tracts and Systems rather then in regulating our Lives, and more frequently appears in Fiddling and Dancing, then in noble Deeds: were it not useful in Teachers for the Instruction of others, we should scarce reckon it in the number of Vertues" (*CE*, p. 24). Even though scarcely intellectually virtuous according to Traherne, it is, nevertheless, hoped that this book will be of interest not only to theologians, historians, and literary critics, but also to all those who cherish the values for which the seventeenth century is justly famous: an age which successfully linked (perhaps for the last time) faith and life, revelation and reason, art and science. I have come to agree with Traherne who thought there never was "so much clear Knowledge in any Age: Learned Ministers, multitudes of Sermons, excellent Books, translated Bibles, studious Gentlemen, multitudes of Schollers, publick Liberty, Peace and Safety: all great and eminent Blessings" (*CE*, p. 283).

This study, which makes use of theological, historical, and literary-critical methodology, has characteristics both of the thoroughness of a dissertation and the proof of a thesis. It depicts Traherne's theology in its entirely and indicates that a knowledge of his theology is indispensable for understanding the man and his writings.

Upon its initial completion, this work was submitted as a dissertation at the University of Heidelberg in 1972 to three distinguished professors for official evaluation. Upon completing his review Prof. Dr. Martin Schmidt, Church Historian, known for his studies in English thought and as the author of the standard work on John Wesley, wrote:

The Metaphysical poets in general combine a high degree of reflection, theological knowledge, allegory, and poetic style. Theology has conventionally not been concerned with this kind of poetry, which is to be regretted in the interest of scientific illumination. The Faculty of Theology of the University of Heidelberg can therefore rejoice that a work of this rare kind has been submitted. This work delineates the cultural background, the methodological difficulties, the societal presuppositions, the other theological systems of the time, and Traherne's unique model or system. Especially interesting is the chapter on 'Natural' theology or philosophy which is seldom pursued in German theology; in fact there is no suitable German expression for it. The entire work shows clarity, care, objectivity, and methodological exactness: all evidences of first-rate work. I recommend a cum laude or magna cum laude as an appropriate evaluation.

Prof. Dr. Friedrich Heyer, Direktor of the Konfessions-kundlichen Seminar wrote:

Traherne was a philosopher, an ethicist, an historian, an author of devotional literature, a poet, and a minister. His system shows an underlying autobiographical theology arranged in three stages: childhood felicity, felicity lost, and felicity regained. This work emphasizes with good reason how for Traherne ancient ecclesiastical, dogmatic, and Calvinistic positions have paled. The valuation of the quality of the work would fit a magna cum laude as well as a cum laude.

Prof. Dr. Rudolf Sühnel, Faculty of English Literature, wrote:

As a literary historian, it was interesting for me to be also instructed so competently about the theological and ecclesiastical import of the writings of Thomas Traherne. The achievement of this study rests upon a wealth of ideas; he does excellent work. Besides, the work has the 'literary' merit of being especially readable, since the clear, fluid presentation of the text is separated from a very substantial documentation in the notes which contain the actual scientific ballast and which should be fully considered as a surprisingly well-informed report on research in the field.

I am especially grateful for their encouraging evaluation of this dissertation I had submitted to the University of Heidelberg in partial fulfillment of the requirements for a doctorate.

Writing this work enabled me to become familiar with international scholarship, and the benefits have been not only professional but personal. I am especially indebted to Professor Martin Schmidt for his friendship, example, and advice; to the Institute of International Education for arranging Austrian and Bavarian State Scholarships, the William and Tona Shepherd Travel Grant, and *Deutsche Akademischer Austauschdienst* fellowships; to the World Council of Churches; to the Lutheran World Federation; and to the Aid Association for Lutherans for their generous support for this research project. Among the many who have encouraged me in my studies through the years are Professors Erhardt Essig, Warren Rubel, Henry Reimann, Walter Oetting, Arthur Carl Piepkorn, Donald Deffner, Norman Habel, Richard Hazelton, Joseph Summers, Joseph Marotti, Wilfried Joest, Jörg Baur, Wilhelm Maurer, Adelbert Voretsch, Fairy von Lilienveld, Paul Hoffman, and Robert Schnabel. James M. Osborn of Yale University graciously permitted me to consult and quote from the manuscript of the Select Meditations in his personal possession.

To Study Things therfore under the Double Notion of Interest and Treasure, is to study all Things in the Best of all possible Maners. Becaus in Studying so we Enquire after GODs Glory and our own Happiness…to Study Object[s] for Ostentation, vain Knowledge or Curiosity is fruitless Impertinence. tho GOD Himself, and Angels be the Object. But to Study that which will Oblige us to love Him, and Feed us with Nobility and Goodness toward Men, that is Blessed (III *Century* 40).

New York, New York
March 2007

Textual Abbreviations

AN & Q	*American Notes and Queries*
ARG	*Archiv für Reformations Geschichte*
Bush	Douglas Bush, *English Literature in the Earlier Seventeenth Century* (Oxford, 1962) unless otherwise noted.
C	*Centuries*
CB	Commonplace Book
CE	*Christian Ethicks*
Clements	A. L. Clements, *The Mystical Poetry of Thomas Traherne* (Cambridge Mass., 1969) unless otherwise noted.
Curtis	Mark H. Curtis, *Oxford and Cambridge in Transition: 1558-1640* (Oxford, 1959).
CYB	Church's Year Book
DA	*Dissertation Abstracts*
ELH	*English Literary History*
ELN	*English Language Notes*
Eustache	Eustache de Saint-Paul
HEX	*Hexameron*
HLQ	*Huntington Library Quarterly*
JEGP	*Journal of English and Germanic Philology*
Library	*'A Library for Younger Schollers' Compiled by an English Scholar-Priest about 1655*, ed. Alma de Jordy and Harris Francis Fletcher. *Illinois Studies in Language and Literature*, vol. XLVIII (Urbana, 1961).
Marg	*Centuries, Poems and Thanksgivings*, ed. H. M. Margoliouth
MLN	*Modern Language Notes*
MLQ	*Modern Language Quarterly*
N & Q	*Notes and Queries*
Papers	*Papers of the Bibliographical Society of America*

PMLA	*The Publications of the Modern Language Association of America*
PQ	*Philological Quarterly*
RGG	*Religion in Geschichte und Gegenwart*
RES	*Review of English Studies*
RF	*Roman Forgeries*
Select	Select Meditations
SP	*Studies in Philology*
Stewart	Stanley Stewart, *The Expanded Voice* (San Marino, Calif., 1970).
Thanks	*Thanksgivings*
TLS	*Times Literary Supplement*
Wade	Gladys Wade, *Thomas Traherne* (Princeton, 1944) unless otherwise noted

Chapter I

Introduction

In the midst of the multifarious thought currents of seventeenth century England (Puritanism, Anglicanism, Arminianism, Quietism, Neoplatonism), Thomas Traherne formulated an original and provocative theology which he expressed in fine poetry and prose. His reputation as a poet and a writer is established, whereas his reputation as a theologian is not.

For someone who had been forgotten for more than two hundred years, Thomas Traherne, since his rediscovery at the beginning of the twentieth century,[1] has provoked surprisingly widespread and varied responses. It seems as though an attempt were being made to compensate for previous neglect. In spite of this renaissance, there remain a host of unresolved problems and unstudied issues, of various misinterpretations, misplaced emphases, and misreadings. This is particularly problematical with regard to his theological thought.

A. The Problem of Definition

Most of those who are familiar with Traherne's writings probably agree with Thomas Good's seventeenth century characterization of Thomas Traherne: "one of the most pious ingenious men that ever I was acquainted with."[2] Later critics express vastly differing interpretations of precisely how and why he is "pious" and "ingenious." In fact Traherne is labeled almost everything on the theological spectrum from orthodox[3] to heretical:[4] a practical Anglican,[5] an enthusiast,[6] an Agnostic,[7] an Anglo-Catholic,[8] a Puritan,[9] an Arminian;[10] a Pelagian,[11] a prophet,[12] a Pantheist;[13] a gentle

---

1. See ch. ii B below.
2. Reprinted in *Centuries, Poems, and Thanksgivings,* ed. H. M. Margoliouth (Oxford, 1958), I, xxviii, hereinafter abbreviated Marg I or II depending upon the volume. Traherne may also refer to Thomas Good, Master of Balliol and formerly Prebend of Hereford in the Select Medications. See ch. ii C below.
3. Elizabeth Jennings, "The Accessible Art," *Twentieth Century,* 167 (February, 1960), 140-151.
4. Robert Uphaus, "Perception as Process," *University of Windsor Review,* 3 (Spring, 1968), 19.
5. John Malcolm Wallace, Review of Louis L. Martz's *The Paradise Within, JEGP,*64 (1965), 748

fanatic,[14] a visionary, a theosopher,[15] a Gnostic,[16] a Rosicrucian,[17] a mystic,[18] a devout hedonist[19] and the "truest Christian that ever lived."[20] In the secular realm the categories are just as diverse and confusing, with critics disagreeing an almost every point.[21] Traherne characterizes himself as a "Philosophical Poet" in one place[22] and a "Philosopher, a Christian and a Divine" in another.[23]

B. The Problem of Limited Sources

Most critical comment is based on the poetry and the *Centuries,* almost to the exclusion of his other writings, perhaps because critics think these the

---

6. K. M. P. Burton, *Restoration Literature* (London, 1958), p. 150. Helen White refers to Traherne as a "Seeker" in her *Metaphysical Poets* (Oxford, 1936), p. 42. J. M. Wallace calls him an "Anglican enthusiast" in his "Review," p. 751.

7. Margaret Willy thinks he was an agnostic while at Oxford. *Life was their Cry* (London, 1950), p. 75.

8. M. Willy, p. 79.

9. Hoxie Neale Fairchild, *Religious Trends in English Poetry* (New York, 1939), p. 568.

10. Rosalie Colie, "Thomas Traherne and the Infinite," *HLQ,* 21 (November, 1957), 82.

11. Ernst Lehrs, *Der rosenkreuzerische Impuls im Leben und Werk von Joachim Jungius und Thomas Traherne* (Stuttgart, 1962), p. 37.

12. Stanley Stewart, *The Expanded Voice* (San Marino, California, 1970), p. 108.

13. See Hans Oskar Wilde's discussion of the problem in his *Beiträge zur Englishen Literaturgeschichte des 17. Jahrhunderts* (Breslau, 1932), p. 18.

14. Hugh Kenner, ed., *Seventeenth-Century Poetry* (New York, 1964).

15. *Centuries of Meditations,* Intr. by John Hayward (London, 1950), p. 568.

16. Malcolm Day, "Traherne and the Doctrine of Pre-existence," *SP,* 65 (1968), 88.

17. Lehrs, p. 37.

18. See ch ii D.

19. Stewart, p. 63. Willy states he "gave himself up wholly to an orgy of hedonism," p. 70. S. T. H. Parker calls Traherne "a devout hedonist" in "The Riches of Thomas Traherne," *The Living Age,* 314 (July 22, 1922), 223-225.

20. *Centuries of Medications,* ed. Bertram Dobell (London, 1908), xxxi. James Leishman calls him slightly heterodox in *The Metaphysical Poets* (Oxford, 1934), p. 192. Patrick Grant thinks Traherne is a liberal in "Original Sin and the Fall of Man in Thomas Traherne," *ELH* (March, 1971), 46.

21. See Jean-Jacques Denonain's discussion of Traherne as a "Metaphysical" poet in *Thèmes et Formes de la Poésie Métaphysique* (Paris, 1956), 67ff. Traherne is also called a "royalist," *CE,* p. 374n; a "romantic," Willis Barnstone, "Two Poets of Felicity," *Books Abroad,* 42 (1968), p. 16; a "reactionary," a "voluntarist," a "libertarian," by Stewart, pp. 14, 62, 124; a "solipsist," by Malcolm M. Ross, *Poetry and Dogma* (New Brunswick, 1954). See Robert Ellrodt's discussion of Traherne's egocentrism and subjectivism in *L'inspiration personelle et l'esprit du temps chez les poètes métaphysiques anglais* III, pt. 1, pp. 282-306.

22. *CE,* p. 181.

23. IV *C* 3.

most interesting and literary as well as the least religious and orthodox.[24] This concentration of research may be also partly the result of the unavailability of manuscripts. The poetry and the *Centuries* were the first writings of Traherne published in the twentieth century (1903, 1908, 1910). It was not until 1942 that two chapters of *Christian Ethicks* were reprinted.[25] The *Thanksgivings* were first reprinted in 1958,[26] *Christian Ethicks* in its entirety in 1962 and 1968,[27] and the *Hexameron* in 1966.[28] Five manuscripts have yet to be published,[29] and *Roman Forgeries* is available only in the original 1673 edition. Moreover, studies have often been made of a particular writing with little attempt to relate ideas expressed to other writings of Traherne.[30] See the Appendix, pp. 213–215.

C. The Problem of Limited Themes

Although religious aspects of the thought of Traherne have attracted the interest of commentators since his rediscovery, research has concentrated primarily on his mysticism[31] or his understanding of the nature of man.[32] Few bother to delve into other aspects of his theological thought. In fact, much Traherne interpretation tends to be content with one-sentence generalizations.[33] No one has yet attempted to investigate his theological thought on the basis of all of his writings.

Only Beachcroft[34] and Husain[35] indicate the interconnections of Traherne's thought, that there is a system of sorts. Beachcroft, however, refers to Traherne's philosophical system rather than to his theological system, and Husain does not indicate the scope of Traherne's "systematic exposition of his philosophy" (by which he means theology). Although they do not elaborate on particulars, these two scholars point the way.

---

24. See, for example, *CE*, p. 371n.
25. *Of Magnanimity and Charity* (two chapters of *Christian Ethicks*), ed. John Rothwell Slater (New York, 1942).
26. Marg, II, pp. 214-331.
27. *The Way to Blessedness:* Thomas Traherne's *Christian Ethicks* (London, 1962), modernized version with an intro. by Margaret Bottrall. Marks and Guffey's edition (1968) is standard.
28. *Meditations on the Six Days of the Creation,* Intro. by George Robert Guffey (Los Angeles, 1966). Augustan Reprint Society Publication 119.
29. Commonplace Book, Church's Year Book, Early Notebook, Ficino Notebook, and the Select Medications.
30. See, for example, the works of G. Willett, K. W. Salter, A. Russell. See, however, the Appendix to this volume.
31. See ch. ii D below.
32. See chs. v and vi below.

Unfortunately, these early observations were bypassed by later criticism which was concerned with other matters and which tended to see Traherne as an unorganized thinker of limited scope, who was unconcerned with traditional theology.[36] A reviewer of one edition of Traherne's writings is representative of the majority opinion: "We shall probably be disappointed if we expect from Traherne a consistent system of religious thought.[37]

D. The Problem of Description

Interest in Traherne focuses generally on problems of literary criticism,[38] biography,[39] influence,[40] and religion. The bibliography in the first three areas is fairly extensive, perhaps because Traherne's prose and poetry first

33. For example: "Traherne's religion may almost be reduced to the simple belief that by the recollection of his innocent childhood the Christian can recreate about himself the happy childhood of the world." P. E. More, "Thomas Traherne," *The Nation*, 88 (February 18, 1909), 161. "His concern is only with the positive, with acceptance, with vindicating and revealing life, not analyzing it." Haerald Massingham, "A Note on Thomas Traherne," *The New Statesman,* 4 (Dec. 19, 1914), 271. His "Cardinal doctrine" is the "unbounded delight in all created things." J. W. Proud, "Thomas Traherne: A Divine Philosopher," *Friends Quarterly Examiner,* 51 (January, 1917), 80. "The Love of Nature is the central theme of Traherne's life." Hilda Queenie Iredale, *Thomas Traherne* (Oxford, 1935), p. 1. "The cornerstone of Traherne's concept of life is his unfaltering belief in the immanence of God." Elbert N. S. Thompson, "The Philosophy of Thomas Traherne," *PQ,* 8 (April, 1929), 98. Ernst Christ sees only two experiences as decisive for Traherne's life and work: infancy and the Bible. *Studien zu Thomas Traherne* (Tübingen, 1932), p. 20. Rosalie Colie sees "Infinity as the key to Traherne's total devotion." *Paradoxia Epidemica* (Princeton, 1966), p. 146.
34. "Traherne is on his own scale and after his own way as much a theologian with a system as, say Origen." T. O. Beachcroft, "Traherne and the Cambridge Platonists," *The Dublin Review,* 186 (April, 1930), 278-279.
35. "Traherne alone of all the mystical poets of the seventeenth century has tried to give us a systematic exposition of his philosophy." Itrat Husain, *The Mystical Element in the Metaphysical Poets of the Seventeenth Century* (London, 1948), p. 264.
36. See Gladys Wade, *Traherne,* p. 140; *CE,* xlvii; and ch. iv below.
37. M. W. Lloyd, Review of Anne Ridler's edition of *Poems, Centuries and Three Thanksgivings. RES,* 18 (1967), 201.
38. Some of the bibliography is surveyed in ch. iii below. See also A. L. Clements, "Thomas Traherne: A Chronological Bibliography," *The Library Chronicle,* XXXV, n. 1, 2 (Winter-Spring, 1969), 36-51. For a good, general introduction to all of Traherne's writings as literature, see S. Stewart, *The Expanded Voice.* See Carol Marks' careful studies of the EN, CB, CYB, FN, and her intro. to the *CE.* On the poetry see A. L. Clements, *Mystical;* on the *Centuries* see L. Martz, *The Paradise Within* (New Haven, 1964); on the *Hex* George Guffey's intro. There is no full-scale study of the *Thanks.*
39. Biographical research is surveyed in ch. ii below, and see G. Wade, A. Russell, and Marg I.

caught the public's fancy. There is proportionately far less written comment on Traherne's religious thought. Only a few theologians, for example, have ventured into Traherne research, and the literary critics who have done so have had little or no theological training or interest. Thus there has been little extended discussion of Traherne's theological thought.[41] Hilda Vaughan, commenting on the *Centuries*, expresses what is apparently the general consensus of critical opinion regarding his writings: they are "no quarry for theologians" because they are a "work of art."[42]

Yet of the authors of the seventeenth century, an age noted for its religious preoccupation, Traherne is one of the most thoroughly religious.

---

40. Research on influences and affinity is surveyed in the notes and excursuses below. See especially chs. ii D and vii C.

41. Early commentary on Traherne's theological thought tended to be reductionist, appellative (see notes 2-24, 33 above), and disparaging. There are those who think Traherne is not a theologian at all. P. More writes that "He has almost nothing of theology, as it was practised in those days, or the church." *Nation*, p. 161. The Dobell manuscript is "wholly lacking in anything that is exclusively Christian." A Gilbert, "Thomas Traherne as Artist," *MLQ*, 8 (1947). Traherne's "dogmas are elusive" and "are often prescriptive." Ronald Hepburn, "Thomas Traherne: The Nature and Dignity of the Imagination," *Cambridge Journal*, 6 (1953), 733ff. Traherne is more a Christian than a theologian. R. Ellrodt, *L'Inspiration*, p. 291.

Three studies of Traherne in German (F. Löhrer, E. Christ, and H. Wilde) in the early 1930s were primarily concerned with his mysticism but more helpful theologically than most previous research. J. Denonain presented the first overview in French of Traherne's thought in 1956. Because of the scale of the work (which treats mystical, sociological, metaphysical, philosophical, and theological aspects of the Metaphysical poets) only a few paragraphs are devoted to Traherne as theologian, although a broad range of doctrines are mentioned. He thinks that it is too much to speak of a system of philosophy in Traherne. R. Ellrodt in 1960 was more comprehensive.

Due to seven landmark articles and books, Traherne criticism since G. Wade has become more detailed, comprehensive, and scholarly (reflected also somewhat in the quality of theological comment). (a) G. Wade's, *Traherne* (1944) surveys primarily biographical and literary critical issues. The last chapter, entitled "Thomas Traherne, the Divine Philosopher," describes his thought under the categories of "Christian, Platonist, and Mystic." (b) Perhaps the best study of Traherne's religious philosophy to date, although it is brief and based on only a few works, is that of I. Husain who stresses *The Mystical Element in the Metaphysical Poets* (also the book's title) in 1948. His premise is that "these poets cannot be criticized on purely literary grounds; one has to take into consideration their theological beliefs and the mystical tradition," p. 93. A Russell in her dissertation on *Christian Ethicks* examines Traherne's "position not so much has a poet, but as a religious writer" (Oxford, 1952). (c) Margoliouth's edition of the *Poems, Centuries, and Thanksgivings* in 1958 provides the basis for research based on reliable texts, as does (d) the critical edition of *Christian Ethicks* (1968). (e) In connection with the latter work reference should also be made to C. Marks' studies of Traherne's notebooks and CYB. (f) A. Clement's close study of the Dobell folio of the poetry indicates the wrong directions of previous research, as well as the depth and breadth of Traherne's thought (1969). (g) S. Stewart's work has superseded Wade's.

All of his known writings are on theological topics, and almost all seventeenth century references to him, primary and secondary, have to do with religious matters.[43] That can be said of few writers of his own or any other age. It would seem, then, that Traherne would wish to be read for his theological ideas, and not so much for his literary style, for the events of his life, or for what influenced him.

E. Procedure

This study attempts to describe, to analyze, and to define the theological thought of Thomas Traherne as it is expressed in his known writings. This entails at times contributory discussions of biography, influences, and literary critical problems. The primary thrust, however, of this study is to indicate that Traherne is a theologian whose thought is interrelated and to describe his theological thought on the basis of the outline he uses in the third *Century* (42-45).

---

42. *Centuries*. Intro. By Hilda Vaughan (London, 1960). Some early articles and books devote sections to particular aspects of Traherne's theology, although these sections are often subservient to other interests. See G. Willett on Traherne's doctrine of the church and Trinity; F. Towers on nature; E. Thompson on eternity and creation; Beachcroft on felicity, pantheism, and Pelagianism; and J. Leishman on original sin. Studies relating to individual doctrines are summarized under the appropriate sections of Traherne's theological thought.

43. See T. Beachcroft, "Traherne," *Criterion*, 9 (January, 1930), 392 and ch. ii B, C, D.

Chapter II

Background

Never so much clear Knowledge in any Age; Learned
Ministers, Multitudes of Sermons, excellent Books,
translated Bibles, studious Gentlemen, multitudes of
Schollers, publick Liberty, Peace and Safety: all great and
eminent Blessings (*CE*, p. 283).

A. Milieu: 1600-1689

In many ways the seventeenth century marked both the end of the Middle
Ages and Renaissance and the beginning of the Modern Age. Yet it was not
simply a transitional period, it was itself a century of great religious
movements,[1] meetings,[2] men,[3] and monuments.[4] In fact, although it has
been identified by such secular names as the Age of Reason,[5] the Age of
Baroque,[6] and the Classical Period,[7] religion was a dominant concern of

---

1. For extended discussions of seventeenth century milieu see: Maurice Ashley, *England in the Seventeenth Century* (Harmondsworth, 1961); Basil Willey, *The Seventeenth Century Background* (Garden City, N. Y., 1933); Douglas Bush, *English Literature in the Earlier Seventeenth Century* (Oxford, 1962); Gerald R. Cragg, *The Church and the Age of Reason* (Harmondsworth, 1966); Martin Schmidt, "*Christentum und Kirche in Grossbritannien,*" *Englandkunde* (Frankfurt, 1960); H. Daniel Rops, *The Church in the Seventeenth Century* (London, 1963), trans. J. B. Buckingham. Among seventeenth century religious movements in England are: Puritanism, Arminianism, Independency, Quakerism, Cambridge Platonism, Latitudinarianism, and Deism; in France: Jansenism, Quietism, and Gallicanism; in Germany: Federalism, orthodoxy, and Pietism.
2. Among the major meetings of the seventeenth century are: the Synod of Dort, the Savoy Conference, the Peace of Westphalia, the Westminster Assembly, and the Council of Jerusalem.
3. Donne, Herbert, Milton, Paul Gerhardt, Johann Crüger, Heinrich Schütz, Purcell, Bach, Mozart, William Byrd, and Isaac Watts are active in religious poetry and hymnology; and Arthur Dent, Augustine Baker, Lewis Bayly, George Fox, John Bunyan, Thomas Browne, St. Vincent de Paul, Pascal, Bossuet, Johanne Scheffler, and Molinos are writers of devotional and theological classics.
4. Van Dyck, Rubens, Rembrandt, Velasquez, Murillo, Nicholas Poussin at times painted religious pictures; and Versailles, Saint Sulpice, St. Peter's in Rome, and St. Paul's in London were built in part in the seventeenth century.
5. See Stuart Hampshire, *The Age of Reason* (New York, 1956).

the age. Religion, politics, and culture were still inextricably intertwined.[8] Statesmen and poets wrote theology, and theologians wrote poetry and were statesmen.[9]

On the dark side, wars continued to be fought over religious questions. The Irish War began the century. The Thirty Years War on the Continent and the Civil War in England dominated its first half. Religious persecution and witch hunts flourished almost everywhere.[10] It was as though Western Europe were unwittingly reacting against the decline in the importance of institutional religion by magnifying its jots and tittles.

Institutional religion experienced the challenge and questioning that many institutions and doctrines generally received in the seventeenth century. Scholasticism, monarchy, episcopacy, nothing seemed beyond criticism,[11] and even many who would not have questioned religion as such went on to express their religion in unconventional ways: in mysticism, in quietism, in pietism.[12] The age was indeed buffeted by "every wind of doctrine" (Ephesians 4:14).

It was surprising, then, that a counterpoint to this unrest and revolt was a corresponding desire for order and right reason, a shift from the external to the internal.[13] Many of the religious classics and much of the religious thought of the age may owe their genesis to an attempt at comprehending the upheavals shaking every sector of life.[14]

---

6. See Geoffrey Brereton, *A Short History of French Literature* (Harmondsworth, 1968), pp. 190ff.

7. See Daniel-Rops, *Seventeenth*, pp. 235ff.

8. A survey of book publishing statistics for the period is one indication of the importance of religion. Three-fourths of the books listed in William Jagerd's *Catalogue* (1619) were religious. See Bush for more statistics, pp. 310ff.

9. *Basilikeon Doron* by King James I (1599) and the influence on politics of Archbishop Laud during the reign of Charles I are two examples.

10. The last execution for witchcraft in England was probably in Exeter in 1685. There is one reference to witchcraft in Traherne (IV C 89). Prynne, Bastwick, and Burton were pilloried, mutilated, and imprisoned in 1637, the date of a famous witch trial and the probable date of Traherne's birth.

11. For a discussion of "The Rejection of Scholasticism" see Willey, *Background*, pp. 5ff. Puritanism, Sectarianism, and Independency questioned all three institutions on biblical and pragmatic grounds.

12. John Everard, John Saltmarsh, Gerrard Winstanley, George Fox were active in England, and Molinos, Guyon, Spener on the Continent. See Bush, pp. 346ff, and Schmidt, *Christentum*, pp. 24ff.

13. The philosophy of Hobbes, the Cambridge Platonists and Traherne may indicate these desires. See *CE*, p. 96; Bush, pp. 36ff; and E. Christ, pp. 39ff.

A number of important religious movements graced the beginning of the century. Traherne has often been characterized as a later Metaphysical poet who were active in the first third of the century, among them: John Donne (1572-1631), George Herbert (1593-1633), Henry Vaughan (1621/2-95), and Richard Crashaw (1612/13-49).[15]

Another movement which permeated the entire century has been loosely labeled latitudinarianism. Though often not as liberal as Lord Herbert of Cherbury (1582-1648), sometimes called the father of deism, the latitudinarians were, like him, not rigid on doctrinal matters.[16] In the 1630s a group consisting of Willliam Chillingworth, [17] John Hales,[18] John Earle,

---

14. As Traherne says, "It is an easie observation, that Troublous Times are the Seasons of Honour, and that a warlike-Field is the Seed-Plot of great and Heroical Actions" (*CE*, p. 188). See Rops-Daniel, pp. 235ff.

15. See the Introduction for some definitions of "Metaphysical" (note 21) and the studies of G. Willett, E. Christ, and R. Ellrodt who compare and contrast Traherne with other Metaphysical poets. Traherne copies four poems of Quarles into his EN (reprinted in Marg, II, pp. 204-205). There may also be a reference to Quarles' *Job Militant* in the *CE* (p. 181). Traherne uses a few passages from Donne's Pentecost sermon (CYB 51v-52), and Hand C copies a brief passage from Donne's 1930 Easter sermon (CYB 11v). Most of the changes made are stylistic. Traherne concludes the CYB with Herbert's poem "To all Angels and Saints" (CYB 112) making only four slight alterations. There are also reminiscences of Abraham Cowley (Marg II, p. 152; see 388n); Richard Crashaw (Marg II, pp. 110, 122; see 370n, 374n); and John Milton (*CE*, p. 298; see p. 359n). Some scholars find similarities to Henry Vaughan. See W. L. Jones "Religious Poetry," *QR*, 376-382; Malcolm Ross, *Poetry*. However, the writings of the Metaphysical poets are more helpful in providing a context for Traherne's poetry than as sources of ideas.

16. G. R. Cragg has a good historical overview of Latitudinarianism, *Age of Reason*, pp. 61, 70-72, 153, 157-160, 169. See also "Broad Church Party" in the *RGG*. Lord Herbert is the author of *De Veritate* (1624) and *De Religione* (1645) in which he expounds his views on natural religion. See Basil Willey, *Seventeenth*, pp. 125ff, and *RGG*, III, 232-233. Traherne may refer to Samuel Butler's *Hudibras* (1662) in his poem "Author to the Critical Peruser"; to Dr. Hammond, whom Traherne calls a "Great Divine" (*CE*, p. 213, but see note); and to Thomas Fuller's *Holy State* (Marg, II, p. 129 and see 378n). Traherne's references to *The Whole Duty of Man* are few, without acknowledgment, and altered (see *CE*, pp. 140-142, and 348-349). In the intro, to the *CE* Traherne states that his work has a different purpose from *The Whole Duty*. Traherne does not intend to treat virtues as though they are "Duties enjoyed by the Law of GOD" which "the Author of *The Whole Duty of Man* hath excellently done" (*CE*, p. 130). There is only one reference to "the learned" Richard Hooker (CYB 24v) which Traherne borrows from Sparkes.

17. Chillingworth (1602-44) is the author of *The Religion of Protestants a Safe Way to Salvation* (1637). Tillotson calls him "the glory of this Age and Nation." He is a philosophical theologian who defends "The Bible only" as "the Religion of Protestants," but the Puritans suspected him of heresy. See *RGG*, I, 1653.

18. Hales (1584-1656) attended the Synod of Dort (and bade "Calvin goodnight") and like the others of the Falkland circle was anti-Roman Catholic. See *RGG*, III, 33-34.

and perhaps Thomas Hobbes,[19] sometimes called early latitudinarians, met at the home of Lord Falkland (Lucius Cary).[20]

Arminianism, which has both doctrinal and institutional significance in England, can be traced back perhaps to Peter Baro's lectures in sixteenth century Cambridge. After the Synod of Dort, Arminianism gained strength but did not become widespread until the 1640s.[21] The Caroline Divines (often considered Arminian in their day) were the leading churchmen and theologians during the reign of Charles the First: men like Lancelot Andrewes (1555-1626), Jeremy Taylor (1613-1667), Nicholas Ferrar (1593-1637), and William Laud (1573-1645).[22] The Continent, too, was experiencing this flourishing of religious life and thought, and perhaps more than at any time before or since, England and the Continent were interrelated.[23]

The short life of Thomas Traherne spanned the tumultuous middle third of a lively century. He was probably born in 1637, the year considered to be the turning point in the reign of Charles the First.[24] He died in 1674,

---

19. John Earle (1600?-65) was tutor to Prince Charles and author of *Microcosmography,* a book of characters (one of which, on childhood, is similar to Traherne's picture of childhood). See Bush for a description of others of the Falkland Circle, pp. 342ff. Traherne labels the *Leviathan* of Hobbes "arrogant," "Debauched and unreasonable," "blind," and "impious" (*CE,* p 163). He implies that Hobbes is an "Atheistical fool" and deserves to be "burnt as an enemy" (*CE,* pp. 261ff). Yet Traherne agrees with Hobbes that self-love is natural and not totally wrong. One must, of course, rise above self-love to love of others and God (*CE,* pp. 260ff; see *CE,* pp. 28, 45; *Thanks,* II, 222 for other allusions to Hobbes). Traherne probably reacted negatively to Hobbes' cynicism, materialism, rationalism, empiricism, and determinism. However, it is doubtful whether Traherne read Hobbes carefully, if he read him at all. For discussions of Hobbes' thought, see: Willey, *Seventeenth,* pp. 99-124; E. Austin, *Ethics of the Cambridge Platonists,* pp. 8ff; and R. Brett, *English Mind,* pp. 30-54. Most theologians of the time took exception to self-love. "Self-love is an hindrance to this Charity," according to the *Whole Duty,* p. 367. "By such reflections and comparisons we may, I think, competently understand the nature of that bastard self-love, which is so vicious in itself, and productive of so many vices" according to Issac Barrow in his *Sermons.* See T. Gale, *Court,* I, ch. iv.

20. There were Oxford Men in contradistinction to the Cambridge Platonists. They met at Great Tew at the home of Lord Falkland, author of *Of the Infallibility of the Church of Rome.*

21. The Remonstrants rejected predestination, limited Atonement, irresistible grace, and perseverance. The English church was concerned primarily with the questions of election and predestination. Arminius (1560-1609) was a Professor at Leiden. See A. W. Harrison, *The Beginnings of Arminianism* (London, 1926); *RGG,* I, 619-622; Bettenson, pp. 375-377 for the Five Articles. Traherne stresses foreknowledge rather than predestination, Christ's death for all rather than limited atonement, free will, and the possibility of falling from grace rather than perseverance. See chs. vii-ix for a further discussion of these issues.

22. See below, ch. vii C, for Traherne's indebtedness to Andrewes and Taylor. Traherne uses Taylor's *Great Exemplar,* for example, in the CYB 75v.

considered to be the turning point in the reign of Charles the Second.[25] The Civil War, the Commonwealth, and the Restoration with all that these events meant to the spiritual, cultural, and political life of England intervened between these two dates. Traherne made only a few references to any of these events, but this in itself is also significant.[26]

In 1637, when Charles I and Archbishop Laud attempted to impose the *Book of Common Prayer* on Scotland, they set in motion the events which eventually led to the Civil War (1640-49). Traherne was about five when the war broke out, and Herefordshire, where he was probably reared, had Royalist sympathies.[27] Traherne alluded to the Civil War a few times, always negatively.[28] In 1641 the Long Parliament was convened and the *Grand Remonstrance* issued, in 1643 the Westminster Assembly met and issued the *Directory of Public Worship* in 1645 to replace the *Book of Common Prayer* and the Westminster Confession in 1646. Little Gidding was sacked in the same year.[29] Charles I, whom Traherne called "the Martyr" (I C 61),[30] was executed in 1649. Christmas Day celebrations and church marriages were forbidden in 1651, and the Commonwealth began

---

23. See note 3 above. Reference may be made to Johannes Scheffler, Quirinius Kuhlmann, Jan Lueken, Jakob Boehme, Johann Arndt, and Paul Gerhard who have certain affinities with Traherne. See Schmidt, *"England und der deutsche Pietismus," Evang. Theol.* 13 (1953), 205-224 for relations between England and Germany; and Rosalie Colie, *Light and Enlightenment* for relations between England and Holland.

24. In 1637 Charles I and Archbishop Laud attempted to impose the *Book of Common Prayer* on Scotland, which resulted in a riot in Edinburgh, in the *Solemn League and Covenant*, and eventually in the Civil War.

25. In 1674, Charles II prorogued Parliament, an act called the "dividing line" of his reign by M. Ashley, *England*, p. 135. Robert Herrick and John Milton also died in that year.

26. See sections B and C in this chapter for further examples of Traherne's omission of specific references to place, people, and time. C. Marks notes a passage in which Traherne specifically avoids a reference to a person. In his Early Notebook Traherne changes Bacon's comparison of King James and Solomon not, as might be expected, into a comparison of Charles I and Solomon but into a praise of Solomon and kings in general. "Early Studies," *Papers.*

27. In 1637 Laud wrote "For Herefordshire I find not much amiss." Hereford was easily taken in the first battle, but in the second it withstood six weeks of siege by the Scots. Traherne was about eight years old at the time. See Wade, pp. 19.

28. "...the Soldiers turn Counsellers and every Counsellor deposes the King, nothing but Confusion can follow in such a State" (*CE*, p. 96). "...deliver us from...Civil insurrections" (CYB 31v). See also *CE*, pp. 280-281; SM I 88.

29. Most of the texts of these acts are reprinted in Bettenson. Little Gidding, which was a Protestant religious community, was founded in 1625 by Nicholas Ferrar. It kept a rule of prayer until 1637. The Puritans disliked its similarity to monasticism. G. Wade thinks Mrs. Hopton's home served a similar function, but there is no tangible evidence for this assertion.

with Oliver Cromwell as Lord Protector in 1653. Traherne studied at Brasenose College, Oxford from 1652 to 1656 (B.A.), and in 1661 he received the Master of Arts degree, in 1669 the Bachelor of Divinity degree.

The winds of change blew not only in the religious but also in the political sphere. On the political left the Levelers reached their peak at Putney Church in 1647, and the Diggers emerged in 1649.[31] On the religious front, Anglicanism was disestablished and forbidden, and Presbyterianism was not yet completely in control. This left a vacuum soon filled by a wide variety of other options. There were Independents,[32] Behmists,[33] Rosicrucians,[34] as well as perfectionistic,[35] chiliastic,[36] individualistic,[37] and quietistic sects.[38] At the Restoration as much as one tenth of the population may have been sectarian.[39]

---

30. The execution day of Charles I was commemorated by the Church of England from 1667 to 1859. Traherne may allude to the reaction of Charles II to his father's death in *CE* (p. 218).

31. The Levelers, led by such men as William Walwyn, Richard Overton, and John Lilburne, had some connections with the Independents and their pamphlets on toleration. The Diggers have been seen as an early Communist movement. Gerrard Winstanley (1609-1660?) led the common farmers in their fight against the landlords.

32. "Dissenting bretheren" (Thomas Goodwin among them) petitioned the Westminster Assembly for the right to have independent congregations, an act which led to a pamphlet war.

33. The works of Jakob Boehme were translated into English many times between 1644 and 1692. Boehme was an apprentice to a shoemaker, Traherne's father's and George Fox's profession. Boehme died in 1624, the year Fox was born. Henry More thinks that Ranters and Quakers originated from the Behmist and Familiast movement. *Enthusiasmus Triumphatus* (1656), p. 49 (quoted in Braithwaite, p. 40).

34. E. Lehrs devotes his book to the thesis that Joachim Jungius and Traherne were influenced by Rosicrucianism.

35. The Adamites wished to return to man's Estate of Innocence. They worshipped in the nude. The Grundletonians thought Scripture was only for novices. Once God dwelt in the soul, they thought there could be no more lust and sin. The Family of Love thought that the resurrection was fulfilled in them. See William Braithwaite, *The Beginnings of Quakerism* (London, 1912), pp. 20ff.

36. The Fifth Monarchy men applied Dan. 1:44 to themselves and to their own time. The Muggletonians were another group of chiliasts. Traherne evidences little interest in this kind of eschatology. See ch. vii D below.

37. The Ranters (some of whom are thought to have been Pantheists and free lovers) and the Seekers believed in revelations and visions. Sometimes the Bible was disparaged, and the truth was thought to come from within. A few critics (H. White was perhaps the first) have seen Traherne in connection with this movement. There are tantalizing similarities in Traherne's writings to some of these various seventeenth century sectarian movements but no concrete connections.

38. The Quakers were the best example of this strain, although they encompassed some of the above ideas as well. See below.

Quakers were active in England in the 1650s and 60s, including the Hereford region. Although Traherne copied Bacon's arguments against Quakers and Enthusiasts into his Early Notebook (p. 103) and may have read and approved of Henry More's *Enthusiasmus Triumphatus* (1656), there are traces of Enthusiasm in his writings. These appear not only in his tendency to perfectionism, his positive evaluation of childhood, and his stress on internal experience, but also in his choice of words. For example, he uses words like "inner light" or "divine spark" associated with Fox and other Enthusiasts. In the third *Century* Traherne writes that we are "Born to be a Burning and Shining Light, and whatever men learn of others, they see in the Light of others Souls: I will in the Light of my Soul shew you the Univers." This light, Traherne goes on to say, is "Sweet" and a "Gift of GOD" and perhaps "Celestial." It may also prove to be a "Clear, and familiar Light" to his reader (III C 6).[40] In the "Circulation" Traherne writes, "No Fancy painteth foule or fair/But by the Ministry of Inward Light,/That in the Spirits Cherisheth its Sight" (154).

When George Fox was twenty-four, he wrote that "All things were new, and all the creation gave another smell unto me then before, beyond what words can utter. I knew nothing but pureness and innocence and righteousness, being renewed up into the image of God by Christ Jesus, so that I say I was come up to the state of Adam, which he was before he fell." Moreover, like Traherne, the creation was opened to Fox, so much so that Fox wondered whether he "should practice physic for the good of mankind, seeing the nature and virtues of the creature were so opened to me by the Lord." Furthermore, Fox states that those who were faithful to God "in the power and light of Christ, should come up into the state in which Adam was before he fell, in which the admirable works of the creation and the virtues thereof may be known...".[41]

---

39. Cominges, a 17th c. French Ambassador to England, estimated that there were some sixty sects in England, and Roger L'Estrange in 1681 estimated there were 170. See C. E. Whiting, *Studies in English Puritanism from the Restoration to the Revolution* (London, 1931), p. 233 and Bush, p. 9.

40. Traherne writes, "The first Light which shined in my Infancy in its Primitive and innocent Charity was totally eclypsed" (III C 7; see also "Fullnesse" 58). George Fox (1624-91) writes that when he was eleven, he knew "pureness and righteousness; for while I was a child I was taught how to walk to be kept pure. The Lord taught me." Compare Traherne's statements in this chapter and in ch. vii A. See Braithwaite, *Beginnings*, pp. 29, 38ff; and Rufus Jones, *Spiritual Reformers*, pp. 327ff.

41. *Ibid.*

Cromwell died in 1658, and Charles II returned to England in 1660 to the relief and joy of most of the populace. Traherne was twenty-one at the time and may refer to the coronation (April 23, 1661) in his poem "The Person" (74). It has been noted that Traherne had only a dim recollection of the "eleven years of tyranny" of Charles I but vividly experienced the eleven years of the Commonwealth. The few references in his writings to the times indicate royalist and Anglican sympathies.[42]

A flurry of activity followed the Restoration, particularly in the religious sphere. The Savoy Conference met in April of 1661. Twelve bishops and twelve Puritan divines attempted to reach an agreement on a modified *Book of Common Prayer,* but the conference was foredoomed to failure. [43] The Corporation Act of the same year rooted out Puritans and Independents from governing bodies. In 1662, the Act of Uniformity required the use of the *Book of Common Prayer,* and those who dissented had to give up their livings.[44] In December of that year, the King's First Declaration of Indulgence went against the feelings of the House of Commons and was withdrawn in 1663.[45] The Conventicle Acts (1664, 1670) penalized those who worshipped differently from the way the *Book of Common Prayer* prescribed.[46] The Five Mile Act (1664) prohibited nonconformist preachers from visiting their former parishes. The king's relationship to Roman Catholicism was also suspect and brought forth a spate of anti-Roman Catholic writings like Traherne's *Roman Forgeries*.[47] These religious upheavals were paralleled by the natural calamities of the Plague which swept through England again in 1665 and the Fire of London

42. "In these because they are maintained by the care of Kings, who themselves with their Magistrates have offer'd up their Scepters at the feet of Christ" (SM II 23; see also SM III 25; CYB 51r).
43. Among those present were Richard Baxter, Edward Reynolds, and Edward Calamy. The Anglicans saw no reason to make concessions, since they were in a position of power.
44. It is estimated that between one and two thousand ministers lost their livings (Ashley, p. 146).
45. The Declaration allowed public worship in chapels to Nonconformists and private worship in homes to Roman Catholics. Sir Orlando Bridgeman refused to grant the Privy Seal which led to his dismissal as Lord Keeper in 1672.
46. The Acts state that it is illegal for anyone over sixteen to attend an "assembly, conventicle, or meeting, under colour or pretence of any exercise of religion, in other manner than according to the liturgy and practice of the Church of England...."
47. See, for example, Thorndike's *The Reformation of the C. of E. better than that of the Council of Trent* (1670).

(1666) which necessitated Christopher Wren's plans for the rebuilding of the city.

The Restoration (1660) was the watershed of the century in England. The cultural, political, and religious character of seventeenth century England after the Restoration was quite different from that before the Civil War or during the Commonwealth, although many Englishmen thought that things had returned to the way they were with Charles I. After the Restoration, religion, both institutional and personal, became less important in English affairs. There was, for example, less religious art and architecture except for Wren's reconstruction of London, and what there was of a different quality. Baroque was giving way to Rococo on the Continent, and there was a definite process of secularization at work both in England and on the Continent.[48] There was also less religious verse written after 1660 (Milton, Traherne, and Henry Vaughan are major exceptions), and theological thought was far less rigid and orthodox. Toleration was more or less accepted as the century wore on, except for minor setbacks.[49]

The Cambridge Platonists were at their peak at the time of the Restoration; most of them did not publish until after 1660. They opposed both Calvinism and Laud, stressing freedom, reason, and ethics.[50] Most of them were connected in some way with Emmanuel College, Cambridge; the chief exception was Henry More (1614-87) of Christ College.[51] Benjamin Whichcote (1609-83) was a major influence, though he published very little. Nathanael Culverwel (1618-51) and John Smith (1616-52) were two of his pupils. Ralph Cudworth (1617-88) was a fellow and tutor at Emmanuel; later he became Professor of Hebrew and a Master of Christ's College. John Norris and Peter Sterry have also been included in this group. Traherne has been called an "Oxford Platonist" or the poet Laureate of the Cambridge Platonists because of his similar ideas.[52]

The term "Latitude-men" or "Latitudinarians," though used at various times in the century to identify various men and movements, including the Cambridge Platonists, more strictly applies to men such as Edward

48. Daniel-Rops points out that the chapel at Versailles, for example, is not so much to the glory of God as to the glory of the king (pp. 318ff).
49. See Bush, pp. 340ff.

Stillingfleet (1635-99), John Tillotson (1630-94), Gilbert Burnet and Simon Patrick. Some of these men were students of the Cambridge Platonists.[53]

There was also a wave of scientific inquiry which brought into question much which had been commonly accepted, including religious issues. Many of the scientists of the time (such as Newton, Bacon, Boyle

---

50. Traherne had various direct and indirect contacts with the Cambridge Platonists. His patron was an Oxonian whose home was a meeting place for progressive thinkers of the time. Traherne's predecessor, Hezekiah Burton, was a Latitudinarian divine. Traherne read More, and he could have read Smith and Culverwel. Most of the other Cambridge Platonists, however, did not publish until after Traherne's death. Although Traherne was an Anglican at Oxford, he read many of the same influential works as the Platonists at Puritan Emmanuel College in Cambridge. Traherne may refer, for example, to Plotinus in *CE*, pp. 45, 126; "Shadows in the Water" and "Nature." Q. Iredale lists a number of similarities in their points of view, some of which seem speculative. I. Husain thinks that Traherne borrows his concept of the Trinity and his minimization of evil from Plotinus. *Mystical,* pp. 293ff. Traherne's philosophy, however, is in many ways very different from that of Plotinus, who is said, for example, to have been so ashamed of having a body that he refused to sit for a portrait. Bullett, *English*, pp. 41ff. See Plotinus, *The Enneads,* revised ed., trans. S. Mackenna (London, 1957); *CE*, pp. 321n, 346n.

   C. Marks compares Traherne with the Cambridge Platonists and finds similarities in the stress on reason, free will, the new learning, the immanence of God, infinity, eternity, plenitude, activity, goodness, and appreciation. Traherne is more positive about the soul, free will, and infinity. He is also more concrete and more affirmative about the material world, physical creation, and the potential of man. While Traherne rejects dualism (like Whichcote), Sterry, Smith, and Culverwel seem to tend in that direction. Cudworth and More hold a position between Traherne and dualism. See C. Marks, "Cambridge Platonism," *PMLA,* 521-534. Anthony Tuckney, a Puritan critic, but also a friend of Whichcote, describes Cambridge Platonism in the 17th c.: "The power of nature in morals too much advanced. Reason hath too much given to it in the mysteries of faith…Mind and understanding is all; heart and will little spoken of. The decrees of God questioned….The philosophers and other heathens much fairer candidates for heaven than the Scriptures seem to allow of." See Wade, p. 226, but compare S. P., *A Brief Account of the New Sect of Latitude-Men Together with Some Reflections upon the New Philosophy* (London, 1662), a more favorable account.

51. Traherne copies three extended notes from Henry More's *Divine Dialogues* (1668). In one of them Traherne disagrees with More's definition of God as infinite space ("Deitie" 33-33v). They share excitement for the new theories of space (see *CE*, pp. 67ff; II C 24, 81; V C 3, 4). Moreover, H. More as a child had an "exceeding hail and entire sense of God which nature herself had planted deep in" him, and he was "enlightened with a sense of the noblest theories in the morning of his days." See Willey, *Seventeenth*, pp. 163ff; G. Sherer, "More and Traherne," *MLN,* 498-50; F. Colby, "Traherne and More," *MLN,* 490-492; and Aaron Lichtenstein, *Henry More* (Cambridge, Mass., 1962).

52. See the studies of Traherne and Cambridge Platonism by J. W. Proud (1917); E. Thompson (1929; T. Beachcroft (1930); G. Wade (1946); F. Colby (1947); R. Ellrodt (1966); G. Cragg and S. Stewart (1970). Good general studies include those of J. Tulloch (1874); M. Carré (1949); G. Cragg (1968); H. Baker (1952); E. Cassirer (1932); and B. Willey.

53. See note 16 above.

and Ray) were good churchmen and interested in theology. The Royal Society received its charter in 1662.[54]

Thomas Traherne died in 1674, the "dividing line" in the reign of Charles II. In that year the king prorogued Parliament.[55] The English Revolution (1688), the Toleration Act, and the Bill of Rights brought to an end the middle period of the seventeenth century and ushered in another era, but one not as lively, productive or religious as that in which Traherne lived.

B. Seventeenth Century Biography

A major part of Traherne research is a quest for biographical data, partly because so little is available.[56] The few seventeenth century references to Thomas Traherne record primarily religious details: his entrance into Brasenose to study for the ministry, his Puritan presentation to the living at Credenhill, his episcopal ordination, his parish records, his charity. In addition, two of the three contemporary references to his death reflect theologically on existence: "poor worm," "fiat voluntas Dei." Moreover, late seventeenth century biographical material focuses on Traherne as a clergyman or a seer of apparitions. [57]

The date and place of Traherne's birth and baptism are unknown.[58] According to the Brasenose College Register, Traherne entered at the age of fifteen on March 1, 1652/3, which would place the date of his birth between March 2, 1636/7 and March 1, 1637/8.[59] He received his Bachelor of Arts degree in 1656. Nothing else is known of the early life of Traherne until his presentation on December 30, 1657 to the living at Credenhill, four miles northeast of Hereford, where he was Rector (only nominally after 1669) until his death. His "Certificates" were from seven clergymen, some of

---

54. For a detailed discussion, see ch. viii.
55. Ashley, p. 135.
56. See, for example, the work of G. Wade, A. Gilbert, A. Russell, V. Huntington, A. Ridler, K. Salter.
57. Most of these references have been conveniently reprinted by Marg, I, xxiii-xxxii. Only those with direct theological significance or those not reprinted there are elaborated upon in this chapter.
58. Perhaps they were in the records of St. John's parish in Hereford which are missing for the years 1635 to 1638. See Hopkins, p. 694.
59. See Russell, p. 35.

whom were leading Puritans in Herefordshire.[60] On October 20, 1660 (the year of the Restoration and not quite three years after his Puritan equivalent of ordination) Traherne received episcopal ordination at the hands of Robert Skinner, Bishop of Oxford.[61]

The Credenhill Parish Registers indicate that Traherne occasionally visited the parish even after he moved to London in 1667 or 1669.[62] The Parish records also indicate that Credenhill was small. The most active year, 1667, lists two baptisms, three marriages, and three burials. A Parliamentary survey states that Credenhill had a parsonage and an income of fifty pounds a year.[63]

In addition to the brief references to Traherne in the *Brasenose College Register* and the *Brasenose Buttery Books*, the *Brasenose Book of Benefactors* lists a donation of Traherne to the college in 1664.[64] His will, dated September 27, 1674, indicates that he had very few possessions and was able to dispose of them verbally.[65] Not mentioned in his will, however, are five tenements on Widemarsh Street in Hereford which he gave to "the successive ministers and churchwardens of the parish of All Saints" for the poor of that parish.[66] The exact day of Traherne's death is uncertain, and there are only three known seventeenth century references to it. The parish register of St. Mary's in Teddington indicates that he was buried under the reading desk on October 10, 1674. On October 21, 1674 Sir Edward Harley of Brampton Bryan in Herefordshire in a "Retrospect on the Completion of his Fiftieth Year" reflecting on the deaths of his niece, sister, cousin and

---

60. His presentation is recorded in the *Commonwealth Book of Augmentation*. The clergymen were W. Voile, W. Lowe, S. Smith, G. Primrose, R. Breton, B. Baxter, and J. Cholmley. Lambeth MS 10, f. 117. Marg, I, xxiv.

61. Robert Skinner ordained a number of clergymen secretly during the Commonwealth which may indicate that Traherne was not old enough (23 years) to be ordained before the Restoration, that he did not desire episcopal ordination, or that he did not desire it in secret. See Bodleian MS Oxford Diocesan Papers, f. 106, and Marg, I, xxiv.

62. The entries for the years 1664, 1665, 1666 were signed by Traherne; those for 1667 and 1668 were written and signed by him; those for 1669, 1670, 1671, and 1673 were written and signed by churchwardens, but that of 1672 was signed by Traherne. Dobell, Wade and others think that Traherne became Bridgeman's chaplain in 1667, but see A. Russell, pp. 39ff.

63. Lambeth MS 10, f. 177 (January 8, 1654/5), reprinted by Russell.

64. Reprinted by Marg, I, xxiv.

65. Traherne willed two rings to the Bridgemans, a few pounds to the servants, his best hat, clothes and books to his brother, Philip, and the rest of his possessions to a Philip Landmann. Reprinted in Marg, I, xxvi.

66. Duncomb, *Hereford* (1804), i, p. 410; corrected in Marg, I, xxvii-xxviii.

"my worthy friend Mr. Thomas Trahern" was moved to comment "I, poor unprofitable worm, am still spared."[67] Thomas Good, Master of Balliol and sometime a prebend of Hereford Cathedral wrote to William Thomas, Dean of the Worcester Cathedral, "Tom Traherne is dead, one of the most pious ingenious men that ever I was acquainted with, it has pleased the divine providence to take him out of this uneasy troublesome world, to a better place, *fiat voluntas Dei.*"[68]

Some fifteen years later, the first real biography of Traherne appeared in Anthony à Wood's *Athenae Oxonienses.* First published in 1691/92, Wood's account forms the basis of most of what is known about the life of Traherne. Besides giving his father's occupation as shoemaker (in the second edition) and his home, Herefordshire, most of Wood's information is also more of theological interest than biographical. Wood wrote that after Traherne took his degree in Arts in March 1652, he "left the house for a time, entered into the sacred function." In 1661 Traherne was created Master of Arts and "About that time became rector of Credenhill...near Hereford." Most critics have thought that he went to Credenhill in 1656, but there is also a possibility that he carried on the "sacred function" elsewhere, perhaps even in Oxford, where he would have had opportunity to continue using the library.

Later, probably in 1669, he became chaplain to Sir Orlando Bridgeman, Lord Keeper of the Privy Seal. At the same time he served as minister in the Teddington parish, near Hampton Court. In 1669 he received the degree of Bachelor of Divinity. Wood ascribes only *Roman Forgeries* and *Christian Ethicks* to Traherne. Wood notes the place of death, Bridgeman's home, as well as the date and place of burial, October 10, 1674, under the reading desk of the Teddington church, and concludes that Traherne "always led a single and devout life, and was well read in primitive antiquity as the councils, fathers, etc."[69]

In 1696 John Aubrey, in a section of his *Miscellanies* entitled "Apparition of the Man's Own Self," asserts that Traherne in bed one

67. *Letters of Lady Brilliana Harley,* ed. T.T. Lewis, Camden Society (1850), p. 24. Reprinted in Marg, I, xxviii. Sir Edward Harley may provide a connecting link between Traherne and Henry Vaughan who visited Harley's home frequently. See White, pp. 321ff.

68. Undated Worcester Cathedral Library, MS D. 64, quoted in a letter to the *T.L.S.,* October 27, 1927. This letter is not complete in Marg, I.

69. See Marg, I, xxiii for the complete text.

moonlit night saw "the phantom of one of the apprentices" who was really asleep at the time. At another time Traherne saw "a basket sailing in the air, along by the valence of the bed." Apparently Aubrey had spoken to Traherne about these matters. These are evidences of what Aubrey calls "Hermetick Philosophy."[70] Dean Comber in the Introduction to his *Roman Forgeries in the Councils* (1689) refers to Traherne's previous work on the councils, though Comber does not mention Traherne by name.

The longest, but not necessarily the most trustworthy because it is schematicized, biographical reference to Traherne in the seventeenth century is that in an unsigned Preface to the *Thanksgivings*, published anonymously in 1699. "A LETTER Concerning this Book from the PUBLISHER to the BOOKSELLER" preceding the Preface states that "A worthy Gentleman of the Author's acquaintance" had written the Preface. The work was recommended to the Publisher "by a devout Person, who was a great Judge of Devotion, having given the World one already, which had been well received in three Impressions, and would in time furnish it with more."

According to the Preface, the *Thanksgivings* were written by a "very devout Christian" who had "long since removed to the Regions of Beatified Spirits," and who had joined them in worship "in which he was very vigorously employ'd" while on earth. The author of the Preface states that to identify the writer would serve no purpose, and he only gives his profession as a minister "of a very comprehensive Soul...very acute Parts," committed to his office, "transported with the Love of God to mankind." The author, according to the Preface, "dwelt continuously among these thoughts and spent much time writing. When he was with others he was rather insistent about discussing these matters which led some, perhaps, to think him troublesome." The Preface also asserts that he was not infected with "Enthusiasm," but was in "love with the beautiful Order and *Primitive* Devotions" of the Church of England. He almost "never failed" either in public or in private "to make use of her publick offices." He was, according to the Preface, cheerful, sprightly, not sour or formal, affable, pleasant, ready to do good, and charitable "almost beyond his ability."[71] After this

70. Reprinted in Marg, I, xxviii-xxix.
71. See Marg, I, xxx-xxxii for the complete text.

anonymous tribute, which does not mention Traherne by name, he sank into oblivion for more than two hundred years.

Traherne's name entered literary and theological discussion again when William T. Brook bought the manuscripts of the *Centuries* and the Dobell folio of poetry at a Farringdon Road bookbarrow in London in 1896. The complicated and rather romantic subsequent attribution of these works to Traherne by Bertram Dobell has been called one of the most exciting literary tales of the twentieth century.[72]

Scholars began almost at once to sift through parish records, college registers, and correspondence of the time for more information on this "new" metaphysical poet. Much subsequent research has been done in the area of biography but has often been merely elaboration and conjecture based on very few facts.

C. Post-Seventeenth Century Biographical Conjecture

While extant seventeenth century biographical data tends to stress the religious, later interest in Traherne tends to concentrate almost entirely on the secular: his birthdate, his family, his source of funds, his advancement, and even his romantic interests. Some of this secular biographical data is also relevant to a discussion of Traherne's theological thought.

Thomas Traherne's brother Philip, who is thought to have been two years older, was also a clergyman and an author. He served as his brother's amanuensis and edited many of the writings of Thomas Traherne. Ordained before May 23, 1664, he was made perpetual curate in Aldersgate on May 23,1664. He was a chaplain of the Levant Company in Smyrna

---

72. When William T. Brooke found the manuscripts at a Farringdon Road, London, bookbarrow, he thought they were by Henry Vaughan. Dr. Alexander Grosart agreed, purchased them, and prepared to issue a new edition of Vaughan with this new material; both died before he could accomplish this task. Brooke had mentioned his find to Bertram Dobell, a bookseller. Dobell bought Grosart's library and carefully studied the manuscripts. He decided they could not be by Vaughan and spoke to Brooke again, who remembered that he had once used a poem in the anthology he had edited from a book entitled, *A Serious and Pathetical Contemplation of the Mercies of God,* which was similar to some of this new poetry. From that source they noted the name of Sir Orlando Bridgeman and located the *Christian Ethicks* by Thomas Traherne. An excerpt of a poem in that work was identical to one in the poetry manuscript (coincidently the same passage which indicated the authorship of the Select Meditations in 1964). In 1910, while searching for something else in the British Museum, Dr. Bell discovered the Burney manuscript of the "Poems of Felicity." See Wade, pp. 5-10; Dobell, Intro. to the *Poems* (1903); and *Centuries* (1908); and Richard Altick, *The Scholar Adventurers* (New York, 1950).

(1670-74). Philip returned to England only after his brother's death with the *Codex Ephesus*. This may explain why some of Thomas Traherne's poems were in the Burney collection in the British Museum, since Burney also owned the *Codex Ephesus*. From 1675 to his death in 1723 Philip was engaged in pastoral duties.[73]

Nothing definite is known of Thomas Traherne's early education. He may have attended the Hereford Cathedral School which traditionally had close ties with Brasenose.[74] Neither of the brothers is mentioned in the school's records, which are, however, only partially complete for this period. Traherne entered Brasenose College as a commoner, and he may have paid his own fees, although the majority of students received financial aid.[75]

Anthony à Wood, a contemporary of Traherne at Oxford, in his *Life and Times* describes the religious life at the university as strict and severe. According to Wood there were frequent disputations, lectures, catechisings, and too much preaching and praying. The doctrines of Arminius and Socinus were considered scandalous; formal prayers or the Lord's Prayer prayed kneeling were unacceptable to the Puritans of the time. Wood was known to have disliked Presbyterians and Independents, which may have colored his description of the religious life at Oxford during the Commonwealth.[76]

Brasenose may have been the most Puritan of the colleges in Royalist and Anglican-sympathizing Oxford. Its principal, Dr. Daniel Greenwood, had a reputation for being a "severe and choleric" Puritan.[77] S. Stewart, however, thinks that Brasenose was "violently royalist," at least in 1648 when two thirds of the college opposed Parliament.[78] Since the principal was appointed by Cromwell, he was bound to be a Puritan. Traherne's

---

73.   See Marg, I, xxxiii-xxxvi for a fuller discussion of Philip Traherne. Philip authored *The Souls Communion with God her Saviour* which some have thought he adapted from a manuscript of his brother, Thomas. See Wade, pp. 112ff.

74.   See Wade, p. 38.

75.   A commoner, according to C. N. Wakeling, was not necessarily the lowest class of student. He was, at times, a gentleman's son with some financial means. The bateller was the lowest class. "History of the College: 1603-1660," *Brasenose College Quatercenterary Monographs*, vol. II, Part I, Sect. xi, p. 17.

76.   Anthony à Wood, *Life and Times*, ed. A. Clark, I (Oxford 1891), p. 300; reprinted in Russell, p. 10.

77.   See Wade, p. 49.

78.   See Stewart, p. 216n.

years at Oxford coincided approximately with the last eight years of the Protectorate, when the scholastic curriculum, while still in force, was increasingly under attack by Milton, Bacon, Descartes and Locke.[79]

Traherne was appointed and ordained twice as the rector of Credenhill: Puritan under the Commonwealth in 1657 and Anglican after the Restoration in 1660. There is no evidence that he actually took up residence there until 1661. According to Margoliouth, his studies were possibly financed in part from the revenues of Credenhill parish.[80] There is also no indication of what he did in the years between 1657 and 1661, except study for his Master of Arts. He may have stayed in residence at Oxford or become an assistant in a parish.[81]

Even these scanty details create a host of problems. For example, how was Traherne able to be ordained first a Puritan minister and then an Anglican priest in so short a time. Some have thought that he was not aware that any principles were at stake,[82] others that the Parliamentary ordinance for ordination (enacted in November of 1645) was seldom put into practice.[83]

Traherne's writings suggest that his sympathies were more Anglican than Puritan, and thus, perhaps, when the opportunity presented itself, he obtained episcopal ordination. It does not appear, however, that he laid inordinate stress on peculiarly Anglican doctrines which would have created a clear conflict of conscience. Though his writings indicate that he accepted an Anglican view of orders, for example, his primary concerns lay elsewhere.[84]

His apparent ordination opportunism is not the only problem. There is also the question of absenteeism and pluralism. Traherne was appointed to Credenhill in 1657 but apparently did not take up residence until 1661.

79. Stewart, p. 10. Joseph Glanville, John Locke, and Theophilus Gale were contemporaries of Traherne at Oxford. Traherne may refer to Gale in his Select Meditations: "O my T. G." or the reference may be to Thomas Good, Master of Balliol (SM II 38).

80. Marg, I, xxvi.

81. Wood states that he "left the house for a time, entered into the sacred function, and in 1661 he was actually created Master of Arts" (Marg, I, xxiii).

82. G. Wade, p. 50.

83. The applicant was asked to present to a presbytery "certificates of having taken the *Solemn League and Covenant,* of his studies and degrees; to be examined touching the grace of God in him and his call to the Ministry, his knowledge and power to defend the orthodox doctrine; to preach before the classes, and then before his intended flock three days…" Russell, pp. 38ff.

84. See ch. vii C for Traherne's understanding of ministry.

During some of those years no one seems to have been in residence, and for other years there is no indication of how or if the income and duties were divided. Edmund Quarrell, who was appointed to the living by the Hereford Parliamentary Committee, was replaced at the Restoration by William Carpenter. The latter had been appointed by the Crown, but he vacated in 1661. The Earl of Kent, a new patron, then appointed Traherne.[85] Traherne may thus have received the revenues from 1657 to 1661 in absentia and again from 1669 until his death in 1674 while he was chaplain to Sir Orlando Bridgeman and curate of the Teddington parish (a type of pluralism).

There has been much speculation on the silent years of Traherne's life, particularly those of his youth and ministry, periods for which there are almost no biographical data. Much is based on seemingly autobiographical details in his writings, especially in the *Centuries* and poetry. Statements are also often used from works of doubtful authorship, and the literary critical methodology seems equally doubtful.[86] In meditational writings, for example, the author's personality can not be read indiscriminately into what he has written, especially when the writings are meant for the use and benefit of a general audience.

Important on several levels was his friendship with Mrs. Susanna Hopton (nee Harvey) who lived in Kington about fifteen miles northwest of Credenhill. She was the aunt and godmother of Susan, the wife of Philip Traherne, Thomas's brother. It was probably Mrs. Hopton who first gave Traherne the notebook which he later returned or meant to return with the unfinished *Centuries* written on its pages. The 'hundred miles distant' mentioned in the first *Century* (80) may refer to the distance between

---

85. Marg, I, xxxv.

86. G. Wade lists his personal faults, for example, as: "a hot tongue, impatience with stupidity, resentfulness of contradiction, covetousness of money, a tendency to compromise in order to win popularity, vacillations of moods, waverings on his hard path of self-imposed discipline" (p. 71). She cites no precise sources for this list, but elsewhere she quotes at length from the *Life of Christ* and *Daily Devotions* which are, for the most part, not Traherne's writings. See Wade, pp. 129-137, 156-168, and cf. *Life of Christ*, p. 257. See ch. ii. Hayward writes: "During adolescence…he confesses to having been something of a libertine; and it is presumably to this period we should refer to ambiguous hints he drops of sexual and other adventures." Hayward also thinks Traherne a "somewhat worldly priest. He was on his own admission 'a sociable creature, a lover of good company,' and his enjoyment of the good things of life which, he assures us, were plentifully provided for him in London, he ingenuously described as 'Christian Epicurianism.'" Intro., *Centuries* (1950).

London and Kington. It may also have been Mrs. Hopton who recommended that the *Thanksgivings* be published in 1699 after Traherne's death.[87] Other manuscripts may well have remained in her library, complicating the question of the authorship of several works. She was related to the Bridgeman family by marriage, which may account for Traherne's appointment as chaplain.[88]

Most of what Traherne wrote appears to have been written or completed while he was chaplain to Sir Orlando Bridgeman. After Sir Orlando's death in 1674 and shortly before his own, Traherne referred to his patron in *Christian Ethicks* as one who thought of himself as a "Steward of his Estate," one who prayed for forgiveness for the misuse of his funds, and one who lived a charitable life, though one perhaps unnoticed by the world (*CE*, p. 239).

Important for understanding the theological thought of Traherne is Bridgeman's anti-Romanism and his theological contacts. Sir Orlando, as an ardent anti-Roman Catholic, disliked the increasingly evident Roman Catholic tendencies of the Royal Court. He declined, therefore, to give the Seal for the Declaration of Indulgence or to approve grants for the mistresses of the king.[89] He was dismissed as Lord Keeper in 1672, and

---

87. See part B above.

88. The following details are a summary of G. Wade's research. Born in 1627, "never bred in Scholastick education," converted to Romas Catholicism during the Protectorate, Mrs. Hopton became an ardent Anglican at the Restoration. Wealthy and owner of several homes, her husband was a chief justice. Wade thinks Mrs. Hopton was the center of a "family" or religious society such as the one at Little Gidding. However, the sources may refer to a normal family circle. Spinckes refers to her "constant Course of Devotion," five times a day for worship. Not only did she keep the feasts and fasts, but she was "much scandalized at the generality of those who profess themselves members of the Church of England for showing no more regard to such Days..." She was said to have given liberally of her time and money to the church. She seems to relish Roman Catholic/Anglican religious controversy, her knowledge of which was thought to have been "not much inferior to the best divines." Her own authorship (or adaptation) of several popular devotional authologies (for example *Devotions in the Ancient Way of Offices*), and her close friendship with Traherne have complicated the question of the authorship of several books. She died at the age of eighty-two. Wade, pp. 79-88. The relationship between Traherne and Mrs. Hopton may be likened to that of Henry More with Lady Conway or that of Francis de Sales with Madame de Chantal in the 17th c.

89. For a fuller description of Bridgeman see *CE*, xxvi-xxxi. Traherne may refer to Bridgeman in the CYB (56): "thou that bearest the Privy Seal of God." Traherne also copies a section from Bacon into his Early Notebook: "Learned men may sometimes apply themselves to men of power or get riches as also to submit to the necessity of the times" (93). See also Russell, p. 42.

Roman Forgeries may have gained some of its inspiration from the cause of Traherne's patron. It was printed in 1673 and dedicated to Sir Orlando.

Traherne's predecessor as Bridgeman's chaplain, Hezekiah Burton, had been, like Bridgeman, a Cambridge man. Burton was a Latitudinarian divine in contact with many of the leading theologians of the day and in correspondence with Henry More. Bridgeman's home was known as a meeting place for the open discussion of theological issues,[90] and Bridgeman and his chaplain, Hezekiah Burton, played major roles in the discussion of ways to right the wrongs of the Ejection of 1662. They met in 1668 with the leaders of both sides: Latitudinarian divines such as John Wilkins, John Tillotson, and Edward Stillingfleet and Nonconformists such as William Bates, Thomas Manton and Richard Baxter. Although the meeting ended in bitterness and failure, at least one seventeenth century commentator thought that although Bridgeman was "always on the side of the church...he had great tenderness for the nonconformists...."[91]

D. Traherne's Theological Autobiography

Traherne's autobiographical statements confirm the thoroughly theological cast of what secondary sources reveal of his life and thought. The term "autobiography," as S. Stewart points out, has inherent pitfalls. In general, most autobiographical writing aims at delineating "the exact qualities of a particular individual." Seventeenth century autobiography in particular tended to be "univocal," like a diary, and "closely concerned with the details of a single life."[92] Traherne, however, refers to few precise places, people, events, dates. It is, furthermore, a questionable practice to equate even these statements with fact (the poetic fallacy). For example, in the third *Century* which describes "his Enterance and Progress in Felicity" (IV C 1) there is no logical chronological sequence. Instead, apparently, Traherne allegorizes, mythologizes, symbolizes, poeticizes, and theologizes the events of his own life and by extention the life of man (see III C 14).[93] What is more, Traherne not only writes these reflections for others, but he also intends at least the *Centuries* to be completed by another person. He

---

90. See Russell, p. 41, and *CE*, xxvi-xxxi.
91. Burnet, *History*, I, p. 454, quoted in *CE*, xxix. See also parts A and B above for additional background material.
92. Stewart, pp. 105, 132.

draws upon the experiences of others, particularly the Psalmist David, to confirm and parallel his own experience. He seems to attempt to transcend the limits of his own life creating something like a personalized history of salvation.[94]

Further complicating the autobiographical issue is, as S. Stewart notes, Traherne's inclusion of Adam, David, and perhaps his own pre-existence in the purview of his autobiography. He attempts to see his own experience as a pattern, example, and guide for another and others. Traherne conceives of himself as a mentor (I C 1; *CE*, p. 3) and a prophet (I C 3). These roles may in part account for his use of the third person singular in the fourth *Century* which tends to objectify, generalize and almost fictionalize the contents of the third *Century*. This undergirds Traherne's stress on his "principles" and not his "practices" (IV C 30), the processes and not the product.[95] For these reasons, in this study Traherne's autobiography has been separated from his biography and qualified with the adjective: theological.

There is yet another way critics have tried to get at the "real" Traherne besides through primary and secondary sources or through autobiographical statements, and that is through a form of psychological literary criticism: conjecturing on the basis of what he wrote and how, as to what kind of person he was.[96] There are apparently introspective passages, but it is not always possible to distinguish the autobiographical from the meditational voice. In the *Thanksgivings*, for example, he praises God for making "thy Servant a sociable Creature…a lover of company," and he asks that this "inclination" be replenished (p. 326). The passage cannot refer to

93. In contrast to G. Wade, who often equates everything Traherne wrote as factual autobiography, see Stewart and Clements. Stewart thinks that only the preface to the *Roman Forgeries* can be seen as "strict narrative" (pp. 110, 113). M. Dawson says, "No man's writings ever furnished a clearer or more faithful mirror of their author's personality than do those of Thomas Traherne. But of the outward incidents of his life he is singularly reticent" (1927).

94. A. Russell notes that the "autobiographical passages in the *Centuries*…are concerned only with Traherne's spiritual awakening and growth" (pp. 36ff).

95. L. Martz thinks that Traherne tried to "project an ideal image of his best possible self" or a picture of "unfallen Adam" (*Paradise,* pp. 95-98).

96. On the basis of such criticism, G. Wade is led to assert that Traherne "became one of the most radiantly and most infectiously happy mortals the earth has ever known" (p. 3). S. Stewart is much more cautious, but he too finds unpredictability (p. 17), flexibility, openness (p. 210), stridency, skepticism (p. 56), humility (p. 105), freedom and spontaneity (p. 97) in Traherne's character on the basis of a study of Traherne's style and content.

David, and perhaps not to the reader, but since the passage is meant as a meditational exercise it is not possible to say for certain that Traherne thought of himself as a "sociable man." In the Select Meditations he may list introspection, "Reservation and silence" among his desires and "Too much openness and proneness to speak," "Too easy and complying a Nature," and a tendency to speak in the first person singular as his diseases (SM III 65). Elsewhere he may lament his "Levity" and may ask to be "Weighty" in all his deeds (SM III 96).

More likely to be autobiographical, however, are passages with a particular referent or those which refer to something attested to in another source: i.e. his ejaculation "O my T. G. O My S. H. O my brother" (SM II 38); his parenthetical statement "as I have often experienced" in relation to others entrusting their wives and children into his hands (*CE*, p. 200); his description of the "Little Church Environed with Trees;" his calling "to teach immortal Souls the way to Heaven, to sanctify his Sabbaths, to instruct them in the love of a glorious Saviour," and his own education "at universities in Beautiful Streets and famous Colleges" (SM III 83, II 15).

The third *Century* which Traherne says describes "his enterance and progress in Felicity" (IV *C* 1; see III *C* 6) is a condensed yet thorough interpretation of his own life. The essentials and major movements of a theological autobiography or autobiographical theology are sketched in the first three meditations of the third *Century*: 1) *childhood felicity*, 2) *felicity lost*, and 3) *felicity regained*. This progression parallels his use of estates in his outline of theology.

Felicity is a recurrent theme and keynote of Traherne's theological autobiography and his theology, and it is intimately related to his theme of infancy or childhood. It was in his infancy that he possessed felicity, and to regain felicity he must "becom. . .a little Child again" (III *C* 3). Thus to describe felicity he is led to describe his childhood. This ability to remember childhood felicity he calls a gift of God, a favor (III *C* 1).

1. Childhood Felicity

When Traherne is referred to, it is taken for granted that his speaking voice is meant, indicating that all statements are not to be taken as literal fact but as interpretation and are not to be automatically ascribed to the historical person Traherne. The essence of *childhood felicity*, according to Traherne, is the possession of "Pure and Virgin Apprehensions" (III *C* 1). Traherne uses a multitude of adjectives to describe how things appeared to him as an infant: new, strange, rare, beautiful, delightful, eternal, and infinite (In C 2, 3). Traherne thinks that as a child he saw things as they actually were, not as they were commonly apprehended (III C 62*).*

His knowledge, too, was divine, and he knew by intuition things which he later had to collect "again, by the Highest Reason." These things were "unattainable by Book." Thus the reader of the *Centuries* must learn them by "Experience" (III C 1, 2). He likens his childhood to the "Estate of Innocence" and compares himself with Adam in Eden.[97] As a child everything for him was spotless and pure, glorious and precious, free and immortal, and all was *his.* His strong sense of personal possession is perhaps an outgrowth of his vivid awareness of being the heir of the world. The parallels to paradise are heightened by his list of what he did not know as a child: sin, laws, poverty, contention, vice, tears, sickness, property, boundaries, death. In addition, he thought he was "ten thousand times more prone to Good. . .then evil" (III C 8).[98]

In the third *Century* Traherne implies that not all children are as favored as he was, but some of the poetry seems to generalize and include others under the umbrella of childhood felicity. It is "our" childhood ("Approach" 36) and "Thy blessed Infancy ("Instruction" 24), but he asks rhetorically in the "Inference" (140) "How many Thousands see the Sky/ The Sun and Moon as well as I?" Complicating the issue is his admission that there may be some exaggeration involved in his depiction of infant felicity. "Oh! the Vigor of mine Infant Sence/Drives me too far: I had not yet the Eye/The Apprehension, or Intelligence" ("Improvement" 30). In addition, there is a negative side to childhood. He quotes St. Paul favorably "with little Understanding we are but children" (IV C 6).[99]

How to account for Traherne's conception of childhood has been a constant feature of Traherne research.[100] Plato and Aristotle do not exalt childhood, but there is a good case to be made for some of the biblical

---

97. Traherne's identification of himself as a child and as Adam is more explicit in his poetry: "I was an Adam there" in paradise ("Innocence" 18). He beheld only what Adam did in his first estate ("Eden" 14). See "Silence" 46, and ch. vii A.

98. Traherne's other writings add a few emphases to these affirmations of the essence of childhood felicity. See ch. vii A.

99. In "Blisse" Traherne points out that there are those who take notice of baubles "With Greedier Eys, more Boys tho Men" (171). "Shadows in the Water" opens with the assertion that "In unexperienced Infancy/Many a sweet Mistake doth ly:/Mistake tho false, intending tru/" (F 127). See "Walking" F 135-136.

100. See especially E. Christ, G. Wade, J. Leishman, and G. Boas.

literature providing the basis for later positive evaluations of the child (see Psalm 8:2; Luke 2:42-49; 9:47).[101] Perhaps one of the main sources for Traherne's positive evaluation of childhood is Hermes Trismegistus who states that the child's soul "sees it self beautiful, as not having been yet spotted with Passions of the Body." However, Hermes thinks it is the body which "distracteth the Soul" whereas for Traherne it is customs and sin.[102]

The Church Fathers evidence a tension with regard to childhood, similar to that in Traherne. Boethius (commonly considered a Church Father) thinks that his condition is "due to the loss of the memory of his true nature," but his memory is clouded and, though his soul is naturally attracted to the good, it is often deflected.[103] Augustine writes that as a child he had being, life, senses, and care of his own well being, all due to God's impression of unity on his inward senses. As a child he was delighted even in little things and the truth, avoiding sadness, dejection, and ignorance. All of these were, of course, gifts of God.[104] Yet elsewhere Augustine writes that everyone knows the ignorance and vain desires with which men enter the world.[105]

Traherne does not follow the common seventeenth century French practice of referring to the childhood of Jesus nor does Traherne use it as a basis for his own infant state.[106] The seventeenth century was heir not only to the classical, biblical, hermetic and Catholic traditions, but also to the Calvinist point of view. Pascal views the child as close to an animal.[107] Lewis Bayly calls an infant a "brute having the shape of a man."[108] However, there are positive evaluations of childhood in the seventeenth century. Henry Vaughan is often compared to Traherne in this respect.[109] George Herbert could say that "Childhood is health," but he is stressing baptismal grace which Traherne evidently does not.[110] Henry More writes

101. Diodati lists 147 interpretations of Matthew 11:25 in his *Pious and Learned Annotations upon the Holy Bible*, trans. N. Fussell, 2nd ed. (London, 1948). See G. Boas for a fuller discussion.

102. See C. Marks, "Traherne and Hermes," *Renaissance News*, 124ff. Fisch thinks Rabbinic Judaism insists on the innocence of children (p. 180).

103. Boethius, *The Consolation of Philosophy*, trans. by V. E. Watts, pp. 22ff.

104. Augustine, *Confessions*, Loeb Library I: 20-22.

105. Augustine, *City of God*, Loeb Library XXII: 22.

106. See Daniel-Rops, p. 244.

107. G. Boas, p. 29.

108. L. Bayly, *The Practice of Piety*, p. 46.

109. See "Henry Vaughan and the Theme of Infancy," *Seventeenth Century Studies* presented to Sir Herbert Grierson (Oxford, 1938), pp. 243-245.

110. See E. Christ, p. 30.

that even as a child he had "an inward sense of the divine presence."[111] Thomas Jackson parallels the properties of infants and of Christians.[112] In a more secular vein, John Evelyn in his diary (1658) writes of his five year old son who is, he thinks, "a prodigy for witt and understanding." Evelyn stresses the linguistic abilities of his son, an emphasis which is quite foreign to Traherne.[113]

Perhaps the best known description of childhood in the seventeenth century is that of John Earle who includes a sketch of a child in his *Microcosmographie* (1628). The child, according to Earle, "is the best copy of Adam" and "nature's fresh picture." The child's soul is like "white paper." He is happy and does not know evil. The child can be an example to the Christian. However, as he grows older, he moves farther from God. Time and activity deface his happiness.[114]

Because of his views on childhood, Traherne has been accused of the Romantic heresy and Pelagianism, which hold that the child is basically good until he is corrupted by civilization. There is some basis for this point of view in Traherne's writings, but he defies simplistic categorization. Traherne was not a post-Pelagian, pre-Rousseauean, or pre-Romantic.[115] It may be less severe and bizarre to see in his depiction of childhood strands of real experience, but experience magnified, idealized, interpreted by hindsight. It is, after all, the adult Traherne who is reflecting back on his childhood. This approach would stress his poetic nature.

In addition to a poetic interpretation of Traherne's understanding of childhood, seeing the child as a symbol might be more compatible with his other writings and with his theological thought. Traherne refers to Matthew 18: 3: "Except ye be converted, and become as little children, ye shall not enter into the kingdom of heaven" (III *C* 5). Traherne, like Jesus, may be attempting to convey a truth by using the image of a child. Not everything Traherne says about his own childhood is meant to be taken merely as literal fact but also as poetry and theology.

---

111. Wade, p. 231.
112. Thomas Jackson, *Works*, ch. xxix, pp. 579ff.
113. Notation on January 27, 1658, quoted in Leishman, *Metaphysical,* pp. 168ff.
114. John Earle, *Microcosmographie* (London, 1638), 6th ed.
115. See chs. vi-x. G. Boas lists direct intuition, anti-authoritarianism, anti-intellectualism as traits of the mystic which can be compared to childhood (pp. 23ff).

2. Felicity Lost

Traherne *lost* his childhood *felicity*, however. The child was corrupted and lost his infinite felicity (III *C* 3). Thereafter the world became a comfortless wilderness for Traherne, and he said he lived like the Prodigal son (III *C* 14). The loss was not the sudden one which Adam experienced in Paradise, but it resulted gradually from various causes. Traherne thinks his fall was due to the customs and manners of men, to vulgar and worthless objects, to a torrent of wrong desires, and to the evil influence of a bad education (III *C* 7; see III *C* 13). The corruption, according to Traherne, came more from "outward rather then from any inward corruption or Depravation of nature." It is not so much "our Parents Loyns. . .as our Parents lives, that Enthrals and Blinds us." Yet all of man's corruption has derived from Adam since all evil examples and evil inclinations arise from his sin (III *C* 8).[116]

As he grew up, Traherne says he investigated various possible sources of help to regain his infant felicity, but he found them all wanting. "Schools were a burden," and he did not understand "what churches were for." No teacher taught felicity and nothing was studied for enjoyment but only as *aliena*. Men studied for knowledge but did not know the end for which they sought this knowledge. Thus they "Erred in the Maner" (III *C* 37). To study for interest and treasure is to study "in the Best of all Possible Maners." One is not to study for ostentation, vain knowledge, or curiosity but for the glory of God (III *C* 39, 40). Traherne thinks that his education was not altogether useless for he received the seeds of knowledge which he later improved (III *C* 37). His own suggestion for educating children is to "talk of God" to them and "remove silly Objects from before them" because truth is easily taught (III *C* 11).[117] In "Solitude" (an F poem) he indicates that public worship in itself gives him no relief unless the people participating move his soul with divine love (100).

What was apparently a personal experience of these years of lost felicity indicates the feelings he had. He was once alone in a field and felt the horror, silence, and "wideness" of his condition as a weak and little child. Yet his "Hope and Expectation comforted" him and taught him that he was a part of the world (III *C* 23).

---

116. See "Apostacy" F 95, "Speed" 40, "Silence" 46, "Dreams" F 138, for other metaphors describing the extent of the loss, as well as ch. vii B.

117. See ch. iv for a fuller discussion of Traherne's educational philosophy.

3. Felicity Regained

The movement from felicity in childhood through a loss of felicity leads to *felicity regained*. Traherne "unlearned" the customs of men and became a little child again so that he might "enter into the Kingdom of God" (III C 3). He sketches the movement of his theological autobiography or spiritual growth in the first three meditations of the third *Century* and elaborates upon it in the rest of the third *Century* and his other writings.

According to Traherne, Jesus' use of the childhood metaphor: "You must be born again and become as a little child to enter the Kingdom of Heaven" is more profound than most people realize. To become a child again does not merely mean to rely on Providence, not to be very angry, to have simple Passions. It means also to have peace and purity of soul, to "disrobe our selvs of all fals Colors," to "unclothe our Souls of evil Habits," and to have "Infant-like" thoughts disentangled from the customs and conceits of men. Things should appear as they do to children. Thus childhood remained his teacher and guide (III C 4, 5).

Traherne attributes his own return to felicity to God, who "talks" with men's thoughts and minds even though men often send him away (III C 4).[118] God also plants a desire for felicity in men so that they might "labor after it" (III C 56). Traherne also had a desire to know, a curiosity which he saw leading him to live in communion with God (III C 17, 18). These desires and partial answers which he experienced as a child, he considers emanations of the "highest reason" but not fully realized "till a long time afterwards." In effect Traherne restates Augustine's assertion that the "heart is restless till it finds its rest in God." Yet all things were not perfectly known in childhood (III C 22). Traherne's early thirst for God and his curiosity are intimately connected with his doctrine of the "Liveliness of interior presence." His spirit, he said, was able to be present in all ages and enter into all kingdoms. The child Traherne received all news with greediness and delight, because he expected that his happiness was concealed in it. That the news of salvation first came from Jerusalem proved that his expectations were not in vain (III C 24, 25).[119] Traherne's curiosity led him to desire a book from heaven, but he discovered that God had already sent the Bible before he was born. He found that thousands in shops, schools, or trades were enjoying a felicity he himself had not seen

---

118. In "The Approach" God is not only sent away, he is also received with cold acceptance, "sleighted," or met with hardness of heart (38).

119. See ch. v for a discussion of preexistence.

(III C 28). He was amazed to find that the thoughts he believed no one else had had before were not only in the Bible but also in the writings of the Church Fathers (III C 66). But rather than a direct contribution to his recovery, the *Centuries* imply that the Bible was a confirmation of what had already come to pass in his own life.

When he went to the country (possibly Credenhill), Traherne resolved to search for happiness and satisfy the "thirst" nature had instilled in him from his youth (III C 26). Traherne states that he would rather have lived upon ten pounds a year and have worn leather clothing (eliciting the image of John the Baptist or George Fox) so that he might have his time to himself than have a lot of money in a position where his time would be devoured in care and labor. God had been so pleased with his decision to search for happiness, that all things were plentifully provided for him. He lived a carefree life as if the world had been turned into an Eden (III C 46, 47).

When Traherne first came to the country, he states that he did not know where to begin his study of felicity (III C 52). In general he was guided by an implicit faith in God's goodness. This led him to study the most "Obvious and common things." The value of things was to be measured by their serviceableness. He was led by their fame to such invisible and common things as the laws of God and the soul of man, but even though they were generally discussed, their value was unknown. He indicates that he studied for ten years before his self-love was satisfied (IV C 55). In studying these things he was brought to all the treasures of heaven and earth (III C 55).

He began to believe that every creature was as it had seemed in his infancy, not as it was commonly apprehended (III C 62). It is a matter of perception (III C 68). Thus he came to see that everything was in its "Proper Place," and only he was out of frame and needed to be mended (III C 60). Traherne admits that sin often assailed him and that sin alone could spoil his joy and disturb his advance toward felicity (III C 47-49). However, in Jesus Christ, according to Traherne, sin may be escaped and killed, for grace perfects nature overcoming its perversity (III C 81). Recovery consists of repentance, regeneration, a mystical experience, unlearning the dirty devices of the world, and a return to infancy.[120] Felicity regained, however, is not exactly the same as childhood felicity. It is a wiser felicity (see "Right Apprehension" F 124; IV C 21).

---

120. See ch. vii C for a discussion of felicity regained.

Traherne arrives at approximately twenty five principles in his study of felicity, which he wishes not only to recover but also to exhibit. The core of the principles is: a man should know the blessings he enjoys, prize the blessings he knows, be thankful for the blessings he prizes, and rejoice in that for which he is thankful (IV C 54).

E. Traherne as Mystic

The mixture of influences, affinities, and peculiarities in the writings of Thomas Traherne is probably nowhere so evident as in his mysticism. Previous research in Traherne's mysticism has generally gone through three phases. The first articles were more or less content with a positive response to and a categorization of his mysticism.[121] In the 1920s a few scholars began to question the assumptions of such research. Some responded negatively to the quality of his mysticism, and some even questioned whether he were a mystic.[122] More recently there has been an attempt to reassess historically the question of Traherne's mysticism.[123]

There remain, however, a number of problem areas with regard to Traherne's mysticism.

1) There is not enough data to establish a convincing case. Manuscripts may be missing or Traherne may have chosen not to describe all aspects of his religious experiences.

---

121. Some of the titles of early articles reflect this attempt: "Joyous Mystic" (Willcox in 1911), "English Mystic" (Lock in 1913), "Neglected Mystic" (Wilson in 1925), G. Willett thinks Traherne was a "love mystic" (1919); G. Hodgson, a "nature mystic" (1922); E. Herman, a link between the love and nature mystics (1925); C. Spurgeon, a "philosophic mystic" (1913); J. Proud, a combination of nature, love, theological, and philosophical mystic (1917); G. Wade, a Neoplatonic mystic (1944); and I. Husain, a Christian mystic (1948). This kind of criticism tends to take for granted that he was a mystic and to see Traherne primarily in mystical terms, partly the result of basing most research on the *Centuries* and the poetry alone.

122. F. Towers (1920) states that he is not a nature mystic, and she criticizes the bases of his point of view in general. E. Underhill, perhaps the most influential English scholar in the area of mysticism, places Traherne among the "tasters" rather than among the "seekers" after truth. She finds little evidence of first-hand struggle and experience. She criticizes his "sugary Platonism." G. Willett (1919) notes that Traherne makes "little use of traditional expressions of mysticism." H. White (1936) thinks that the "personal character" of Traherne's revelation and "the nature of his self-consciousness carried him out of the circle of mysticism." Q. Iredale (1935) thinks he did not "attain the last stage of mysticism."

2) The times in which a writer lives or the religious community to which he belongs may dictate his mode of expression as well as prejudice him against certain terminology or themes. For example, seventeenth century Puritanism and Anglicanism would have looked askance at some of the Spanish and French mystical writings of the time. Benjamin Whichcote states categorically that the Christian religion is "not mystical, symbolical, enigmatical, or emblematical."[124] Yet Sir Thomas Browne lists the stages of mysticism as: "Annihilation, Extasis, Liquefaction, Transformation, the Kiss of God, and Ingression into the Divine Shadow."[125] Perhaps the nature and background of the

---

123. The most thorough early discussions of Traherne's mysticism were based primarily upon his *Centuries* and poetry. F. Lohrer (1930) sees three sources of Traherne's mysticism: the Bible, his country stay at Credenhill (nature), and his remembrance of childhood. E. Christ (1932) narrows these sources to infancy and the Bible. In fact he states that all the phenomena which identify Traherne as mystic are connected with his infant experience. He also notes (in Rudolf Otto's categories) that there is more *communio* than *unio* in Traherne. H. Wilde (1932) discusses the possibility of pantheism and the importance of the will. Dean Inge, P. Osmond, F. Löhrer, E. Christ, and others relate Traherne's mysticism to Plato, Proclus, Porphyry, pseudo-Dionysius and others, as well as to sixteenth and seventeenth century mystics like Eckhart, Tauler, Ruysbroek, Boehme, and the English mystics such as Walter Hilton, Julian of Norwich, and Augustine Baker. These comparisons enable scholars to note the similarities as well as the differences in Traherne's style of mysticism. Löhrer, for example, notes that even though Traherne is a nature mystic, he is not a pantheist. He is not a visionary or a prophetic mystic like mystics of the Middle Ages, nor a philosophic mystic like some sixteenth and seventeenth century mystics. Traherne does not use the same concepts or have the same concerns. He is not as subjective or as individualistic as they are. Traherne's concept of God remains biblical. While Leishman links Traherne to the German mystics who stress the spiritual rather than the historical nature of Christ, Lohrer demonstrates the contrary on the basis of I C 54-65. According to Löhrer, Traherne differs from many mystics because he is so interested in nature and the physical body, while others are more interested in the form and the idea.

There are probably as many definitions of mysticism as there are commentators on the subject. While for German scholars Rudolf Otto has set the tone and the terminology, for English scholars, it is Evelyn Underhill. She finds five stages which mystics evidence in their spiritual autobiographies. There are, however, various other listings of the stages. The concept may be most useful for Neoplatonic mysticism. Hugo of St. Victor (1141) lists six stages on the mystic way, Neoplatonism just three (purification, enlightenment, union). The Middle Ages stress purgation. St. Theresa (1515-82) has yet a different ordering of stages. E. Christ thinks that Traherne substitutes four estates (innocence, misery, grace, and glory) for the stages of mystical purification. Discussions of mysticism can easily become a matter of definitions.

Rufus Jones defines a mystical religion as one "which insists upon an immediate inward revelation of God within the sphere of personal experience" (Intro. to Braithwaite's *Beginnings*). Elsewhere, he defines it as "religion in its most acute, intense and loving stage" (*Studies*, 1909). Salter suggests substituting "contemplative" for mystical in describing Traherne.

124. Quoted in G. Bullett, *The English Mystics*, p. 113.

two men contributed to their different points of view. Whichcote was a theologian, preacher and philosopher at a Puritan College at Cambridge, whereas Browne was a layman, writer, and medical doctor from Anglican Oxford.

3) There is a tendency in some research to see mysticism as the dominant characteristic or the key feature of a person's life, but mysticism seems to be just one of many aspects of the life and thought of Thomas Traherne. He was also a theologian, philosopher, ethicist, historian, devotional writer, poet and pastor.

Since there are so many studies of Traherne's mysticism, only a brief sketch of the nature and extent of his mysticism need be outlined. Basic to an understanding of Traherne's mysticism is that it fits no one category. The broader mystical tradition (Neoplatonic, Christian, medieval, sixteenth and seventeenth century) illuminates his mysticism in a way that no one school can. Traherne is not consistently a love mystic, a nature mystic, or a philosophic mystic. Depending upon the context and the audience, his writings take on aspects of one or all the types of mysticism. Furthermore, Traherne's mysticism is not exotic or separatistic but fully within the Christian tradition. He does not dabble in the occult to any great extent as does Henry More. D. Sayers and A. Clements show that Traherne uses both the *via negativa* and *via positiva* to describe his relationship with God.[126] Even using the artificial listing of stages in the mystic way, a number of scholars have demonstrated that Traherne might very well have experienced all the stages.[127] However, forcing his thought into such rigid categories tends to blur his intention, which was usually to lead men to felicity not to mystical experience, and Traherne does not equate the two.

In the earliest tradition of Christianity, the word "contemplation" was used rather than the word "mysticism." The word "mystery" means shutting or closing the eyes or lips, indicating the secret nature of the mysteries. Pseudo-Dionysius was probably the first to use "the word mysticism to describe the Christian experience of God."[128] Since then the

---

125. Quoted in P. Osmond, *The Mystical Poets,* p. 3.
126. D. Sayers, "The Beatrician Vision in Dante and Other Poets," *Nottingham Medieaval Studies,* 2 (1958), 3-23; and Clements, pp. 27-28. I. Husain and R. Ellrodt, however, find no evidence of negative theology in Traherne.
127. Both G. Wade and A. Clements find evidence of all five stages in the writings of Traherne.

term has been used and expanded inclusively and exclusively. What is commonly considered the mystical experience, the sudden flash, the awareness of God's presence, the *mysterium tremendum et fascinans* is not a major issue in most mystical writings, nor is the experience very long in duration or frequent in occurrence.[129] Traherne's experience of childhood and his apprehension of nature are integral to his mysticism, but he does not abdicate reason, tradition, theology, or community because of his experience.

F. Happold indicates a unanimity not in the stages of mysticism but in the results of the mystical experience. As he demonstrates, much of the literature of mysticism is concerned with knowledge, understanding, love, union, and action. If this is the case, Traherne's writings belong in the mystical tradition. There is a passage in the Church's Year Book which approximates mystical terminology. Traherne writes that "Suspension, Admiration, and other Effects of Divine Contemplation" are to be used with moderation because "they are not our last End, but only one Means to Achieve it." Because "Contemplation without Action is not Sufficient," the speaking voice asks to follow God with "desire and obedience, with contemplation and action."[130]

There are also passages which can be seen as evidence for a mystical experience. In Traherne's Select Meditations, he writes that when he first saw "This Endless Comprehension" of his soul, his spirit was "so wholy Ravished and Transported" that he could "scarsly Think or speak or write of any other Thing" for a fortnight. Instead, "like a man Doteing with Delight and Extasie, Talk of it Night and Day as if all the Joy of Heaven and Earth were Shut up in it." He sees the "Divine Image Relucent and Shining," the "foundation of Mans Excellency, and that which made Him a Son of God." He thinks that he will never "be able to forget its Glory" (IV C 3).

128. I. Husain points out that contemplation is the term used by St. Bernard and St. Augustine (p. 24). See F. Happold's discussion, *Mysticism*, pp. 18ff.

129. According to Dean Inge, Plotinus had a mystical experience four times and his disciple Porphyry just once. Most writers have indicated that the experience is a sudden flash of about half an hour in duration (*Mysticism in Religion*, pp. 156ff).

130. Happold, pp. 119ff. See Wade, p. 243; *RGG*, IV, 1237-1262; and Malcolm Day, "Thomas Traherne and the Perennial Philosophy," *DA*, 1964.

In the *Hexameron* the meditational voice exhorts "Up! Up! my Soul," among the angels and "rejoice in their glorious Beings, and more in God that gave it them" (p. 106). In the *Thanksgivings* Old Testament events are described in mystical terminology: "Thy Servant Moses transported into Extasies and Blessings. Joseph on the Brink of Glory, saw the Beauties which Angels Admire" (p. 247). In one poem Traherne writes that "The Union was so Strait" between God and his soul "That all was eithers/His Gifts, and my Possessions, both/our Treasures; He mine." In fact, "The World was more in me, then I in it./The King of Glory in my Soul did sit" ("Silence" 48). Such passages occur not only in his meditational and poetical writings but also in the *Christian Ethicks.* In a chapter on the "Beauty of Gratitude" Traherne devotes an extended passage to his response to God's love:

> My Joy, my Life, my Crown, my Glory; my exceeding great Reward, my Love, my Soul, my Idol, nay the GOD of my Soul! My All in all! This is the language of Love in its Rapture. Seraphick Love! It is Altar, Heart and Sacrifice, Angelical Love! It is Enjoyment, Honour, Praise, Adoration, Thanksgiving, Extasie, Pleasure, Bliss and Happiness (*CE*, p. 275).

Thus Traherne's mysticism, his biography, his autobiography, and his theology are all interrelated.

Chapter III

The Writings of
Thomas Traherne

At that we aim to th'end thy Soul might see
With open Eys thy Great Felicity
("The Author to the Critical Peruser" 2).

A. Chronology and Appraisal of Traherne's Writings

An exact chronology of the writings of Traherne is almost impossible to construct because of the nature of his writings, the lack of internal evidence, and the relative brevity of his life. A few of his writings, however, can be generally dated. Other writings then may sometimes be seen in relationship to them by the way similar materials or ideas are handled.

Parts of Traherne's Early Notebook may be dated as early as 1653, and Traherne added to it at least until 1657.[1] There are indications that Traherne began parts of the *Roman Forgeries*, perhaps as a research project, while he was still at Oxford (1653-1661). Later he may have expanded the material and published it in 1673.[2] The Select Meditations were apparently written between 1660 and 1665.[3] His part in both the *Daily Devotions* and the *Life of Christ* may have been composed and used during his Credenhill period (1661-1669), and they seem to have been written before the *Thanksgivings* (from 1661-1666).[4] Certain passages common to these works are more fully developed in the *Hexameron* which may indicate that it is a later work.[5] The Ficino Notebook was completed around 1669 or 1670.[6] Indications are that they were begun in the early 1670s and

---

1. See B 5 below and C. Marks, "Early Studies," *Papers*, 511-536.
2. See, however, B 1. Traherne makes reference to the Labbé and Cossart edition of 1671/2.
3. See B 4 and A. Clements, *Mystical*, p. 9.
4. See B 2 and G. Wade, *Traherne*, p. 147; C Owen, "Authorship," *MLR*, 1-12.
5. See B 3 and Guffey's intro. to *Hex*; Lynn Sauls, "Puente," *PQ*, 173.
6. See B 5 and C. Marks, "Ficino," *Papers*, 73-81.

somewhat later, the poetry.[7] The Church's Year Book appears to have been completed in 1670, yet parts of it may precede the *Hexameron*.[8] The Commonplace Book was probably begun at about this time.[9] *Christian Ethicks* was the last work Traherne wrote. In it is a reference to Sir Orlando Bridgeman's will (*CE*, p. 239).

Because Traherne often added to or corrected what he had previously written, a description of any possible development of his thought is just as problematical as constructing a chronology. There was too little time for many major developments, but a few changes in emphasis and different approaches will be pointed out in chapters five through nine.

Not all the writings of Traherne are of equal value in describing his theological thought. Of least value, perhaps, are those of his writings which are the most derivative: his studies, notebooks, the Church's Year Book, his part in the *Daily Devotions*, and the *Life of Christ*. Yet even these are of some value in that Traherne seemed to have selected and copied from sources with which he agreed, and he sometimes added his own comments. What is more, his studies are a major clue as to what influenced him. The poetry of the Burney manuscript is also problematical as a source of his thought because Thomas Traherne's brother, Philip, tampered with the manuscript. Traherne's use of an amanuensis for his Commonplace Book, Church's Year Book, and Ficino Notebook pose less of a problem, because apparently Traherne directed, read, and often corrected the work of his helpers.[10]

On a more philosophical and psychological level is the suspicion that there is a private and a public faith with some variations between the two. Merely attributing these differences in thought among his various writings to the age in which he lived (severe censorship and heresy trials) and to the fact that his life spanned the Commonwealth and Restoration, does not totally solve the problem. To go further and say that when Traherne wrote the *Centuries* or the Select Meditations for private use, he stated what he actually believed, and when he wrote the *Roman Forgeries* or *Christian Ethicks* for public consumption, he was less than honest, is too facile. This

---

7.   See B 3, 4 and the note on the poem "Approach" which occurs in the Dobell, F and *Centuries* manuscript. Marg, II, p. 346. The Dobell version seems to be the last written.

8.   See B 3; L. Sauls, "Puente," *PQ*; C. Marks, "CYB," *Papers*.

9.   See B 5; CE, xiii-xiv; and C. Marks, "CB," *Papers*.

10.   See articles by C. Marks: "CB," "CYB," and "FN" all in *Papers*.

misconception may be an unacknowledged factor in the greater critical emphasis placed on the *Centuries* and the poetry with the correspondingly lesser emphasis on his published works, even though some of his poetry as well as the Church's Year Book were apparently also meant for publication. The *Centuries*, for example, also had their audience, and as S. Stewart has shown, Traherne takes various rhetorical stances depending upon his audience and the genre: polemical, devotional, pastoral.[11]

An easier way out of the difficulty is to conclude that Traherne's beliefs vacillated among or perhaps even encompassed the variety of stances he took. Similarly, it might be possible that he had no single position, that he was not sure of what he believed, or that he neither desired a rigid position nor thought one necessary. The appeal to a chronological progress in his thought is further weakened by the fact that Traherne wrote the Centuries and Select Meditations in the middle of his productive period and the greatest differences can be found between the poetry and the *Christian Ethicks*, both later writings.

Perhaps closer to the truth, although it does not account for all the problems, is the possibility that either Traherne was unaware of the paradoxes or contradictions in his thought or that he was able to live with them. The seventeenth century was, after all, in a state of flux on every front, and paradox was a way of looking at reality.[12] Perhaps he felt no driving need to resolve the paradoxes, to dissolve the mysteries. For example, there are often contradictions not only among the different writings of Traherne, but also within the same work and at times even on the same page.[13]

A vital factor to be remembered is that Traherne published or prepared for publication what he wanted to communicate to the general public. In his own time he would have been judged by his published works. These were his considered positions. Thus it is possible to see the *Christian Ethicks*, for example, as containing his most developed and polished theological thought. In any event, the published works ought not to be suspect merely because they were published or meant for publication.

---

11. Stewart, pp. 209-214.
12. See R. Colie, *Paradoxia Epidemica* (Princeton, 1966), and *CE*, xlix-1.
13. See extended discussion in ch. viii.

There is, however, a mediating position by which the works are not played off against one another, nor is one a standard by which all are compared. His position on any point is examined as it is expressed in all of his writings public and private, and if there is a unified point of view, either a collation or the best expression of his position is used to describe his thought. If there are contradictions or differences, the spectrum of his ideas is presented with possible solutions.

B. The Intent of the Writings by and Ascribed to Traherne

1. Published Writings

a) *Roman Forgeries, Or a True Account of False Records Discovering the imposture and Counterfeit Antiquities of the Church of Rome* By a Faithful Son of the Church of England, is the only work of uncontested authorship published during Traherne's lifetime.[14] Various scholars note in this work what they call the distinctive qualities of a thesis[15] or a disputation,[16] but in his introduction to *Roman Forgeries* Traherne implies that it developed out of a private discussion with a Roman Catholic at the Bodleian Library in Oxford. The dismissal of Sir Orlando Bridgeman to whom the work is dedicated could have led Traherne to expand his previous research (represented perhaps in the first twelve chapters) for publication.[17]

Roman Forgeries is, as S. Stewart points out, a response to the kind of need seen by Dr. James in his *A Treatise of Corruption of Scripture, Councels, Fathers, by the Prelats, Pastors, and Pillars of the Church of Rome, for Maintenance of Popery and Religion* (1611). In that work James admits that he was not able to deal adequately with the councils. However, it is a necessary task, according to James, since the Roman Catholic Church ("Adversaries") had published so many collections of the documents of the

---

14. Hereinafter abbreviated *RF*. See the discussion of *Daily Devotions* in B 2.
15. G. Wade, p. 68; Marg, I, xxxviii.
16. Stewart, p. 16.
17. In November 1672 Bridgeman was dismissed as Lord Keeper of the Seal for his opposition to the Catholic policies of Charles II. See *CE*, xxvii; and G. Wade, p. 125, but see C Marks, "CYB," *Papers*, p. 61. Because Traherne refers to Labbé and Cossart does not preclude the possibility that he was expanding previous research.

councils.[18] This was not, however, as Stewart notes, a general appeal for someone to write on this theme. Dr. James had in mind Dr. Ward of Sidney-Sussex College, Cambridge, who had already done some research in this area. It was, however, Traherne who first published what Dr. James desired.[19] Dean Comber continued the work in his *Roman Forgeries in the Councils during the First Four Centuries* (1689), and refers to Traherne (though not by name) in his Introduction. Some "Eminent Men," according to Comber, had begun the work, but no one man could accomplish the task alone. A "Learned and Ingenious Gentleman" (Traherne) who began the work did not "follow the exact order of Time," nor did "he go much beyond the Nicene Council," and "he left out many plain Instances." Dean Comber thus began where Traherne left off.[20] Traherne's book is in a long polemical or apologetic tradition. The first such English work in this genre was that of John Jewel, Bishop of Salisbury, whose *An Apologie or Answer in the Defense of the Church of England* (1562) has been called the "first systematic statement of the doctrinal position of the Church of England."[21]

There is an intimate connection between apologetics or polemics and systematic theology. The writer defends the truth of his own position and elaborates upon it in a criticism of what he believes to be false in the position of his opponent. In much the same way Traherne said he was going to exclude from *Christian Ethicks* a discussion of the vices, yet he treated them by illustrating the contrary of the virtues. Likewise, even though he said he was going to exclude doctrine from *Roman Forgeries*, he expounds it by pointing out the false doctrine of the Romanists.

The fact that sixty-two years separate the works of Dr. James and of Traherne may be accounted for in part by the events of the time. The Anglican church's line of attack had shifted from the Papists to the Puritans. During the Protectorate, of course, even this area of controversy was severely restricted. It was not until the Restoration, amidst fears of the ascendancy of Roman Catholicism in the royal house, that anti-Catholic polemical works were again seen as necessary. *Roman Forgeries* is the most

18. Thomas James, *A Treatise*, II, p. 102. According to Stewart, James is the "primary influence on the subject, tone and structure of the *Roman Forgeries*" (pp. 22ff).

19. Stewart, pp. 22ff.

20. Thomas Comber, *Roman,* Epistle Dedicatory.

21. Stewart, p. 20.

consistently polemical writing of Traherne, but the Church's Year Book also contains polemical passages against the Puritans.[22]

By excluding "the Fathers at large," limiting himself to the "Records...such as Apostles Canons, Decretal Epistles, and Ancient Councils," and by concentrating only on the first 420 years of church history, Traherne is able to keep his book "little for the use and benefit of all."[23] Its 342 pages are the equivalent of a modern pocket book.

The book has twenty-four chapters and an appendix. G. Wade sees the first twelve chapters as a unit, describing the Councils, the rise of the Papacy, and the use of forged documents to support papal claims. Traherne says he examined the collections of Isidore, James Merlin, Francis Turrian, Peter Crabbe, Carranza, Surius, Nicolinus, Binius, and Baronius.[24] Traherne intended to continue "in another volume" his study of the forgeries of "succeeding ages" (*RF*, p. 35).

b) *Christian Ethicks: or divine Morality, opening the Way to Blessedness, by the Rules of Virtue and Reason* (1675), unqualifiedly Traherne's, was sent to the printers during the last months of his life. It is, as C. Marks notes, "the only systematic treatise on ethics intended for the educated layman to appear in English during the thirty years after the Restoration."[25] However, the book fell into comparative oblivion. Discounting demonic forces, there were a number of possible reasons why the book was neglected. Traherne was not alive either to correct the printer's proofs or to promote the book. Furthermore, his literary reputation depended entirely upon the *Roman Forgeries* which was not widely read. *Daily Devotions* was not associated with his name until the twentieth century. Sir Orlando Bridgeman had died

---

22. Stewart thinks *RF* is Traherne's only work in the polemical mode (p. 29). But see, for example, the CYB: "As on the one side we Decline Superstion [sic] on the other side let us avoid Profaneness, Ingratitude, or Forgetfulness of Thee! Make us to follow Antiquity...Save us from Novelty" (16). See also CYB 46v, 20.

23. *RF*, Intro. Stewart thinks that because Traherne concentrates on the first 420 years of church history, he comes "close to the primitivism of the Earl of Shaftesbury" or pre-Romanticism (p. 18). Yet the Anglican principle: "What is at all times, in all places, and everywhere to be believed" was usually also limited to the first five centuries.

24. G. Wade, p. 125.

25. *CE*, xxxiii. C. Marks' Intro. to the critical edition of the *CE* discusses in detail: seventeenth-century ethical thought, as well as the audience, patron, method, philosophy, and style of the *CE*.

a few months before Traherne, closing that avenue to the public. A book with neither a living author nor patron could easily have been overlooked.

Traherne's book may also have appeared somewhat strange in comparison with similar publications of his contemporaries. He thought to deal with the vices would be a waste of time and paper (*CE*, p. 207), nor did he deal in depth with the passions and some of the "less Principal" virtues (*CE*, p. 24). He supplements a scholastic schema with a view of history which is divided into four estates: innocence, misery, grace and glory. This schema is comparable to his suggestion for the study of divinity.[26]

Traherne's primary source is the *Ethics* of Eustache de Saint Paul, which he modifies by omitting the last section which deals with the vices and appending definitions of two cardinal virtues and all the lesser virtues from other works.[27] His intended audience is ostensibly the educated laity, "For Vulgar Apprehension" (*CE*, p. 23), like his own patron, Sir Orlando Bridgeman. It is evidently not his intent to put forward a new ethical theory nor to write exclusively for theologians.[28]

c)   First "Published in 1699 By the Reverend Doctor HICKS [sic] at the request of a Friend of the Authors" in London, *A Serious Pathetical Contemplation of the Mercies of God in several most Devout and Sublime Thanksgivings for the same*, was reprinted in 1941 and 1958. The title, the biblical references, and the final form of the work may not be Traherne's in all details.[29] The authorship of the *Thanksgivings*, like other writings of Traherne, has at times been uncertain. It has been ascribed to Susanna Hopton, Theophilus Dorrington, Brian Dupper and others.[30] Its liturgical

26.   III C 43–45, the outline of this study.

27.   Traherne summarizes Eustache's *Ethica* in his EN (7–21) without indicating his source. C. Marks demonstrates that Traherne simplifies and sometimes distorts Eustache by noting just one of his conclusions or the conclusion of another philosopher which Eustache lists. See *CE*, xix-xxii. Eustache (1573-1640), a member of the Feuillant Order and friend of Francis de Sales and other French religious leaders, wrote *Summa philosophiae Quadripartite* (*de rebus dialecticis, moralibus, physicis, & metaphysicis*) which was published at Cambridge (1640, 1648, 1649). The *Ethica* was published as a separate work in England in 1654 and 1648. He also wrote a *Summa theologica tripartita* (Paris, 1613, 1616).

28.   See *CE*, xxii, and see ch. ix for a fuller discussion of Traherne's understanding of ethics.

29.   Hereinfter abbreviated *Thanks*. Marg, I, xxii. Other "thanksgivings" in the seventeenth century were: Thomas Becon, *Pomaunder of Prayers* (1560); Lancelet Andrewes, *Private Devotions* (London, 1647); and *Institutiones Piae* (London, 1633). See Stewart, p. 98.

30.   See G. Wade, pp. 135ff, and the annotation inside the British Museum copy of the *Thanksgivings*.

character, form, and content indicate that the work was intended for publication. Parts of the work can be dated between 1661 and 1666 because of apparent references to national disasters such as the Great Plague and the Fire of London.[31] The prefatory letter and the Preface to the work contain biographical material on Traherne.[32]

The layout and form of the *Thanksgivings* are problematical. Often it seems as though the contents of one of the *Thanksgivings* could easily be inserted or exchanged with that of another. Yet they may be a unified whole for the title of one, "Appendix to the former *Thanksgiving*," implies some desire for order and linkage. G. Wade thinks that there are two sets of *Thanksgivings* with the first set ending with the "Appendix to the former *Thanksgiving*." She concludes that the first seven are written as a whole,[33] and that the last three are miscellaneous.[34] The fact that "Thanksgivings for God's Attributes" is written in a style different from the others and is the only *Thanksgiving* without bracketing strengthens her arguments.

d) The first part (pp. 1-91) of *A Collection of Meditations and Devotions in Three Parts*, the *Meditations on the Six Days of the Creation*, is the only part of that work certain to be Traherne's. Wade,[35] Margoliouth,[36] Owen,[37] and Guffey[38] have adequately dealt with the problems of authorship. When it was first published in 1717, the publisher, Nathaniel

---

31. The work is not, as Wade asserts, "intensely personal" and "intended for...himself" (p. 147, 150).
32. Reprinted in Marg, I, xxx-xxxi, and see ch. ii C.
33. I.e. "Thanksgivings" for: "the Body," "the Soul," "the Glory of God's Works," "the Blessedness of GOD's Ways," "the Blessedness of his LAWS," "the Beauty of his Providence," and "the Wisdom of his word."
34. I.e. "Appendix," "Thanksgivings for God's Attributes," and "A Thanksgiving and Prayer for the Nation" (Wade, p. 146). Margoliouth's table of contents is somewhat misleading. "A KEY to the Gate" ought to be subsumed under the previous "Thanksgiving for the Blessedness of God's Ways." That is how it is printed in the text, and internal evidence indicates that this is the way it was to be. Compare lines 346-354 of the preceding "Thanksgivings...God's Ways" with the outline of Puente's *Meditations* in II 223-229, 243-244. Traherne shortens Puente's text intensifying his ideas, but he does not alter Puente's style completely. See Sauls, "Puente," *PQ*.
35. Hereinafter abbreviated *Hex*. Wade, p. 155.
36. Marg, I, xvi-xvii.
37. C. Owen, "Authorship," *MLR*, pp. 1-5.
38. *Hex*, Intro., i-vii.

Spinckes, attributed all three parts of the collection to Mrs. Susanna Hopton.[39] There is now little doubt that Traherne wrote the *Hexameron*.

Traherne's work is one of the two hexameral works published in England after 1500. The other is Josuah Sylvester's translation of Guillaume Du Bartas's *Premiere semaine* (1578) which Traherne had read and used. His primary debt both in style and content, however, is to the English translation of Luis de la Puente's *Meditations upon Mysteries of Holie Faith* (St. Omer, 1619).[40] Traherne's work and the seventh book of *Paradise Lost* have been called the finest poems on creation in the English language.[41]

The methodology of Traherne's *Hexameron* is standard for such works. There are six parts corresponding exactly to the six days of the creation, each of which ends with a poem summarizing the key ideas of the meditation.[42] R. Guffey thinks Traherne's meditational pattern is like that of Bonaventura[43] whereas L. Sauls thinks it is Ignation.[44]

The "Meditations on the Sixth Day's Creation" is the most complex of the meditations. It is especially pertinent to a study of Traherne's theological thought focusing as it does on the creation of man. The sixth day's meditation begins, as do all except the second meditation, with the words, "Let the Words of my Mouth, and the Meditations of my Heart, be always acceptable in thy Sight, Oh Lord, my strength and my Redeemer." This prayer is traditionally the prayer of the leader in Christian worship or the preacher as an introduction to a homily. As in all but the fourth meditation, the meditation proper begins with the appropriate text from

---

39. See B 2 below.

40. Lynn Sauls demonstrates that some 56 of the 91 pages of the *Hex* are indebted to Puente in wording and structure. Sauls also notes that Traherne often changes the voice, directing his *Hex* to the soul or to God, whereas Puente addresses his work to the reader. Traherne even alters Scripture passages in this way. Traherne alters and modernizes Puente's facts. "Puente," *PQ*. For its literary evaluations see Wade, p. 156; Guffey, *Hex*, xi; and Sauls, p. 174.

41. In his introduction to the *Hex*, Guffey places "the subject matter of the work solidly within the Hexameral tradition" and its "form" in the meditational tradition. He does not, however, indicate precisely what the differences are between the two traditions. *Hex*, vii.

42. "Traherne begins each series with a contemplation of the nature of the beings God created on the day in question, becomes aware of the providential wisdom reflected in God's supreme craftsmanship, and finally bursts into a song in praise of God's handiwork." *Hex*, ix.

43. *Hex*, x. L. Martz describes the stages of Bonaventura's *Itinerarium Mentis in Deum* thus: "we contemplate God outside through His traces, inside through His image, and above us through His light, which has signed upon our minds the light of eternal truth." L. Martz, *The Paradise Within* (New Haven, 1964), p. 56.

44. L. Sauls, "Puente," p. 166.

Genesis one, followed by a commentary by Traherne of what happened on that day. Several of the paragraphs in this section are prefaced by such phrases as, "Consider now, O my Soul," adding a devotional flavor to what would otherwise be merely a repetition of the biblical account.

As is done elsewhere in the *Hexameron*, additional passages of Scripture are cited which parallel or illuminate the Genesis text. Often these passages are followed by an exhortation or prayer of praise. In the sixth day's meditation, the meditational voice asks, "O Lord, make me to magnify thy Works" (p. 67). An integral part of these meditations is the discussion of the "Uses, Benefits, Blessings" of all that God created on that day. Sometimes this is followed by a section which explores the allegorical or emblematical significance of what was created, for example, "From the laboring Beast, teach me to be laborious in thy Service..." (p. 68). Prayers and praises are liberally interspersed throughout the meditations, conveying a liturgical flavor.

Usually the appropriate verse of the canticle *Benedicite Omnia Opera Domini* (The Song of the Three Children) is cited in each meditation. For example, after the creation of the beasts, he quotes almost as a final refrain, "Praise ye the Lord, ye Beasts and all Cattel, Worms and feathered Fowls: Let everything that hath Breath praise the Lord" (p. 70). Traherne does not follow this canticle slavishly but freely adapts and reconstructs it according to his needs. The subsection of the sixth day (which is the only labeled subsection in the entire work), "The Creation of Man," is the finest part of the *Hexameron*, but it is not typical enough in structure to allow generalizations on the meditational method of the whole *Hexameron*.

2. Published Writings of Disputed Authorship

a) The transcripts of the Stationers' Registers indicate that another book was submitted to the printer, Jonathan Edwin, on the same day (September 25, 1673) as Traherne's *Roman Forgeries*. This is the same press which later was to print *Christian Ethicks* and which printed a total of only thirty eight books between 1671 and 1679. That book, *Daily Devotions*, consisting of "Thanksgivings, Confessions and Prayer" probably also contains sections written by Traherne. It went through six editions. The Preface to the 1673, edition states that the work is "the Devotions of a Learned, and pious Christian. . . ." The 1703 Preface alters this somewhat saying that it is "By a Late Reverend Divine of the Church of England." Dr. Hickes writes, however, in his *A Second Collection of Controversial Letters* (1710) that it "was printed from a MS. of a venerable deceased Clergyman of Herefordshire." Mrs. Hopton states that "she had Intimate Correspondence" with him. Yet the *Daily Devotions* was attributed to Mrs. Hopton. [45]

Much of *Daily Devotions* is derived from Austin, Augustine, and Andrewes. A close examination of the contents of the *Daily Devotions* indicates that perhaps only parts of "The Paraphrase of the Objective Hymn of Praise," the "Thanksgivings for all Persons and Times" and "A Daily Thanksgiving" are Traherne's in entirety or in part.[46] Mrs. Hopton either reflects Traherne's ideas in her own writings or incorporates some of his writings into her anthology. Because of the work's dependence on secondary sources and the problems involved in its authorship, references to it will be carefully qualified.

b) The evidence that Traherne wrote the *Meditations and Devotions on the Life of Christ* like that of *Daily Devotions* (parts II, pp. 92-322, and III, pp. 323-423, of a *Collection of Meditation and Devotions in Three Parts*, 1717) is too inconclusive to permit this work in its entirety to be used with confidence as a statement of his theological thought. G. Wade ascribes it to Traherne,[47] A. Russell surmises that the *Life of Christ* and *The Soul's Communion With her Saviour* by Philip Traherne derive from a common manuscript written by Traherne.[48] C. Owen, however, demonstrates convincingly that only the material between pages 232 and 241 bears any resemblance to anything else Traherne wrote, and that this work can be used "only with great reservations as an indication of his thought." [49]

It seems necessary, then, to ascribe the *Life of Christ* to Mrs. Hopton. Dr. Hickes in his *Second Collection of Controversial Letters* states that it is in her hand.[50] What is more, there are references to a husband, and

---

45. Discussed in Wade, pp. 129ff.
46. See *Daily Devotions*, pp. 336, 347, 354, 361 for distinctive Traherne terminology. G. Wade, however, thinks a larger part of the *Daily Devotions* is Traherne's.
47. Wade, p. 157.
48. Russell, p. 49.
49. Owen, p. 12. The sections which Owen thinks Traherne wrote or strongly influenced are entitled: "Reflections upon our Saviour's Sermon after the Sacrament, before his Passion based on John 15" and "On our Saviour's Prayer, John 17."
50. Quoted in Owen, p. 6.

indications that a layman with a high regard for the clergy wrote it.[51] Furthermore, Philip Traherne was still alive in 1717 when the work was published and ascribed to the "First Reformer of the Devotions in the Ancient Way of Offices" (i.e. Mrs. Hopton). He would certainly have indicated that his brother's work had been ascribed to someone else. Because this work may reflect or incorporate some of Traherne's ideas, passages from the *Life of Christ* will be used to illuminate ideas from his other works.

3. Writings Possibly Intended for Publication

a)   Traherne probably intended to publish the Church's Year Book. Still in manuscript, there are numerous corrections, inserts, and passages marked for alteration.[52] It appears to be a rough draft, written rapidly by various people (probably from April to November 1670) with later corrections. C. Marks demonstrates that there are three different handwritings in evidence in the manuscript: Thomas's, Philip's, and an unknown person's. To complicate the matter, Thomas Traherne, himself, uses various styles of handwriting.[53] Some of the material is meant for the public and for the private use of a specific audience or patron, perhaps the household of Sir Orlando Bridgeman. Asides in the Pentecost section: "concerning which we shall speak more on Trinity Sunday" (CYB 5Iv), and an extended section in the "Meditations. . .on St. Peter's Day:" "I shall briefly entertain you with Repentance" (CYB 76v) indicate the public character of at least some of the devotions.[54]

Traherne's major source is Luis de la Puente's *Meditations upon the Mysterie of our Holie Faith*. L. Sauls demonstrates that some fifty two of the 204 pages of the Church's Year Book contain borrowings from Puente. Traherne alters his source in places because he disagrees with Puente's narrower doctrine of man, his attitude toward the Virgin Mary and some of

---

51.   *Life of Christ*, pp. 50, 112, 113, 163, 305. According to Owen, there are "no allusions to ancient philosophy or the Patristic writings, and it presupposes no academic background..." Thus there is no inherent reason Mrs. Hopton could not have written it. Owen, p. 9.

52.   Herein abbreviated CYB. Bodleian MS. Eng. th. E. 51. See CYB 10v, 35vff, 50vff, 52v, 57v, and a notation between paragraphs on 49v "Insert Paper." Marg has printed a table of contents and a description of the work in "CYB," *Papers*, 31ff.

53.   According to C. Marks, a Hand C (not yet identified) wrote in a brief prayer in a section devoted to the Resurrection: "Give them victory over all their sins and temptations. Deliver us from all Iniquity to obey the same" (15r). "CYB," *Papers*, 31ff.

the saints and apostles, the Holy Spirit, prayer, and avoiding evil. Traherne is also less abstract.[55] Edward Sparke's *Scintillula Altaris* (1652) is another source which is similar in form and content.[56] Traherne also borrows from Anthony Sparrow's *A Rationale upon the Common Prayer of the Church of England* (1653),[57] Daniel Featley's *Ancilla Pietatis* (1626),[58] and William Austin's *Devotionis Augustinianae Flamma*,[59] There are also less extensive borrowings from Jeremy Taylor's *The Great Exemplar* (1649),[60] John Gerard's *Meditations* (1627),[61] Lancelot Andrewes' *A Manual of Private Devotions and Meditations* (1648), and *Private Devotions* (1630).[62]

The first part of the Church's Year Book may be missing,[63] but missing notebooks, manuscripts, pages are a continuing aspect of Traherne scholarship. However, Traherne may simply have begun the CYB at Easter or at the beginning of his duties as chaplain to Sir Orlando Bridgeman, without ever completing it. There are too many explanations of the concept of the church's year in the manuscript to make it likely that the manuscript

---

54. Dobell, however, asserts that "This volume…is his private book of Meditations and Devotions." G. Wade thinks Traherne has a three-fold purpose, "to provide High Church Anglicans with information about the origin of certain church festivals and with the life history of certain saints so commemorated; to furnish suitable prayers and meditations for use on these festivals; and to attack the Puritans and Low Churchmen who opposed their observance" (p. 241). C. Marks, however, seems to be closer to the truth: "It embodies a composite production of Traherne as vicar, chaplain, private Christian, friend." "CYB," *Papers.* The polemical aspects of the CYB should not be overemphasized. Traherne writes: "I shall not wander into the Maze of Disputation…Desiring not to interrupt the Sweet Methods of Meditation with the Harsh Touches of Accents of Contention" (CYB 76v).

55. See L. Sauls article on "Puente."

56. Traherne includes more material on worship and devotional response than Sparkes, and he uses Sparkes infrequently as a stylistic source, according to C. Marks. "CYB," *Papers*, pp. 46-47.

57. Traherne borrows Sparrow's summaries of the ideas of Durandus, Gemma, and Micrologus, according to Marks. See CYB 22 and C. Marks, "CYB," *Papers*, p. 45.

58. Traherne acknowledges his debt to Featley only once (CYB 39v), but see also CYB 55v-56, 13, 14v. He also uses Featley as a stimulus of ideas, according to Marks. See "CYB," *Papers*, 34, 48.

59. Traherne uses Austin's discussion of angels in the *Hex*, pp. 6-9. See also CYB 31-33, 34v-35v, 36, 36v, 96v-97. C. Marks, "CYB," *Papers*, 48-50.

60. Traherne acknowledges his source (CYB 75v).

61. CYB 89v-90. The translation Traherne uses is by Ralph Winterton.

62. Traherne uses Richard Drake's translation and wonders how "much Exercise. . . of Phancy, & by Consequence. . . little Certainty" there is in Andrewes' elaboration on the nine orders of angels ("CYB," *Papers*, 56-58 and L. Sauls, "Puente," 163). R. Daniels in his intro. to the facsimile reprint of the *Thanks* contrasts Traherne's thought with that of Andrewes.

63. See Marg, I, xvii and C. Marks, "CYB," *Papers*, 34ff, but see CYB 100r.

is the second half of an already completed first half. A section from "For Trinity Sunday" is missing (58-68).

Due to the vastly varying moods of the season from Easter to All Saints, Traherne has no rigid outline which he follows for each day's meditation.[64] The general format for a saint's day is to begin with an expression of praise to God for giving the church the particular saint, followed by an exposition of the saint's life and work, and, if he is an evangelist, an explanation of the intent of his Gospel. Prayers, applications of the life of the saint to the lives of other Christians, biblical quotations, and praises to God for the saint follow in no particular order. Usually the meditation ends with the proper collect for the day. The format for a feast or festival is usually more elaborate and structured: e.g. on Ascension Day he prays for "Grace to consider in it, the Person ascending, The Time when, The Manner how, The place from Whence, The place Whither, The ends for which besides the Benefits already Enummerated" (CYB 31r).[65]

Traherne's primary concerns in the CYB seem to be liturgical, but he is also interested in the historical, the allegorical, the polemical, the moral, and the historical. He includes meditations for all major liturgical days for the half of the church year covered by the CYB, except for the Sundays after Easter. That these are omitted is strange, because the propers for these Sundays (particularly *Cantate* and *Jubilate*) reflect major emphases of Traherne's thought.

b) Of Traherne's writings, the poetry along with the *Centuries* has received the most scholarly attention. In addition to that which is scattered throughout his other works (in the *CE*, *Centuries*, *Hex*, *Thanks*, and CYB), the poetry is found primarily in three manuscripts: the Dobell, the Burney, and the Early Notebook.

The Dobell manuscript is named after the man who first discovered the authorship of the poetry and who printed it in a modernized version in 1903.[66] The thirty-seven poems are neatly written out at the beginning of the manuscript which includes Traherne's Commonplace Book. G. Wade

---

64. C. Marks thinks she sees a recurring Ignatian devotional method in the CYB, particularly evident in the "Meditations. . . on the Resurrection." "CYB," *Papers*, 35ff.

65. See also CYB 41v-44v.

66. Bodleian MS. Eng. Poet c. 42. This manuscript also contains Traherne's Commonplace Book. See B 5 below.

suggests that there are three main but non-sequential groupings of poetry in this manuscript: childhood, need of God for man, and the nature of the mind.[67] J. Denonain, J. Wallace, and A. Clements discern a sequence of thought. Clements, for example, develops the thesis that the poems progress "from childhood innocence through fallen adult experience to redeemed Felicity. . . ".[68] The second collection of poems occurs in the Burney manuscript (MS 392) which was found in the British Museum by H. I. Bell and published by him in 1910. This manuscript, containing sixty-one poems, has been in the British Museum since 1818. The title page lists as the author, "Tho. Traherne. B.D. Author of the *Roman Forgeries* and *Christian Ethicks*." Surprisingly no one had noticed the manuscript until after the publication of the Dobell edition of poetry. The poems in this manuscript, however, have been tampered with and rearranged by Philip Traherne, and thus are not reliable as direct sources for the thought of Thomas Traherne as are those in the Dobell folio. Philip had prepared these poems for publication under the title: *Poems of Felicity* with the subtitle *Divine Reflections on the natural objects of an Infant-Ey*. The subtitle may have been Traherne's title. Some of the poems are found in both manuscripts enabling the critic to examine the extent and kind of alterations Philip made.[69]

The third major source of poetry is the Early Notebook which contains only a few early poems.[70] The Margoliouth edition has reprinted most of Traherne's poetry from all available sources except for the Select Meditations.

These then are the writings of Traherne and those ascribed to him which were published or most probably meant for publication. There are other writings of a more private nature which are also useful for describing the theological thought of Traherne. The *Centuries* and the Select

---

67. Wade, p. 169.

68. J. Denonain, pp. 254ff; J. Wallace, pp. 5-7; A. Clements, book jacket. A Clements' schema is similar to the one used for Traherne's theological autobiography in ch. ii above.

69. G. Wade demonstrates that Philip "revised toward greater correctness of form and stricter conventionality of thought," and that he has arranged the poetry into two sequences, each of which tells of "infant felicity lost and infant felicity regained." Wade, pp. 176-178. E. Christ attributes the differences to the fact that baroque was giving way to classicism (p. 17). See Stewart for another suggested sequence (pp. 156).

70. Bodleian Lat. Misc. f. 45. See C. Marks, "EN," *Papers*, 511-536.

Meditations were sent to at least one ether person to read or perhaps to circulate among a small circle of friends, a not unusual practice of the time.

4. Private Writings

a) The *Centuries* are contained in a small notebook Brookes acquired together with the Dobell manuscript of poetry. It had no indication of authorship or title. Apparently the manuscript incorporates material written previously with new material. Particularly in his commentary on the Psalms, there is evidence that Traherne is copying from a previously written document. The title given to the *Centuries* may be Traherne's own idea.[71] The "century" format was used by others in various ways in the seventeenth century.[72]

The *Centuries* are written in a notebook which had been given to Traherne probably by Mrs. Hopton. He writes, "Love made you put it into my hands." He has "a mind to fill it with Profitable Wonders. And with those Truths you Love without Knowing them. . ." (I C 1). He intends the person to whom the notebook is addressed to continue the writing, "That she may write my Makers Praise therein" ("Presentation Quatrain"). The *Centuries* have been the most enthusiastically received of Traherne's writings in the twentieth century and are valued even above his poetry.[73]

Traherne wrote four divisions consisting of one hundred sections of meditations each plus ten completed sections of a fifth *Century*. The notebook ends with the number eleven. There are a number of theories as to why the *Centuries* break off at the number eleven.[74] However, Traherne may simply have stopped near the beginning of the fifth Century to invite

---

71. Abbreviated *C* in textual references and the notes. Bodleian MS Eng. th. e. 50. Marg thinks that "If Traherne had given the work a title, he might very well have called it, 'The Heir of the World,'" I, p. 238, see x-xi. However, since the Select Meditations appear to be an earlier version of the *Centuries*, it seems that Traherne uses the century format intentionally.

72. Compare Joseph Hall who writes in his Intro., "The intent of this Labor is to put some good Thoughts (Reader) into thy minds, which would not otherwise perhaps have tendered themselves to thee; such as I hope may not a little further thee on thy journey to Heaven." *Select Thoughts: One Century* (London, 1648), p. 9. He adds five "Supernumeraries" (pp. 296ff), which may be compared to Traherne's tenth section of the fifth *Century*. See also Alexander Ross, *A Centurie of Divine Meditations* (London 1646). A "century" can also mean *saeculum* or a lifetime. Stewart, p. 120.

73. G. Wade, for example, asserts that the *Centuries* "contain the most complete expression of Traherne's philosophy." p. 183. F. Löhrer thinks they are his chief work and evidence the last phase of his spiritual development in its fullness and perfection. p. 4.

his reader to complete this *Century* and perhaps add more of her own. Traherne may also have intended to contrast the perfection and infinity of God who leaves nothing unfinished (V C 4) with man who is finite and incomplete.

The question of completeness is intimately connected with that of internal structure. Various theories have attempted to explain the inner logic of the *Centuries*. [75] Traherne apparently has a general outline in mind. In the fourth *Century* he provides a rough sketch of a plan: "Enterance and Progress in Felicity. . .Principles. . .to enjoy it" (I).

b) Select Meditations, the most recently discovered manuscript of Traherne (1964), is now in the James M. Osborn collection at Yale University. It closely resembles the *Centuries* and appears to be an earlier version of the same idea. There was no hint that such a manuscript existed before it came to light in 1964.

The discovery of this manuscript is as interesting as that of the Dobell poetry and the *Centuries*. On a visit to England Mr. James Osborn's attention was drawn to a manuscript for sale in a book catalogue. He bought the manuscript by telephone, sight unseen, and had it sent to his office at Yale University for examination. There Prof. Louis Martz was asked for his opinion. Coincidently, the poem, "As in a Clock" (*CE*, p. 186; III C 21) which led Dobell to ascribe the poem and *Centuries* to Traherne also appears in the Select Meditations. It provided the final proof that this too was another long lost work of Thomas Traherne.

The bookseller refuses to disclose where he had secured the manuscript. In the front of the manuscript, however, there is a puzzling note (not of recent origin): "Bought near Montgomery." Montgomery is about fifty miles from Hereford. The manuscript contains the Select Meditations, a discourse on the soul, a "Meditation for Ash Wednesday" (229-230), and a "Meditation" (231-232). [76] Much of it appears to be fair

---

74. G. Wade thinks they were cut short by illness (p. 188); B. Dobell by death (*Centuries*, 1908, intr.); Marg that v. 10 is "a triumphant and perfect conclusion... The *Centuries* are not unfinished (I, xi)."

75. Whereas Löhrer thinks there is no inner grouping for classification of the *Centuries*, L. Martz sees them as "Augustinian in theme, in style, in method of meditation" and uses the *Itinerarium* of Bonaventura to explain the progression of thought of the *Centuries*. *Paradise*, pp. 54ff. See Marg, I, pp. 235-237, 253-256, 268-271, 281-284, 295 for detailed outlines of the *Centuries*.

copy in various styles of handwriting with comparatively few corrections. There are a number of pages left blank to which Traherne apparently intended to return (see SM III 86 and II 63). There are also many pages missing and misnumbered, as well as several procedural changes.[77]

5. Notebooks

There are also three notebooks which Traherne used for private study. Often derivative, seldom original, they are worthwhile in that they indicate what he read, what he thought was important in that reading, and with what he agreed.

a) The Early Notebook seems to have belonged to Thomas Traherne's brother Philip who made notes on the first five pages before Thomas took over the notebook and then again on pages 237-240 after Thomas's death. Thomas Traherne probably began to use the notebook while at Brasenose College (1653-1656).

In this notebook are Traherne's Latin epitomes of Eustache de Saint Paul's *Ethica*, [78] a geometry textbook (perhaps by Peter Ramus), and Justin's *History*. The remainder of the notebook may have been written later, perhaps while he was at St. Mary's, Credenhill. This latter part includes lengthy extracts from Francis Bacon's *De augmentis scientarum*, which is important for Traherne's ordering of knowledge, a quote from Bacon's *Apophthegmes* and one from his *Essays*.[79] Other works cited are Edward Reynold's *Treatise of the Passions and Faculties of the Soule of Man*,[80] an unidentified Latin religious text, and early poems, all of which reflect Traherne's early intellectual interests.[81] While Traherne's notes on

---

76. C. Marks thinks that the "Prayer for Ash Wednesday," "The Meditation," and SM III 89 are written in the same handwriting. "CYB," *Papers*, p. 32.

77. Among the misnumbered meditations are: II 25, 66, 78; IV 65, 87, 94; crossed out: II 17; omitted: II 41, 63; missing: IV 16, 17; I 95-100; II 68-71; III 18; skipped: III 39, II 63; blank: 220-228. As a procedural change, see SM II 59, 60 which Traherne indicates are to be reversed.

78. See discussion under part B 1 above.

79. Traherne's notes on *De Augmentis* comprise the longest section in the EN (69-170). They were probably copied after Traherne received his B. A. and thus mirror his own interests. Most of the notes are in English. C. Marks demonstrates that he summarizes, condenses, and selects what he is most interested in. Often he ignores Bacon's main points. He omits most of Bacon's scientific comments, his discussions of the soul, and of moral and civil knowledge. His notes reflect his concerns as a clergyman, according to C. Marks. "EN," *Papers*, 511-536 for a fuller discussion.

Eustache in his Early Notebook formed the basis of his *Christian Ethicks*, his notes on Bacon, Justin, Reynolds, and the Latin work on religion are seldom used or referred to elsewhere in his later writings.

b) The Ficino Notebook is so called because it consists mainly of extracts from Marsilio Ficino's Latin epitomes, his translations of Plato, and the "*Argumentum*" appended to Ficino's translation of Hermes Trismegistus.[82] There are also notes from "*Stoicismus Christianus*" and a Latin life of Socrates from an unknown source. Traherne's amanuensis copied into the notebook two passages from Gale's *Court of the Gentiles* (57v, 59v).[83]

c) The Commonplace Book, which includes the Dobell series of poems, was probably written in the last four years of Traherne's life during which he was aided by at least one amanuensis. It consists chiefly of notes in English from five works roughly in alphabetical order: Theophilus Gale's *Court of the Gentiles*, Part II (1670),[84] the *Divine Pymander* of Hermes Trismegistus in John Everard's translation (1657),[85] Henry More's *Divine Dialogues* (1668),[86] Isaac Barrow's sermon *On the Duty and Reward of*

---

80. C. Marks has shown that most of Traherne's notes on Reynolds are elaborations of statements of Bacon: Bacon's call for an orderly history of ancient philosophy (EN, p. 140); the relation of body and soul (EN, p 143); the relation of the fancy to the will and reason (p. 154). There may also be a reference to Reynolds in the *Centuries*. See II C 16.

81. See below.

82. Marsilio Ficino, the leader of the Platonic Academy in Florence, made Neoplatonism a major force in Western thought. Pico della Mirandola, Pomponazzi, and Zabarella were others in the movement. Ficino appreciated the Greek Fathers (particularly Origen) and thought that Platonism and Christianity were basically in agreement. He translated the *Corpus Hermeticum* (see below) and wrote the *Theologia Platonica*. Traherne simplifies, alters, and omits passages with which he does not agree. See C. Marks, "FN," *Papers*, 73-81. See Patrides, Intr.; P. O. Kristeller, *The Renaissance Philosophy of Man* (1947), p. 16; and Kristeller, *The Philosophy of Marsilio Ficino* (New York, 1943). There are also extended references to Pico della Mirandola, who wrote the *Oration on the Dignity of Man*, in IV C 73-78, 81. Traherne seems to agree with Pico's praise of man, but he also criticizes him. As Traherne puts it, there are important things "hidden under his free and luxuriant language" (*CE*, p. 225). There may also be echoes of Pico in the CYB (24v and 94) and the *Hex* (pp. 82-84). See *CE*, p. 340 and the bibliography cited above.

83. See footnote 84.

84. Traherne's notes on Gale were apparently written in part by an amanuensis who copied what Traherne directed. Traherne sometimes corrected his work. Traherne's notes seem freer than those of the amanuensis. Traherne condenses, paraphrases, and reworks Gale's book. Gale is the source of many of Traherne's classical references used elsewhere in Traherne's writings. See C. Marks, "CE," *Papers*, 459, 461-463. I have been unable to locate J. W. Proud's article "Traherne and Theophilus Gale," *Friends Quarterly Examiner* (April, 1916).

Bounty to the Poor (1671).[87] and Thomas Jackson's *Commentaries on the Creed* (1625, 1628, 1629, 1657).[88] There are shorter passages from many unidentified works, and some original passages. It was probably begun in 1670 and has close connections with *Christian Ethicks*.[89]

6. Missing Manuscripts

Roman Forgeries, Christian Ethicks, Daily Devotions, Life of Christ, Thanksgivings, and the *Hexameron* exist only in their original printed editions. (*Christian Ethicks,* the *Thanksgivings,* and the *Hexameron* have been reissued within the past thirty years.) There are holographs of the poetry, *Centuries,* Select Meditations, Church's Year Book, Early Notebook, Ficino Notebook, and Commonplace Book. Except for Milton, Traherne is the only major seventeenth century poet "whose works exist in their author's own handwriting." [90] The poetry and *Centuries* were not printed until the twentieth century.

There are a number of manuscripts known to be missing and perhaps there are others, like the Select Meditations discovered in 1964 about which

---

85. Most of the notes on Hermes are short. Traherne's amanuensis wrote ten entries, probably marked by Traherne for copying, and Traherne wrote twenty. Some of the material is used again in the *CE*, pp. 225-227, 228, 230, 290, especially the sections on "Man" and "Capacity." Ficino calls Hermes, the "*Primus. . . Theologiae Autor*" which Traherne copies into his FN (58). Traherne calls him "Magnum" (IV *C* 74). Ficino repeats many of the myths which had grown up around the Hermetic material: that Hermes was a contemporary of Moses, that he delivered laws, philosophy, and letters to the Egyptians, and that this knowledge was passed on through Orpheus, Pythagoras, and Plato. This information was later discredited by Mornay and Casaubon. Traherne reflects these doubts (*CE*, p. 230). Traherne agrees with certain aspects of Hermes' thought. There are contradictory passages in the CB (cf. "Fall" and "Fate"), but there are also many contradictions in the Hermetic material. Some of the difficulties lie in passages copied by Traherne's amanuensis. There are similarities in Traherne's and Hermes' high regard for man, interest in childhood, imagery, but there are also many differences. Hermes denigrates the body and tends toward asceticism. Traherne also criticizes Hermes because he "did not indicate the end" (*CE*, p. 230). The above information is based on C Marks, "Hermes," *Renaissance News* (1966), 118-131, and see Wade, pp. 217ff.
86. See ch. ii A.
87. Traherne copies Barrow carefully and exactly. According to Marks, Traherne is as interested in content well as form. See "CB," *Papers,* p. 463.
88. An amanuensis made notes on Jackson, except for four lines and a few changes made by Traherne, according to C. Marks. Jackson was considered an Arminian in his time. C. Marks, "CB," *Papers,* pp. 459-460, 463.
89. See C. Marks, "CB," *Papers,* pp. 458-465.
90. Anon., "Manuscripts of Thomas Traherne," *Bodleian Library Record,* 3 (1951), pp. 179-180.

nothing was known. Manuscripts for most of Traherne's printed works are probably no longer in existence. The manuscript of the original version of the poetry Philip revised in the Burney manuscript including the poetry not in the Dobell or Burney manuscript is known to be missing. Approximately forty pages are missing from the Select Meditations, and many critics assume that the first part of the Church's Year Book is missing.[91] A section of "For Trinity Sunday" of the Church's Year Book is definitely missing.

See the Appendix, pp 213–216, for recent scholarship and discovered manuscripts.

---

91.   See, however, part 3 above.

Chapter IV

Traherne and Systematic Theology

And therfore of all Kind of Learnings, Humanity and
Divinity are the most Excellent

(III C 41).

To understand Traherne's theological thought it is necessary first to
look at the theological heritage adapted and transmitted partly by
education, partly by controversy, and partly by practice (sermons,
catechetics, and popular piety).

A. Education and the Theological Tradition

Education plays a major role in forming a man's presuppositions and
approaches to knowledge. Unfortunately, comparatively little is known
about education in seventeenth century England.[1] Since it is not clear what
kind of elementary and secondary education Traherne received, only his
university education is discussed. Oxford and Cambridge were about the
same size and had approximately the same curriculum in the 1650s and
60s. Traherne's college, Brasenose, was the fourth largest college at Oxford.
Undergraduates of the time received most of their education in the college
rather than at the university, although they were supposedly required to
attend lectures and disputations at the university.[2]

---

1. Three of the most helpful works on this topic are those of W. T. Costello, *The Scholastic
   Curriculum in Early Seventeenth-Century Cambridge* (Cambridge, Mass., 1958); M. Curtis,
   Oxford and Cambridge in Transition 1958-1640 (Oxford, 1959); and H. Kearney, *Scholars and
   Gentlemen* (London, 1970). See also, James William Johnson, *The Formation of English
   Neoclassical Thought* (Princeton, 1967).
2. See Kearney, pp. 40ff and C. Wakeling, "The History of the College," *Brasenose*, vol. II, Part I,
   pp. 6ff.

After 1649 the *Directory of Worship* replaced the *Book of Common Prayer* in chapel services and the Covenant was made a test of orthodoxy, forcing some tutors to leave Brasenose.[3] There is no evidence of any change in the kind and quality of education during the Commonwealth from that immediately before or after. The student's notebooks of the 1650s are almost the same as those of the 1640s. In fact much of the core reading list remained the same until the early eighteenth century. Suarez, Aquinas, Burgersdicius, Eustache, Baronius, Scheibler are quoted in notebooks throughout the century both at Cambridge and Oxford. Ramus, Locke, Hobbes, Milton, and the other critics of scholasticism evidently had little influence.[4]

M. Curtis describes the prerequisites for the B.D. degree in the early seventeenth century, but he adds that the requirements may not have been faithfully observed in all areas. Traherne's B.D. degree may have had something to do with his appointment as chaplain to Sir Orlando Bridgeman in 1699. Normally, the B.D. degree was conferred on those who had had an M.A. for seven years. (Traherne's M.A. was conferred in 1661; his B.D. in 1669.) The candidate was presumed to have been in residence, to have attended lectures in divinity, and to have taken part in the disputations at the end of the term. He should also have responded once and have been an opponent once in two different disputations.[5] Seventeenth century education in general and theological education in particular remained scholastic, meaning, according to Costello, that it was "dialectical, Aristotelian, and highly systematized."[6] Scholasticism profoundly influenced both the curriculum and the mental habits of the age. As an undergraduate Traherne would have studied metaphysics, which was thought to be based on reason and not revelation. He would have learned to define the common attributes of being (the one, the true and

3. C. Wakeling notes that thirteen Brasenose fellows were expelled, two submitted and one stayed. p. 53.
4. Burgerdicius was read until 1744 and Eustache until the early eighteenth century. John Locke in his *Some Thoughts concerning Education* writes that the Burgersdicius's and the Scheibler's did not "swarm" in Seneca's era as they did in the seventeenth century. See Kearney, p. 161. Pierre de la Ramee (1513-1572) in his *Scholarum Metaphysicarum* denounces the "inexpiable crimes in certain Christian scholastics...to whom the metaphysics of Aristotle is a veritable pillar of the Christian Religion." See Kearney, p. 49.
5. See M. Curtis, p. 161.
6. Costello, p. 36; see also M. Curtis and M. Carré.

good) and would have been trained to use such terms as essence, form, substance, and nature. The scholastic principles of being (potency and act) are also essential in understanding aspects of Traherne's thought, as are the four causes (material, formal, efficient, and final). Even some of the ten categories or predicaments find their way into his theology.[7]

It is difficult to discover, however, in Traherne's writings any remnants of the three traditional scholastic exercises: lectures, disputations, declamations. One scholar has seen the *Roman Forgeries* as an outgrowth of disputation.[8] Traherne's "Treatise on the Soul" resembles Aquinas' parts, questions, articles; Scotus' parts, distinctions, questions; and Nicolas Felton's question and articles.[9]

Traherne has mixed reactions to his education. In one place he writes that knowledge, religion, piety, and wisdom would have been lost without education. It also improves, according to Traherne, the powers of the soul and awakens men to the dignity of their nature, the value of the creatures, and men's interest in them (*CE*, p. 60). Moreover, "Logick, Ethicks, Physicks, Metaphysicks, Geometry, Astronomy, Poesie, Medicine, Grammar, Musick, Rhetorick, all kind of Arts and Mechanicismes" of which he received a "Taste and Tincture" at Oxford "pertained to felicity" (III C 36). But elsewhere, Traherne attributes his loss of felicity in part to "the evil influence of a bad education" (III C 7). He castigates the manner and matter of his education (III C 37, 38), and he calls the scholastic disputes, *"De Ente De forma materiali, De Quid Dictate,"* empty and dry (SM III 30). However, he was able to build upon some of his earlier education in later years (see III C 36).

Traherne also openly disagrees with scholasticism. He thinks, for example, that all attributes are communicable, in contrast to the scholastics who think that some are incommunicable (SM IV 8). He considers the "Schoolmen's" definition of the divine image (true righteousness and holiness) too facile (SM III 30). Traherne thinks that it consists in ability, capacity, and power (which ironically is also scholastic terminology). Scholasticism was mediated to Traherne through his education and

7. The ten categories are: substance, quality, quantity, relations, actions, passions, where, when, site, and habit. See Costello, pp. 71ff and 77ff; and *CE*, pp. 23, 25, 125, 126; "Anticipation"; SM III 52; and Traherne's "Treatise on the Soul" in the SM.

8. Stewart, p. 16.

9. W. Costello, pp. 11-12.

reading. His notebooks indicate that he knew Aristotle, Aquinas, and Eustache.[10] The scholastic character of Traherne's ethical system is obvious, and scholastic thought is also integral to the ordering, terminology and content of his theology.[11]

The traditional bases of Christian theology, the creeds and confessions, were also influential in his age. The Anglican church of the seventeenth century accepted three ecumenical creeds (Apostolic, Nicene, and Athanasian), the four ecumenical councils, and was heir to a huge body of Catholic and Protestant (Calvinist, Arminian, and Lutheran) continental theology.[12] Traherne calls the Nicene Creed an Anglican <u>and</u> a Roman Catholic confession. It is, Traherne says, a confession of Protestants "for its own sake," and for its "conformity to the Scriptures." It is a "great authority," in fact "next to the Bible, the very first, and most indisputable there is" (*RF* Sig A 7). Distinctively Anglican are the Thirty-nine Articles, which also influenced his thought. However, Traherne's structuring of theological knowledge in the third *Century* is not patterned on that of the creeds, confessions or Thirty-nine Articles. A number of the subjects in the Articles are not treated in his known writings nor does he reflect the order in which they occur in his outline. He does adhere to their content (in contradistinction to their form).[13]

---

10. G. Wade asserts (perhaps too enthusiastically) that "Traherne knew the *Summa Theologica*; he was thoroughly master of that immense mass of material. It would not be too much to say that Traherne took from St. Thomas the whole scientific framework of his system of ethics." "St. Thomas Aquinas and Thomas Traherne," *Blackfriars*, 12 (1931), 666-673. Traherne is not an isolated instance of the influence of Aquinas on seventeenth century thought. John K. Ryan in *The Reputation of St. Thomas Aquinas Among English Protestant Thinkers of the Seventeenth Century* develops the thesis that the "works of Thomas Aquinas were known and widely used throughout the seventeenth century."

11. *CE*, xxxi-xxxvi. See Traherne's outline of theology (III C 41-45) where he retains the traditional categories of the powers, inclinations, and faculties of the soul, and develops the concept "Natural Philosophy" in terms of nature, quality, affection, relations, causes, and ends.

12. Article VIII of the Thirty-nine Articles states that the Nicene, Athanasian, and Apostles creeds ought "to be received and believed, for they may be proved by most certain warrents of Holy Scripture." John Cosin in his *The Religion, Discipline and Rules of the Church of England* (London, 1707) writes that after the Scriptures, the Church of England holds as authorities the three creeds, the four Councils, and the first five centuries, reflecting widespread Anglican belief of the time.

13. See chs. v-vii for discussions of the Thirty-nine Articles and Traherne's theology. Traherne does not include sections on the creeds, oaths, free will, works, descent into hell, purgatory, speaking in tongues, and excommunication in his outline of theology.

B. Systematic Theology in Seventeenth Century England

There are only a few extant writings by Traherne's lecturers and tutors. An examination of the few theological works of the lecturers he is likely to have heard reveals very little influence or similarity in theme or style. Perhaps the most similar in theological structure is that of Thomas Adams (1633?-1670), lecturer in Humanities in 1656 and Greek in 1655. His *Main Principles of Christian Religion in 107 Articles* is a solid and somewhat formalistic work, but it bears some resemblance to Traherne's suggestion for the ordering of theology. Adams' other work *Protestant Union, Principles of Religion wherein the Dissenters agree with the Church of England* is very different from Traherne's public attitude toward dissent. Adams was removed in 1662 for Nonconformity.

Writings of other lecturers at Brasenose during Traherne's time such as John Burscough,[14] Richard Adams,[15] Thomas Frankland,[16] Richard Duckworth,[17] bear little relation to his theological thought. Traherne's thought shows some affinities to Brasenose men before his time such as Robert Burton,[18] Edward Fisher,[19] and Jeremy Taylor,[20] as well as to contemporaries in other colleges at Oxford.[21] Particularly interesting are the varying attitudes toward Nonconformity among some of his contemporaries.[22]

In addition to knowing the approximate contents of the curriculum, the doctrinal sources and standards of the time, and some of his teachers, various reading lists for theology students of the time are in existence. Particularly useful is the one attributed to Thomas Barlow[23] or Richard Baxter[24] entitled *A Library for Younger Schollers* which though compiled perhaps in 1655 reflects earlier lists. The reading list is evidently intended

---

14. Burscough was Vice Principal in 1656 and wrote *England's Great Happiness* (London, 1677).
15. Adams was Senior Bursar in 1654 and wrote *The earthly and Heavenly Building opened* (London, 1699).
16. Frankland was Latin lecturer in 1655 and later was infamous for his imposture as a medical doctor. He wrote *The Annals of King James and King Charles the First* (London, 1681).
17. Duckworth was lecturer in Humanity in 1654-55, and in Natural Philosophy in 1653. He wrote *Tintinnalogia or the Art of Ringing* (bells) in 1671.
18. 1577-1640. See Bush, pp. 295-301.
19. Fisher wrote *The Marrow of Modern Divinity* (1645).
20. 1613-67. See Bush, pp. 329-325.

for the younger clergy of the Anglican church. The author advises that to be a "knowing, & wel grounded Divine," a "matter of sweat & Industrie," one should study natural and supernatural divinity.[25] To accomplish this it is necessary to "get an exact Systeme of Theology."[26] That advice is echoed in a note of Bacon which Traherne copied into his Early Notebook, "it is more profitable to read systems of Arts and Sciences. . .and to lay aside polemical tracts and scattered Digressions" (*EN*, p. 96).

These suggestions would not necessarily have been welcomed by all students of divinity. John Donne thinks that "Moral divinity becomes us all, but natural divinity and Metaphysic divinity, almost all may spare."[27] Lest such sentiments be attributed only to a poetic nature, it should be noted that Benjamin Whichcote, the central figure of Cambridge Platonism, also detests "Divinity methodized."[28]

---

21. Admitted the same year as Traherne (1653), James Arderne wrote The *Kingdom of England the best commonwealth* (1660); *True Christians Character and Crown* (1671); and *Directions concerning the matter and style of sermons* (1671). Henry Hesketh, who also matriculated in 1653, wrote *The Dangerous and almost desperate state of religion*; *Piety the best rule of orthodoxy*; *The charge of scandal*; and *The importance of religion to young scholars.* Matriculated in 1654, Joshua Stopford wrote *The way and methods of Rome's advancement* (1672) and *The several ways of resolving faith in the Roman and Reformed Churches* (1677), the first of which is somewhat similar to Traherne's *Roman Forgeries*. Other Brasenose men of the time were Elias Ashmole, matriculated in 1644, who founded the Ashmolean museum and William Petty, matriculated in 1649, lecturer in anatomy and math and renowned scientist of his age. William Earbury or Erbury, matriculated in 1620, was a noted sectarian, perhaps a Seeker, and later an army chaplain. John Locke was the most famous contemporary of Traherne's at Oxford.

22. Thomas Adams was removed for Nonconformity, but Thomas Good (perhaps the "T.G." in Traherne's SM) wrote *Firmianus and Dubitantius or certain Dialogues concerning Atheism, Infidelity, Popery and other Heresies and Schisms* (1674) and Henry More wrote *Enthusiasmus Triumphatus* (1656) against Enthusiasm.

23. Barlow was librarian at the Bodleian from 1642 to 1660. Traherne refers to him in *RF*, p. 90.

24. Baxter was a Presbyterian divine, who with others discussed the problems of the Restoration settlement with Sir Orlando Bridgeman and his chaplain, Hezekiah Burton. Eric Jacobsen attributes the *Library* to Baxter, but Alma de Jordy and Harris Fletcher, editors of the *Library*, attribute it to Barlow.

25. *A Library for Younger Schollers*, ed. Alma de Jordy and Harris Francis Fletcher, *Illinois Studies in Language and Literature*, XLVIII (Urbana, 1961), pp. 18-190.

26. *Library*, p. 39.

27. See McAdoo, p. 13.

28. See Petrides, *Cambridge*, p. 23. John Smith says that Jesus would not "draw [divine truth] into any system or body." *Cambridge*, ed. Cragg, p. 82. Against these criticisms of systematizing, Bacon writes that "all divisions of knowledge be accepted and used rather for lines to mark or distinguish, than sections to divide and separate them." Bacon, IV. 1, p. 373.

The Library supplies the "Younger Scholler" with copious reading lists in dogmatic theology and in other areas. The highly recommended or essential reading list includes the dogmatic texts of Zacharias Ursinus,[29] William Ames,[30] Polyander à Kirchoven,[31] Ludovicus Cappellus,[32] and Ludovicus Crocius.[33] As supplementary reading the *Library* suggests Amandus Polanus,[34] Lucas Trelcatius,[35] John Lawson,[36] Heinrich Bullinger, Peter Martyr, Wolfgang Musculus, Marcus Wendelinus,[37] Johannes Wollebius,[38] Bartholomew Keckermann,[39] Erasmus Sarcerius,[40] and M. Marci Beumleri.[41] Indicating the theological stance of the author of the *Library* is his final suggestion that the young divine should read "Calvin's *Institutions*...that you may know its Doctrine for its Soundnesse."[42] This list can be compared to another list, "A Catalogue of Bookes for a Young Divine to make use of given by Dr. Conant to a Friend, upon his Request," which includes references to Wollebius, Ursinus, Calvin, Wendelinus, and Polyander à Kirchoven. Conant's list includes James Ussher and Heinrich Alting who were not on the *Library* reading list.[43] Neither of the two lists mentions the two Puritans who attempted to write systematic works on the whole range of Christian theology: Dudley Fenner (*Sacra theologia*) and William Perkins (*Armilla aurea*).

A practical suggestion in the Library "for the Improvement of your Reason" sheds light on three Traherne manuscripts. The author of the *Library* suggests that the young divine "Get two Common Place Bookes."

---

29. Ursinus, *Corpus doctrinae orthodoxae* (Heidelberg, 1616 and London, 1646).

30. Ames, *Medulla SS. theologiae*, 4th ed. (London, 1630).

31. Polyander, *Synopsis purioris theologiae* (Leyden, 1625).

32. Cappellus, *Theses theologicae* (Saumur, 1641-51).

33. Crocius, *Syntagma sacrae theologiae*, 4 vols. (Bremen, 1616).

34. Polanus, *Syntagma theologicae* (Hanover, 1609).

35. Trelcatius, *A brief institution of the common places of sacred divinitie* (London, 1610).

36. Lawson, *Gleanings and expositions of some of the more difficult places of Scripture* (London, 1646).

37. Musculus, *Compendium Christianae religionis* (Zurich, 1556); Wendelinus, *Christianae theologiae* (Hanover, 1634).

38. Wollebius, *Christianae theologiae compendium* (Amsterdam, 1633).

39. Keckermann, *Systema theologiae* (Hanover, 1602).

40. Sarcerius, *Methodus in praecipuous scripturae divinae locos* (Basel, 1546).

41. Beumleri, *Hypotyposis theologiae methodice et scholasticae exarata* (Zurich, 1607).

42. *Library*, p. 43.

43. *Library*, p. 50. John Conant. (1608-94). Ussher, *A body of divinitie* (London, 1645). Alting, *Methodus theologiae didacticae* (Groningen, 1645).

One of them should be for reference with author, chapter, and page number of a particular quotation listed under each heading. The other should contain the most important notes of the "Scholler's" reading.[44] Traherne's Commonplace Book follows the first suggestion, although Traherne is, unfortunately, not so precise with regard to author, chapter, and page number of his references. His Early Notebook and Ficino Notebook follow the second suggestion.

Traherne's notebooks provide yet another insight into his ongoing education. Although they do not indicate all his reading, they do provide helpful clues. Traherne read other theological writings which were neither a part of the university curriculum of the time, nor listed in reading lists, nor mentioned in his notebooks. Particularly intriguing is the possibility that Independent, sectarian, or other exotic theological streams of thought influenced him. A study of a sampling of those sources probably available to Traherne has yielded little which approximates Traherne's own method of structuring theology.[45]

C. Traherne's Proposal (III *Century* 42-45): "A Mind in Frame"

The scholastic milieu is evident in Traherne's love of order. One of his recurrent concepts is that of a "Mind in Frame," and he was apparently fascinated by the idea of things in their "proper places."[46] He believes not only in a theology of orders (*Thanks*, p. 223; *CE*, p. 256), but also in an orderly theology. His poetic talent, too, might underscore this aspect of his personality, since rhythm and rhyme also require a sense of order.

Another evidence of Traherne's systematizing mind is his tendency to catalogue, to pile up lists, to exhaust a concept (see *Hex* passim). There are a number of outlines scattered throughout his works,[47] even though he is somewhat disparaging about composing systems, labeling it an "Art" (in contrast to a "Science"). According to Traherne, this "Art" or "Habit" is

44. *Library*, p. 50.
45. See ch. ii A
46. See I C 10; III C 3. 60; *CE*, pp. 255-256. Traherne also uses the concept of the great "Chain of Being" ("Fullnesse" 58).
47. See, for example, *CE*, pp. 4, 5, 7, 23, 24, 41. There is a more traditional outline of divinity at the conclusion of the third *Century* (100) which is not as comprehensive as the one in 41-45.

used in "composing Tracts and Systems," "Fiddling and Dancing," and is "usefull in Teachers for the Instruction of others." He thinks that the regulated life and noble deeds are more important than the practice of this art which is scarcely a virtue (*CE*, p. 24). These statements must be seen in the light of Traherne's practice which reflects a "Homogeneal Learning" (EN, p. 140), an orderly history of ancient philosophies (EN, p. 139), and "systems of Arts and Sciences & continued Discourses." [48]

The frequent catalogues, outlines, and systems scattered throughout Traherne's writings are not intended to display his grasp of scholasticism, his orderly mind, or his ability in academia, but rather to exhibit his ideas so that like the virtues "their Place and Office will appear in their Tendency towards mans last End, his Blessedness and Glory" (*CE*, p. 28).

The most comprehensive and fascinating outline Traherne suggests is found in a section of the third Century devoted to learning. This particular structuring of theology encompasses "Humanity," "Divinity," "Natural Philosophy," and "Ethicks." L. Martz, like C. Stranks (two of the few commentators on this passage), thinks that Traherne is depicting the evolution of thought in the seventeenth century: "Humanity" leading to a study of "Divinity" and then to the study of "Natural Philosophy" and "Ethicks." [49] Whatever else these four sections of the third *Century* might be, they also appear to be a useful way of understanding Traherne's concept of theology. Traherne's system compares favorably in scope with other theological systems of the time. Most of the traditional doctrines of dogmatics are included, but it is what Traherne adds which makes his system so distinctive.

Traherne not only combines the traditional scholastic ordering of the parts of theology with the Calvinist four estates theory, but he also includes "Natural Philosophy," "Ethicks," and "Humanity" in his purview of "the Materials of Religion" (III C 45). His system thus is an amalgam of theology and philosophy (metaphysics, physics, ethics) for which there seems to be little or no precedent. [50]

This is not to say that had Traherne written a "Body of Divinity," he would necessarily have used this third *Century* outline. He revised, for

---

48. Traherne's notes are from Reynolds and Bacon. See also Traherne's note: "strict Methods" by which the "Arts and Sciences are over straitlaced" are to be avoided (EN, p. 100; see p. 102).
49. Martz, *Paradise*, p. 89; Stranks, *Anglican*, p. 113.
50. Traherne does not consider mathematics, which was usually considered a part of philosophy.

example, the outline of *Christian Ethicks* many times (see *CE*, pp. 94, 216). Nor is this to suggest that Traherne intended to write a dogmatics. Nevertheless, the outline he composed in the third *Century* is useful, not only for describing his theological thought, but also for understanding what he thought theology included and how it is to be structured. It provides a perspective, a way of viewing his theology, which is preferable to any externally or artificially imposed ordering. Traherne's ordering of the "Materials of Religion" thus provides the outline for chapters five through nine in this study (slightly revised for the purposes of this study). Significantly, the text of the outline in the original manuscript is remarkably free from any corrections and additions, which might suggest that Traherne had the structure clearly in mind when he wrote it down.[51]

Traherne's fourfold division of "Learnings" or "the Materials of Religion" seems to be unique in the history of theology. On the basis of the seventeenth century curriculum and reading lists, Traherne's notebooks, and a sampling of some of the literature available to him, Francis Bacon's *De Augmentis* could be considered the closest parallel for Traherne's fourfold division. In his *De Augmentis Scientarum* (which Traherne read and noted in detail, see EN, pp. 69-170) Bacon divides all knowledge into divinity and philosophy. By divinity Bacon does not mean natural divinity but sacred and inspired divinity. Bacon further divides philosophy into three areas of knowledge: God, nature, and humanity.[52] In his own studies Bacon omits any major discussion of divinity, because he does not feel competent to comment on theological matters. At least in this respect, Traherne supplements Bacon. In most details, however, Bacon's structuring is not similar enough to Traherne's to be considered a source or an exact parallel. Traherne's very inclusion of "Natural Philosophy" among the "Materials of Religion" transgresses one of Bacon's first principles, that theology and science are not to be mixed.[53] Furthermore, Bacon does not include ethics in his structure.

Another possible source for Traherne's general quadripartite schema might be "Philosophy" in general and "Metaphysics" in particular, as they were traditionally developed in the textbooks of the time. Traherne

---

51. See photocopies prefacing chapters v–ix.

52. Bacon, III, I, pp. 336, 337.

53. See Anderson, *The Philosophy of Francis Bacon* (Chicago, 1948).

probably studied these disciplines and was probably familiar with Eustache de Saint Paul's *Summa Philosophae Quadripartita*.[54] Eustache's *Summa Philosophae* might at least have suggested the quadripartite structure. Eustache's work consists of dialectics (which Traherne omits), ethics (*de rebus Moralibus* upon which Traherne based his *Christian Ethicks*), physics (*De rebus Naturalibus*), and metaphysics. Eustache does not include "Divinity" nor what Traherne calls "Humanity." There are some similarities in the details of the two structures, but there are not enough for Eustache to be Traherne's direct source.

Less comprehensive, but vaguely similar, is the suggestion of the *Library* which divides theology into "Humanity" and "Divinity." However, a comparison of the concept "Humanity" in the two systems shows the preconceptions and subheadings to be quite different. For example, the divine attributes, traditional in scholasticism, belong to "Natural Divinity" in the *Library* but in Traherne to "Divinity" proper.[55] Traherne's section on "Humanity" seems to be something like a "natural" doctrine of man, and a major part of his "Divinity" is a "revealed" doctrine of man. This is different from the *Library* in which "Humanity" is another word for "Natural Theology," as was the case for Bacon and the other systems of the time. Traherne approximates the contemporary understanding of natural theology in a section of his *Christian Ethicks* (p. 118).

Of the four individual sections of Traherne's schema, "Humanity" and "Natural Philosophy" are the most difficult to place in relation to traditional theology.[56] Traherne's section on "Humanity" appears to be virtually a psychology of man with elements of "Divinity."

The first section of "Divinity" (on God) is fairly traditional and trans-confessional with only minor restructuring by Traherne. Useful comparisons can be made to the first part of Lewis Bayly's *Practice of Piety*[57] and Thomas Adams' *The main principles of Christian religion*. Adams includes discussions of the "Principles," the end and means of religion, essence of God, decrees, creation, providence, sin, the covenant of

---

54. Traherne has extensive notes on Eustache's *Ethica* in his EN, and he bases his *Christian Ethicks* on it.

55. *Library*, pp. 18-19.

56. See discussions in chs. v and viii below.

57. Ch. 1 of the *Practice* deals with the essence, persons and attributes of God; ch. II with the miseries of man; and ch. iii with the blessed state.

works and grace, but the book is more traditional in outline and content than anything Traherne wrote.[58]

Thomas Jackson's *Treatise on the Divine Essence and Attributes* (1628) from which Traherne made copious notes in his Commonplace Book, goes into far more detail on God's "Essence and Attributes" than does Traherne, but Jackson is far less comprehensive in scope. Section I "Of the Absolutely Infinite and incomprehensible Essence in General," is followed by four chapters which elaborate on essence and infinity. Section II describes in detail the other attributes of God including a chapter on "the Eternall and Immutable Decree." There is also a section in Jackson entitled "Of Divine Providence in general" of which the doctrine of Creation is a subtopic.[59] Edward Reynold's *Treatise of the Passions and Faculties of the Soule of Man* (1640), whose title approximates some of Traherne's subsections and which Traherne read and noted, is not a source.[60]

Of the various dogmatic theologies Traherne is known to have read none is as close to his outline as two to which he does not refer: those of Aquinas and Wollebius. J. Wollebius' *Christianae theologiae compendium* (Amsterdam, 1633) is a supplemental reading suggestion both of the *Library* and of Conant. It was translated into English by Alexander Ross. It is the closest verbal and structural parallel to Traherne's section on divinity and his entire outline. It is not known, however, if Traherne read Wollebius. Wollebius is not quoted in Traherne's writings, but in a Brasenose, "Pupill Booke of Accounts" of Traherne's time (i.e. a list of books a student bought) there is reference to Wollebius' *Compendium.* [61]

The following parallel columns indicate the similarities of Aquinas and Wollebius to Traherne's section on "Divinity."

Traherne	Wollebius	Aquinas
"the Unity of His Essence"	ch.1 "Of the Essence of God"	"Existence" of God
"the Trinity of Persons"		
"His Manifold Attributes"		attributes of God ["Providence"]

58. Adams has four main sections in his book: the creed, the commandments, the gospel (sacraments), and the Lord's Prayer (London, 1675).
59. See Jackson's *Commentaries on the Creed* (London, 1625-1657.
60. Traherne copied large sections of this work into his EN, but there are no similarities in details with Traherne's outline.
61. See Wakeling, p. 19.

Traherne	Wollebius	Aquinas
"His Works/Internal External,"	2 "Concerning the Works of God, and the Decrees"	
"his Counsels and Decrees"	4 "Of Predestination"	"Predestination"
"the Work of Creation"	5 "Of the Creation"	"Treatise on Creation"
"His works of Providence"	6 "God's Active Providence"	
	7 angelology	"Treatise on the Angels"
"Man"	8 man	"Treatise on Man"

Traherne's other subheadings in his section on "Divinity" are similar to those of other theologies of various confessions and countries of the time, and Traherne does not appear to be following any one school of thought.[62]

The second part of "Divinity" (on Man) is complicated by the combination of the four estates categorization with the traditional scholastic headings for individual doctrines. Most unusual, from both the Protestant and Catholic point of view, is the way Traherne relegates Christology and Scripture to subheadings of his section on man in the "Estate of Grace." Christology was a major part of most traditional and seventeenth century dogmatic theologies, and the first chapters of the works of any Calvinist theologians of the time were devoted to the "Doctrine of the word."[63] Others (Alting and Keckerman, for example) began with the nature of theology and then proceeded to the nature of God.

The "Estates" theory was fairly common in Traherne's day, although among theologians the number and names of the estates varies.[64] One can even find a precedent in Aquinas.[65] The closest verbal and structural parallel, however, seems to be Wollebius. The doctrine of man in the

---

62. See ch. vi.

63. See Ussher; Alting; Polanus; Jackson; and William Perkins, *Bodie of Scripture and Theology* (London, 1621), for examples. Calvin, however, in his *Institutes* devotes his first chapters to the problem of knowledge, as does Robert Barclay (a Quaker) in his An *Apology for the True Christian Divinity* (1678).

64. Traherne also refers to the four estates in the *Thanks* (II 307), the CYB (48v), and the SM (III 37, 53). Polanus works with three estates, but compare Wollebius, Richard Baxter, Ussher, Trelcatius, William Perkins, and Thomas Jackson.

65. *Compendium*, ch. 186: "The Commands laid on the First Man, His Perfection in the Pristine State;" and ch. 187: "The State of Original Justice."

system of Wollebius follows immediately after the doctrine of God, as in Traherne, except that a chapter on angelology comes between in Wollebius (see chart above). Traherne mentions angels only in his last section on "the State of Glory."

Wollebius, like Traherne, elaborates on "the Government of Man in the State of Innocency," "Of the Fall," "Of Original Sinne, and Free Will," "Of Actual Sinne," and "Of the Miseries which follow Sinne" in chapters eight through twelve. However, the intervening chapters (thirteen through nineteen) of Wollebius on the law, the person and office of Christ differ from Traherne's ordering. Chapters twenty through twenty two of Wollebius "Of the common vocation to the State of Grace," "Of the Covenant of Grace," and "Of the Seals or Sacraments of the Covenant of Grace in general" are parallel to Traherne's structure, as are the following chapters of Wollebius on the church and its administration. The remaining chapters of Wollebius' first book are not similar to Traherne. The intention of the second book of Wollebius is similar to Traherne's section on "Ethicks."

"Natural Philosophy," which Traherne defines as "all Humanity and Divinity together," has apparently no prototype in the history of theology.[66] The form of Traherne's third *Century* section on "Ethicks" bears little resemblance to his *Christian Ethicks* which he wrote later, although the presuppositions and content are somewhat similar. Often a section on ethics or virtues was included in traditional dogmatic theologies.[67]

In his outline Traherne omits a number of doctrines which were usually a part of both traditional and seventeenth century dogmatic theology.[68] In this study of Traherne's theology these are subsumed under existing headings with similar themes or inserted where they occur in traditional systems. Although Traherne does not develop in detail every one of the topics he lists in his system, it is striking how comprehensive his theological thought is.[69] What is more, Traherne's somewhat eclectic and

---

66. See discussions in ch. viii.

67. See discussion in ch. ix, and *CE*, xxxi-xxxiii. Compare Traherne's other discarded outline on ethics which he wrote out on the flyleaf of the manuscript of the *Centuries*. See the works of Aquinas, Wollebius, Polanus, and Musculus.

68. See note 13 above. Among them are the doctrine of the Holy Spirit, free will, conversion, sanctification, grace, death, devil and hell.

unconventional system outlined in the third *Century* is best seen in the light of traditional and seventeenth century orthodox dogmatic theologies. At least in structure, his system bears little resemblance to theological works like those of Boehme or Fox which are outside the mainstream of Christian thought.

He recommends that "evry man ought to spend his time, in studying diligently Divine Philosophy" (IV *C* 3) and ought to "dive to the Bottom of true Religion," but not be "Dazled with its Superficial Appearance" (*CE*, p. 35). Religion for Traherne is not merely moralism or activism, but it consists rather in the ten commandments, the two sacraments, the Lord's Prayer, and the "Articles of our Faith" which he calls the "objects of Enjoyment proposed to Speculation which we ought to know as clearly as our faces, as familiarly as our goods as fully as our houses" (SM III 58). Elsewhere he states that the "business of Religion" is the love of God, angels, men and inferiour creatures (*CE*, p. 219). Religion for Traherne is both natural and revealed, and includes both ethics and doctrine (*CE*, pp. 60-61). Traherne also acknowledges that there is false doctrine and heresy (CYB 59v; 17r).

Although doctrine and speculation, law and liturgy are part and parcel of the theological thought of Thomas Traherne, his theology does not accord with Schleiermacher's (1768-1834) description of dogmatic propositions: "doctrines of the descriptively didactic type, in which the highest possible degree of definiteness is aimed at."[70] Due perhaps in part to Traherne's poetic nature, he was seldom overtly didactic or definite, choosing to arrive at the truth experientially. Moreover, the use of the term system to describe the structure of Traherne's theological thought is not to be understood in the same sense, for example, as it would be in a description of the philosophical thought of Spinoza, but rather as "a unified interpretation of the world."[71]

Traherne's approach to theology seems to have been both synthetic (from cause to effect) and analytic (from effect to cause). Essentially it is

---

69.   See the comments in *CE*, xlvii; M. Lloyd in a review of Anne Ridler's edition of the *Poems, Centuries* and *Thanksgivings* writes that "We shall probably be disappointed if we expect from Traherne a consistent system of religious thought." *RES* (1967), 201. G. Wade thinks the CE is "hopelessly bad, full of digressions, incomplete, confused" (p. 140).

70.   F. Schleiermacher, *The Christian Faith*, vol. I, ed. H. R. Mackintosh and J. S. Stewart. Harper Torchbook (New York, 1963), p. 78.

more analytic in that he derives the whole from a particular starting point: felicity. "Felicity is the key that opens all things" (SM III 52) including the theological thought of Traherne.[72] For Luther, perhaps, the starting point is the question, "How can I find a gracious God," for Kierkegaard, the starting point is perhaps paradox, for Schleiermacher, perhaps, the starting point is the absolute feeling of dependence. Traherne maintains that the study of felicity brings one "to the Delineation of God's Kingdom, to the Discovery of His Nature, to a sight of Eternity, to the original of Sin, to the Excellency of Good Works, to the nature of the Soul, to the Reasons of Liberty, to all things in Heaven and Earth...to the House of Wisdom," as well as to the understanding of the "original Nature, Offices, Effects, Consequences" of virtue (SM III 53).

The text of Traherne's outline of the "Materials of Religion" has few corrections or alterations indicating that Traherne had it clearly in mind when he wrote it down. Photocopies of the manuscript precede the relevant chapters pertaining to his outline. A transcription of the manuscript sections of his outline is printed out in its entirety here to indicate its scope and to facilitate comparison.

Third *Century* 42

> By Humanity we search into the Powers and Faculties of the Soul, enquire into the Excellencies of Humane Nature, consider its Wants, Survey its Inclinations: Propensities and Desires. Ponder its Principles Proposals and Ends, Examine the Causes and fitness of all, the Worth of all, the Excellency of all. Whereby we com to know what Man is in this World, What his Soveraign End and Happiness, and what is the Best Means by which He may attain it. And by this we com to see what Wisdom is: Which namely is a Knowledg Exercised in finding out the Way to Perfect Happiness, by discerning Mans real Wants and Soveraign desires. We com more over to Know Gods Goodness, in seeing into the Causes,

---

71. F. C. Copleston's words describing the thought of Aquinas in *Aquinas*, p. 54. Wollebius defines theology or divinity as "that knowledge of God, which a Christian may attain unto in this life out of God's Word." It is a "System or collection of precepts, therefore it is defined by the word Doctrine." pp. 1, 2.

72. Martin Schmidt notes that the equation of holiness and happiness is a constant feature of English theological writings, including: Arthur Dent, *The Plain Man's Pathway to Heaven* (1625), pp. 85, 115ff; Thomas Hooker, *The Soul's Benefit from Union with Christ* (1638), pp. 60-61; Richard Gibbs, *The Saint's Happinesse* (1639), pp. 29ff. Schmidt, *John Wesley*, trans. N. Goldhawk (London, 1962), p. 308.

wherfore He implanted such faculties and Inclinations in us, and the Objects, and Ends prepared for them. This leadeth us to Divinity. For God gav Man an Endless Intellect to see All Things, and a Proneness to covet them, becaus they are His Treasures; and an infinit Variety of Apprehensions and Affections, that he might hav an Allsufficiency in Him self to Enjoy them; A Curiositie Profound and Unsatiable to stir him up to look into them: An Ambition Great and Everlasting to Carry him to the Highest Honors Thrones and Dignities. An Emulation wherby he might be animated and Quickned by all Examples, a Tenderness and Compassion wherby He may be united to all Persons; A Sympathy and Lov to Vertu, a Tenderness of His Credit in evry Soul, that he might Delight to be Honored in all Persons: an Ey to behold Eternity and the Omnipresence of GOD, that he might see Eternity and Dwell within it: A Power of Admiring Loving and Prizing, that seeing the Goodness and Beauty of God, He might be United to it for evermore.

Third *Century* 43

In Divinity we are entertained with all Objects from Everlasting to Everlasting: becaus with Him whose Outgoings from Everlasting: being to Contemplat GOD, and to Walk with Him in all His Ways: And therfore to be Entertained with all Objects, as He is the Fountain, Governor, and End of them. We are to Contemplat GOD in the Unity of His Essence, in the Trinity of Persons, in His Manifold Attributes, in all His Works, Internal and External, in his Counsels and Decrees, in the Work of Creation, and in His Works of Providence. And Man, as he is a Creature of GOD, capable of Celestial Blessedness, and a Subject in His Kingdom: in his fourfold Estate of Innocency, Misery, Grace and Glory. In the Estate of Innocency we are to Contemplate the Nature and Maner of His Happiness, the Laws under which He was governed, the Joys of Paradice, and the Immaculat Powers of His Immortal Soul. In the Estate of Misery we hav his Fall the Nature of Sin Original and Actual, His Manifold Punishments Calamity Sickness Death &c. In the Estate of Grace; the Tenor of the New Covenant, the maner of its Exhibition under the various Dispensations of the Old and New Testament, the Mediator of the Covenant, the Conditions of it Faith and Repentance, the Sacraments or Seals of it, the Scriptures Ministers and Sabbaths, the Nature and Government of the Church, its Histories and Successions from the Beginning to the End of the World. &c. In the State of Glory; the Nature of Seperat Souls, their Advantages Excellencies and Privileges, the Resurrection of the Body, the Day of Judgment and Life Everlasting. Wherein further we are to see and understand the Communion of Saints, Heavenly Joys, and our Society with Angels. To all which I was naturaly

Born to the fruition of all which I was by Grace redeemed, and in the Enjoyment of all which I am to liv Eternally.

Third *Century* 44

Natural Philosophy teaches us the Causes and Effects of all Bodies simply and in them selvs. But if you extend it a little further, to that indeed which its Name imports, signifying the Lov of Nature, it leads us into a Diligent inquisition into all Natures, their Qualities, Affections, Relations, Causes and Ends, so far forth as by Nature and Reason they may be Known. And this Noble Science, as such is most Sublime and Perfect, it includes all Humanity and Divinity together GOD, Angels, Men, Affections, Habits, Actions, Virtues; Evry Thing as it is a Solid intire Object singly proposed, being a subject of it, as well as Material and visible Things But taking it as it is usualy Bounded in its Terms, it treateth only of Corporeal Things, as Heaven, Earth Air Water, Fire, the Sun and Stars, Trees Herbs, flowers, Influences, Winds, Fowles Beasts Fishes Minerals, and Precious Stones; with all other Beings of that Kind. And as thus it is taken it is Nobly Subservient to the Highest Ends: for it Openeth the Riches of Gods Kingdom and the Natures of His Territories Works and Creatures in a Wonderfull Maner, Clearing and Preparing the Ey of the Enjoyer.

Third *Century* 45

Ethicks teach us the Mysteries of Moralitie, and the Nature of Affections Virtues and Maners, as by them we may be Guided to our Highest Happiness. The former for Speculation, this for Practice. The former furnisheth us with Riches, this with Honors and Delights, the former feasteth us, and this instructeth us. For by this we are taught to liv Honorably among men, and to make our selvs Noble and Usefull among them. It teacheth us how to Manage our Passions, to Exercise Virtues, and to form our Maners, so as to liv Happily in this World. And all these put together Discover the Materials of Religion to be so Great, that it Plainly manifesteth the Revelation of GOD to be Deep and Infinit. For it is impossible for Language, Miracles, or Apparitions to teach us the Infallibility of GODs Word or to shew us the Certainty of true Religion, without a Clear Sight into Truth it self that is into the Truth of Things. Which will them selvs when truly seen, by the very Beauty and Glory of them, best Discover, and Prov Religion.

These four meditations of the third *Century*, then, provide the outline for chapters five through nine of this study (slightly modified for outlining purposes).

Chapter V

"Humanity"

42.

By Humanity we search into the Powers & faculties of the Soul, enquire into the Excellencies of Humane Nature, consider its Wants, Survey its Inclinations Proportions & Defires. The Principles Proposals & Ends, Examine the Causes & fitness of ... the Worth of all, the Excellency of all. Whereby we com to know what Man is in this World, what His Sovereign End & Happiness, & what is the Best Means by which He may attain it. And by this we com to see what Wisdom is: ... namely is a Knowledg Exercised in finding out the Soveraign Defires. We com more over to know Mans real Wants & Soveraign Defires. We com more over to know Gods Goodness, in peering into the Caufes, wherefore He implanted such faculties & Inclinations in us, & the Objects, & Ends prepared for them. This leadeth us to Divinity. for God gav man an Endless Intellect to fee All Things, & a Pronenefs to covet them, becaus they are His Creatures; & an infinit variety of Apprehenfions & Affections, that he might hav an All fufficiency in Himself to Enjoy them: of Curiofitie profound & Unfatiable to ftir him up to look into them: Oln Ambition Great & Everlafting to carry him to the Higheft Honors Thrones & Dignities. Oln Emulation wherby he might be animated & Quickned by all Examples, a Tendernefs & Compaffion wherby He may be united to all perfons, of Sympathy & lov to vertu, a Tendernefs of His Credit in every Soul, & He might Delight to be Honored in all perfons: an Ey to behold the ily of the Omnipfience of God, that He might fee Eternity &c. Dwell with in it: of power of Admiring Loving & Prizing &c. feeing the Goodnefs & Beauty of God, He might be united to it for ever more.

III Century 42

"Humanity" appears to be Traherne's synonym for a "natural" doctrine of man; that is, an understanding of man based on reason rather than on revelation.[1] Under this general topic Traherne includes the headings: man, his end, his happiness, the means to attain happiness, the powers, and faculties of the soul, wisdom, and the goodness of God (III *C* 42).

---

1.   See ch. vii for Traherne's "revealed" doctrine of man. Reason is not seen in contrast to revelation but in conformity with it.

In the tradition of Neo- and Cambridge Platonism, Traherne stresses the dignity of man which is discerned in part by knowledge and education (*CE*, p. 60).[2] Traherne calls this a "New Doctrine" (*CE*, p. 195), and states that although there are errors in the Neoplatonist conception of man, some of their ideas are continenced in Scripture (*CE*, p. 226). Because man is in the image of God and redeemed by Jesus Christ, he is great and celestial, divine and glorious, miraculous and mysterious (*CE*, p. 168). Man mirrors and represents God (II *C* 23). He is the epitome, microcosm, sum and end of the creatures, as well as the golden link in the great chain of being.[3]

For Traherne, the *end* of man is important not only because it is the "first intended," but also because it "crowns the Work," and "inspires the soul," and thus it is the "last attained" (*CE*, p. 13). Traherne has various definitions of what the end of man ought to be.[4] The end of man is God (*Thanks*, p. 262), love (II *C* 48), "all kind of Goods in the highest Perfection" (*CE*, p. 66), or the celebration of his praises (*CE*, p. 6). To complicate the issue, Traherne also states that "only God comprehendeth" the best of all possible ends. There is, however, a common thread in all of Traherne's definitions. In the *Centuries* he indicates that "The Best of all Possible Ends is the Glory of God," and the "Glory of God is to make us Happy."[5] Thus the end of man can be seen as felicity, Traherne's central theme.

The "heathen" philosophers, according to Traherne, think felicity consists in apathy, in self-sufficiency, in contentment, in sensual pleasure, or in material things; in fact they have some 288 opinions of what happiness is (II *C* 99), but they fail to discover felicity (*CE*, p. 60).

---

2. Traherne quotes at length from Hermes and Pico della Mirandola in the CB ("Man") and in the *Centuries* (IV 74ff) on the subject of man. See also S. Sandbank, "Thomas Traherne and the Place of Man in the Universe," *Scripta Hierosolymitana*; vol. 17, ed. Alice Shalvi and A.A. Mendilow (Jerusalem, 1966), pp. 121-136.

3. See IV *C* 74; *CE*, p. 84, 85.

4. The *Shorter Catechism* of 1645 asks, "What is the chief end of Man? To glorify God and enjoy Him forever." See also John Bona who writes "Of Man's last end. . . to bring the Reader to Heaven, that is to say, unto that perfect State of Bliss to which we are all directed by a Natural Impulse, as the Principal End of our Being." *A Guide to Eternity*, trans. Roger L'Estrange (London, 1709), 5th ed., p. 1. Traherne's reaction to the frequent criticism of the Jesuits is that the end does not justify the means, it dictates them (*CE*, p. 13). Thomas Adams (perhaps Traherne's teacher) explains that the end of religion is "God's glory and man's happiness, and the means or rule is Scripture."

5. See III *C* 39; *CE*, p. 114.

Traherne's basic definition of happiness approximates that of Aristotle: "The Perfect Exercise of Perfect Virtu in a Perfect Life."[6] Traherne also distinguishes between objective ("all the Goodness that is fit to be enjoyed either in God or in his Creatures") and formal happiness ("an active Enjoyment of all Objects by Contemplation and Love, attended with full complacency in all their Perfections," *CE*, p. 19). These are core definitions which are expanded and elaborated upon in all of Traherne's writings. Felicity has often been a category in Christian theology, but it is seldom the starting point, the central motif, the constant theme, the end as it is in Traherne.[7]

Closely related to happiness as the end of man is Traherne's "Holy Doctrine" of praising and prizing (see "Demonstration" 158). In the first *Century*, for example, Traherne expands his definition of the end of man and connects it to the means. Prizing things "according to their value" is the end for which men are created as well as the means whereby they enjoy (I C 12). The essence of this recurrent theme is that "A Man should Know the Blessings he enjoyeth," "prize the Blessings which he knoweth," be "Thankfull for the Benefits which he prizeth," and "rejoyce in that for which He is Thankful" (IV C 54).[8]

Prizing, appreciating, and enjoying what God has done is the prerequisite for praise, according to Traherne. Right praise is the result of realizing the worth and value of things, praising God for these treasures, and only then enjoying them (*Hex*, p. 32, 86).[9] According to Traherne, the

---

6. See III C 68; *CE*, p. 19, and *CE*, p. 312 for an extended note on the relationship of Traherne's definition to that of Aristotle. Aristotle's was not as compressed as Traherne's.

7. See ch. ii D, vii A and D for other discussions of Traherne's understanding of felicity. Chs. v through ix indicate that much of Traherne's thought is related to felicity. Aquinas devotes two chapters of the *Summa Contra Gentiles* to the thesis "That Man's happiness is not to be found in this life" (ch. xlviii). William Ames writes that man's felicity and happiness should "be regarded and sought for." *The Substance of Christian Religion* (London, 1657). Robert Crofts, who has been compared to Traherne, discusses riches, honor, love, eating, as aspects of arriving at happiness in his *The Way to Happiness on Earth* (London, 1641) and *The Terrestrial Paradise* (London, 1639). In his *The Way to Bliss* (London, 1658) he focuses on long life, health, youth, riches, wisdom, and virtue. Crofts seems to be more secular and interested in an earthly happiness than Traherne. In contrast both to Crofts and Traherne is Grotius's assertion that "the end of all shall be Man's Happiness after this life." *The Truth of the Christian Religion*, ch. xxiv. Traherne differs from many theological definitions of happiness of his time in his stress on the possibility of happiness both on earth and hereafter.

8. See SM III 31; III C 82; IV C 16. Compare the almost identical listing in the *Thanks* (p. 278) and the *Hex* (p. 38).

world and the creatures are of use only because of man for whom they were created and in whom they have their end. Creation is useless of itself because it is unable to offer right praise and to prize. Thus man is meant to express not only praise on his own behalf but also on behalf of the entire creation (*Hex*, pp. 56, 65, 82).

It is not man alone who prizes, praises, and enjoys, according to Traherne, but also God, even though traditionally a basic attribute of divinity is self-sufficiency. Traherne stresses that man is necessary for God's enjoyment of creation. God enjoys the creation only by exercising his goodness to men (*Thanks*, p. 260). Would God enjoy the world without men or if he were not good to men? Traherne leaves this kind of question unanswered, but the implication seems to be that although God does not need the heavens and the earth, he does need man.[10] God needs man not only to enjoy creation but also to see and enjoy, to love and enjoy him.[11] In fact, God was "from Eternity full of want." Before the creation, God wanted worlds, spectators, joys, treasures, "Yet He wanted not for he had them." Because God wanted, he created the world, made man, and manifested his wisdom and power. The heathen deities do not want anything, and, thus, in Traherne's opinion, they are unhappy and have no being (I *C* 41-42).

In addition to anthropomorphisms and weakening God's attributes, Traherne at times disparages the powers of divinity to point out the importance of praise. He labels the power to divide the sea, to command the sun, to raise the dead, "feebleness," "Vanity," and "Childishness," in comparison with a greater power: to praise (*Thanks*, p. 238).

Failure to prize and to praise is a grave matter in Traherne's opinion. If men do not praise God for the light, according to Traherne, they are unworthy of it and deserve eternal darkness (*Hex*, p. 3). Traherne does not, however, use the fear of hell as a motivation to praise, even though on his scale of sins he ranks ingratitude next to pride. According to Traherne, ingratitude is one of the causes of the fall of the angels (*Hex*, pp. 3ff). Prizing is, however, an ethical motivation, for if a man has the proper perspective and the right values, then all else falls into its proper place.[12] Praise is not only an individual act done alone in silent meditation, but also

---

9.   See *Thanks*, p. 311. Admiring, loving, and prizing, according to Traherne, fulfill the law of justice, men's obligations and duties, and are the way to rewards (*CE*, p. 38).

10.   Meister Eckhart states: "You are a thousand times more necessary to him than he is to you."

11.   See *Thanks*, pp. 261-262; I *C* 41; III *C* 82.

a corporate act expressed in community. That may be one reason why Traherne thinks the tongue (or the gift of speech) the most important member of the body (*Thanks*, p. 216).[13] Moreover, men join the angels and the "Saints in the Church triumphant" in the act of praise (*Thanks*, p. 214) and in enjoying God, His creation, and one another (*Hex*, p. 2).

Finally, the cornerstone of Traherne's doctrine of prizing and praising is the first gift: Jesus Christ. Without himself having seen God's goodness in the gift of his Son, Traherne thinks he would not have understood that God gives men all things (*Thanks*, p. 264).

A. The Soul

The last pages of the bound manuscript of the Select Meditations contain Traherne's "Treatise on the Soul."[14] In this treatise he addresses a particular person (perhaps Mrs. Hopton) who desires to learn more about the soul. Traherne responds to the request, because he says he loves the world and cares "about the felicity of all persons." He stresses that knowledge of the soul is not an article of faith, but a matter of speculation which can be investigated on the basis of reason alone.[15] The main theme of the treatise is proving the infinity of the soul. To know why men are redeemed and loved, Traherne thinks it necessary to recognize that the soul is infinite. The soul has no corporeal substance, but it does have infinite inclination, power, capacity and value. It is the best of all possible ends, i.e. the enjoyment of God. The soul is a *tabula rasa* until it begins to think. It is aware of its origin, operations, effects, and properties, and end (*CE*, p. 20). Traherne does not seem to believe in innate ideas.[16] The soul is created in the similitude of God in its extent (omnipresence), duration (immortality), essence (spirit), and value (SM III 28). Other properties of the soul,

---

12. "If thou Weigh thy Dignity, how canst thou choose but prize it? If thou consider the Price that hath been paid for thee, how canst thou return to Beggarly Rudiments, vicious Customs, low and Base Thoughts, Words and Action anymore" (CYB 2v).

13. This seems to be in tension with Traherne's belief that speech corrupts. See ch.ii D.

14. There are also extended discussions on the soul in the *Thanks* (pp. 80-84), the CYB (41vff), the EN (pp. 149-150), and the section from *Stoicismus Christianus* in the FN.

15. In contrast, Bacon believes that the nature of the rational soul is to be a topic only in revealed theology. See F. H. Anderson, *The Philosophy of Francis Bacon*, p. 69.

16. However, R. Colie thinks that Traherne does believe in innate ideas on the basis of II C 80-81. Colie, "Infinite" (1954), pp. 70ff.

according to Traherne, are its liberty, greatness, swiftness, activity, excellency, keenness (SM III 72), subtlety (*CE*, p. 210), invisibility (*Hex*, p. 82-83), ubiquity (*CE*, p. 323), wideness, variety, fullness. These properties make the soul infinitely happy.[17]

Traherne does not seem to have a unified conception of the components of the noncorporal parts of man nor of their interconnections. In the *Christian Ethicks* he distinguishes between the soul (man's immutable essence or the form of his nature employed) and the mind (the soul exerting its power, pp. 231-232); in the Church's Year Book he refers to the heart, soul, and spirit (51v), as well as to the heart, soul, strength, and mind (25v). In the *Centuries* he writes of a trichotomy of body, soul and spirit (I *C* 93-94). His imprecision may be explained in part by his statement that the connections between the soul and the body are "mysterious."[18]

Certain passages in the writings of Traherne (especially in the "Preparative") lead some scholars to surmise that Traherne believes in the preexistence of the soul.[19] Malcolm Day suggests one approach to the problem. He proposes that Traherne identifies the soul, God, and the Son of God. Thus the soul which preexists is God himself.[20] Others postulate that Traherne is referring to the powers of the mind or imagination.[21] Another solution to the problem may be to see poetic license and platonic

---

17. SM IV 27. Traherne does not seem to take a firm position on creationism or traducianism, but he probably believes in the former. Reynolds also believes in creationism. See *Treatise*, pp. 393ff. Traherne uses recurring images to expound the nature of the soul, thought, imagination, and curiosity. The soul is an infinite center (SM I 83; *CE*, p. 40); a comprehensive mirror (CYB 93r); a spiritual sphere (CYB 38v).

18. *Thanks*, p. 226. Traherne makes notes on Bacon's chapters on the relationship of the body and the soul, especially stressing the soul's dependence on the body. EN, p. 143.

19. Lehrs (p. 37), Webber (p. 239), Stewart (p. 172), Christ (p. 24), Iredale (p. 37), and Hall (p. 380) are among the scholars who think Traherne believes in preexistence. I. Husain (pp. 270ff), Doughty (p. 152), Colby (p. 30), Willett (p. 22), and Williams (p. 38) think he does not. H. More, Glanville, and Rust believed in preexistence; Culverwel did not. See *Cambridge Platonists*, ed. Cragg, pp. 337ff. Norris, Vaughan, and Sir Thomas Browne also probably believed in a form of preexistence, but the issue is not easily resolved. Browne, for example, writes "Before Abraham was I am is a saying of Christ; Yet it is true in some sense if I say it of myself; for I was not only before myself, but Adam, that is in the idea of God." *Religio Medici* (Everyman), p. 65. Many of his contemporaries could have agreed with that kind of preexistence. See I *C* 26, 39, 42, 43, 99; II *C* 39, 71-73, 84; III *C* 63; IV *C* 67.

20. M. Day, "Traherne and…Preexistence," *SP*, 65 (1968), 81-97.

21. See ch. ii D on Traherne's doctrine of the "Liveliness of Interiour Presence."

symbolism complicating and confusing an issue which for Traherne is not in doubt.

To undergird his ideas, Traherne draws on images with various levels of meaning. In the "Preparative," often considered the *locus classicus* of Traherne's doctrine of preexistence, though he states that his soul was his "only All," he also speaks of being "clothed with Skin" (20-24). In the "Salutation" he speaks of God's "preparing. . .this Glorious Store" long before he was in his "Mother's Womb." He may be referring to the traditional *creatio* versus the *traducio* theory, thus taking the side of those who think the soul is transmitted in sexual intercourse. The passage could also support the idea that an individual is an idea in the mind of God long before birth: "Before I formed thee in the belly I knew thee" (Jeremiah 1:5). Traherne may simply wish, in addition, to stress the doctrine of creation and providence.

His concept of "Thoughts" sheds some light on the subject. For Traherne thoughts are "Engines of felicity," invisible, infinite, free, by which he is able to summon past and future joys, to make distant objects near, and to enable the soul to be in the "Sacred Presence" ("Thoughts" I-IV). There is no indication that Traherne believes these thoughts exist before the person, but rather that the person is able to be present in all ages, even before his birth by his thoughts. What is more, the poems which tell of beginnings, infancy, and childhood are written by the adult Traherne, reflecting back on his life, entering into and interpreting his early experience.

Another important consideration is the kind of existence of a preexistent soul. For Traherne life "begins" at birth with the existence of a body. Before that all "was silent," in "chaos." The soul had no perception, "was nothing from Eternity" ("Salutation" 4-6). Such an existence would not have been desirable for Traherne who prized the body so highly. The theological point Traherne wishes to make in the "Salutation" is not that his soul preexisted, but that the members of the body are treasures which God prepared for him as a gracious gift long before he was born. In fact in this poem Traherne stresses that the soul, the "I," is nothing without the body.

At times Traherne is almost consciously anti-Platonic in his understanding of the body and the physical universe. He seems to be polemical against Platonism in what he stresses and in what he negates.

The Lord, he states, took pleasure in "creating an earthly Body" and a "visible World" and did not make men "immortal Souls" seating them "immediately in the throne of Glory" (*Thanks*, p. 218). Moreover, man did not fall primarily or only because he had a body. The angels also fell even though they were not "clothed in Bodies,/Nor endued with Senses. For our Bodies, O Lord, for our earthly Bodies, hast thou made the World" (*Thanks*, p. 220).

1. Powers

Traherne does not precisely distinguish between the terms "Powers" and "Faculties of the Soul." Instead, he tends to combine,[22] or equate them (*CE*, p. 107). For Traherne knowledge of self consists in knowing the powers, inclinations, and principles of the soul.[23] The powers of the soul are natural dispositions or graces (inbred inclinations with which men are born, and which men do not choose or acquire). These in turn differ from habits (*CE*, p. 25). Men have freedom to exercise their natural powers in attaining knowledge, wisdom, and righteousness (*CE*, p. 31). The powers may be applied to virtue or vice alike and can be improved upon. They can be compared to the "limbs and members in the Body" (*CE*, p. 6)) and are identical to the substantial parts of the nature of angels. Since the angels do not have bodies, they are essentially powers (CYB 90v). In heaven all the powers of the soul shall be turned into act (III *C* 68).

Traherne's listing of the things "God gav Man" which concludes his section on "Humanity" may be a partial listing of the powers and faculties of the soul, although some of them are also passions. The list includes such things as an endless intellect, a proneness to covet, apprehensions, affections, curiosity, ambition, tenderness, an eye to behold eternity and a "power of Admiring, Loving and Prizing."[24] Traherne includes even such negative characteristics as coveting and ambition in his listing, perhaps because these, too, serve a purpose. He asserts, for example, that without pride "man's humility and modesty would be contemptible virtues" (*CE*, p. 173).

---

22. SM IV 24; CYB 107r; *Daily Devotions*, p. 341
23. II *C* 80. According to Traherne, he who knows the powers of the soul is able to know that he is an infinite treasure, and he that knows their extent, number, and value is able to see himself ordained a king (SM IV 6).

2. Faculties

Traherne is more precise in listing what he considers to be the faculties of the soul: understanding, will, anger, appetite, fear, reason, hope, aversion, love, joy, hatred, boldness, sorrow, and desire. He is apparently aware that this list also includes some passions and powers of the soul, since he ends this listing with the comment: "we are loath to experience the Sence of such Troublesome Passions" (*CE*, p. 29). His listing of faculties, however, is not always consistent.[25] He frequently lists understanding, will and memory as faculties, but he adds such things as: being, life, senses, affection, fancy, judgment, apprehensions, and reason.[26] Theologians of the seventeenth century usually list understanding, will and reason as the faculties of the soul. Traherne uses this particular triad to explain virtuous love (*CE*, p. 49; *Hex*, p. 86).

According to Traherne, the faculties are accidental to man's nature, because they begin in time, may alter, cease, and be perfected (III *C* 68) Traherne even connects the "empty" (because it is "infused") faculty of comprehension with happiness (SM IV).

---

24. III *C* 42. Aquinas lists the powers of the soul as vegetative, sensitive, appetitive, locomotive, and intellectual (memory, reason, and intelligence). Part I, Q LXV-LXXIV, p. 75. Some of this schema may be reflected in the CYB (25) where Traherne states that the animate has life, the sensitive has feeling, the rational has understanding, the virtuous has graces, and the blessed has glory. Charron lists as passions: love, ambition, avarice, sensuality, desires, hope, despair, anger, hatred, envy, jealousy, revenge, cruelty, grief, compassion, and fear. Compare Traherne's list in the *Centuries* (III 42) with that of Charron and that in the CYB: loving, adoring, praising, obeying, admiring, rejoicing, seeing, and pleasing (89r).

25. In the CYB, the faculties of bodies and souls are: being, life, senses, and understanding (25v) or understanding, will, and memory (12v), in the *Hex* they are: understanding, affection, and memory (p. 36); in the *Life of Christ* they are: understanding, fancy, and memory (p. 79); and in the *Daily Devotions*: understanding, judgment, apprehensions, memory, reason, and will (p. 341). Some of the books Traherne is known to have read are helpful in clarifying what he means by the faculties of the soul. Reynold's *Treatise* (London, 1640) lists the same faculties and all but three of the same passions (appetite, aversion and despair) as Traherne does in his outline. Traherne adds appetite to the listing of Aquinas, as does Eustache. Charron defines a passion as "a violent motion of the soul in that which is distinguished by the name of its sensitive part" (p. 168). R. Allestree lists the understanding, will, and affections as parts of the soul in the *Whole Duty*. The faculties, according to Bacon, are understanding, imagination, memory, appetite, will in one place (p. 398), and memory, imagination, and reason in another (p. 292). James Usher lists five faculties: understanding, memory, conscience, will, and affections. Charron lists as the parts of the soul: understanding (which consists of imagination, reason, wit, judgment), memory (imagination and opinion), and the will. Charron's listing of faculties are more like the traditional passions. See *CE*, p. 316n.

26. See CYB 25v; *Hex*, pp. 36, 79; and *Daily Devotions*, p. 341.

Like the Cambridge Platonists, Traherne stresses the place of *reason* though he weakens reason by often placing it on an equal footing with experience.[27] Reason, for Traherne, is the "singular Advantage" man has over the beasts (*CE*, p. 13). It is the essence of the soul of man, and it guides man to desire supreme things (*CE*, p. 265). Reason enables a man to examine his nature and end, his cause and design (*CE*, p. 13). Reason rectifies and directs instinct, informs the senses, and completes man's essence (*CE*, p. 15). It is the transcendent faculty which discovers all the mysteries of heaven.[28].

B. "The Excellencies of Humane Nature"

All of Traherne's writings can be seen to be an elaboration on the "Excellencies of Humane Nature."[29] The subheadings of this section of Traherne's outline (wants, inclinations, propensities, desires, principles, proposals, ends, causes, fitness of all, worth of all, excellence of all) are a mixture of the traditional scholastic passions, faculties, powers, and inclinations. [30]

The subheadings *wants*, *desires*, and a *proneness to covet* are similar enough to be collated. Man is to be aware of his wants so that he might also be aware of his treasures. Unless a man knows his wants, he cannot be happy (I *C* 43). In wanting a man is most like God, because even God wants. Wants are thus a bond between God and man.[31] God implants the desire for felicity in man (III *C* 56), which indicates, according to Traherne, that there is such a place as paradise, and, in turn, this desire leads men to it ("Desire" 177-179).

---

27.   Traherne's understanding of the will and free will is best treated in connection with his discussion of the Estate of Innocency in ch. vii and his treatment of the "understanding" in connection with "wisdom" in ch. v C.

28.   IV *C* 81. See Traherne's notes on "Reason" in the CB which were copied from Gale's *Court*.

29.   In this respect Traherne is similar to Pico della Mirandola who also writes at length on the excellencies of human nature. See I *C* 73ff in which Traherne copies or rephrases long sections of Pico. See also Traherne's notes on Alcibiades, *De Nature Homines*; Philebus, *De summo Bono* in the FN.

30.   The section in minor details and terminology is vaguely scholastic. Metaphysics traditionally devoted a section to similar problems. Eustache, for example, in section two of his *Ethica* discusses *De Principiis humanarum, Quomodo Intellectus, Quomodo Voluntas, Utrum Appetitiis, Habitibus*, etc. The section is, in effect, Traherne's psychology of man.

31.   I *C* 41, 42, 45.

Propensities and *inclinations* are probably Traherne's synonyms for the passions (see II *C* 69). There is a natural desire or inclination in the soul of man, according to Traherne, which draws him toward knowledge, the good, and God (CYB 55ff, 85). Among the inclinations, Traherne lists covetousness, ambition, love of propriety, curiosity, and liberality (SM IV 10; *CE*, p. 29). Although some of these inclinations may have negative effects, they can lead men to treasures, to virtue, and, by extension, to felicity.[32]

Principles like inclinations are infused into men (IV *C* 49). Traherne's reference to *Proposals* in his outline may be a synonym for principles. In the fourth *Century* he lists some twenty four principles of felicity. *Causes* differ in name only from *ends*. Righteous actions, for example, must be "fitted to their ends and Causes" (*CE*, p. 75). As Traherne states in his poem "Anticipation," the end is the cause and needs means.[33]

When wants, inclinations, propensities, desires, principles, proposals, ends, and causes are understood, it is easier to understand the fitness of all things. For anything to be a treasure, "its Place must be found in Eternity" (III *C* 55). Traherne has a strong sense of the fitness and order of everything in its proper place. This sense of balance and harmony, order and stability is not only an "ought," it already is a part of the nature of things for Traherne. It is the order of creation. All things are so constituted "That every one's Glory is beneficial unto all and every one magnified in his place by Service" (*Thanks*, p. 223). To summarize, then, these "Excellencies of Humane Nature" enable man to know what he is in the world, "What his Soveraign End and Happiness, and what is the Best Means by which He may attain it" (III *C* 42): "A Mind in Frame."

C. "Wisdom"

Traherne defines wisdom as a "knowledge Exercised in finding out the Way to Perfect Happiness by discerning Man's real Wants and Soveraign

---

32. I C 23; *CE*, p. 9. Aquinas seems to believe that things have inclinations or propensities to certain forms of behavior. See Coplestone, *Aquinas*, p. 194. Marsilio Ficino writes that "The observed order of created things results from a tendency or desire inherent in the essence characteristic of each species, a tendency to proceed toward a particular end identified with the good of the species." Quoted in Kristeller, *The Renaissance Philosophy of Man*, p. 189.
33. See discussion in ch. viii; Marg, II, p. 159; and "Cause" in the CB.

desires" (III C 42). According to Traherne, God's wisdom, will, and word are one.[34] Happiness is enjoyed, safety established, and life adorned by wisdom (SM IV 56). Wisdom also indicates that eternal treasures are both possible and real. It knows, chooses, does, esteems, and enjoys all that is excellent (*CE*, pp. 68ff). Traherne came to wisdom by studying felicity and not the reverse (SM III 53).

As in the writings of the Neo- and Cambridge Platonists, Traherne has frequent encomiums to knowledge; however, for Traherne, knowledge without action is vain.[35] Knowledge and virtue are interdependent (*CE*, pp. 30ff). Knowledge alone does not bring heavenly joys, just as knowledge alone is not the end of man ("Eden" 12-14). Instead, knowledge is the light in which things are enjoyed, and goodness, according to Traherne, is to be the end, object and means of knowledge.

D. "God's Goodness"

Of the three kinds of goodness (natural, moral, and divine) Traherne strangely chooses to include divine goodness under the heading of "Humanity," perhaps because when he began his own search for felicity, he had been guided by an "implicit Faith in God's Goodness." This principle of God's goodness led him to study "the most Obvious and Common things" (III *C* 53). Traherne equates God's goodness with His pleasure because of the way God promotes the happiness of all created things. God's goodness is also man's felicity, and man's felicity is increased when more people enjoy God's goodness (*CE*, pp. 81ff). Goodness, for Traherne, is an active and eternal principle which does good without obligation or thought of reward. It is the cause of all things (including the creation of the world), and always intends the welfare of others (*CE*, pp. 79ff). It is instructive to note that one of the criticisms raised against the Cambridge Platonists in

---

34. *CE*, p. 179. Traherne describes I Kings 4:29 as an "excellent Praise and Description of true Wisdome" (EN, p. 73). See ch. ix of the *CE* which is devoted to wisdom (pp. 170ff). Scholasticism defines wisdom as an intellectual habit or one of the three speculative habits, and the highest (understanding and knowledge are the other two). Curtis, p. 96.

35. *CE*, pp. 37, 63. See also CYB 56v, 57; *CE*, ch. v which is devoted to the necessity, excellence and use of knowledge; SM IV 56; the notes on "De Sapienta" in the FN; EN, pp. 72-74 copied from Bacon's theory of knowledge. Hermes states that "he that knows is both good and religious & already Divine" (IV 27-28). Quoted in C. Marks, "Hermes" *Renaissance News*, p. 126. See also the first five chapters of Calvin's *Institutes* which are devoted to knowledge.

the seventeenth century was their absorption with the concept of God's goodness "to the neglect of His other attributes."[36]

36. Attributed to Samuel Parker in *An Account of the Nature and Extent of Divine Dominion & Goodnesse* (Oxford, 1666), p. 27.

Chapter VI

"Divinity" (God)

> In Divinity we are entertained with all Objects from Everlasting to
> Everlasting: because with Him whose Outgoings from Everlasting: being to Con
> templat GOD, & to Walk with Him in all His Ways. And therfore to be Enter
> tained with all Objects, as He is & fountain, Governor & End of & We are
> to Contemplat GOD in & Unity of His Essence, in & Trinity of persons, in
> His manifold attributes, in all His Works, Internal & External, in his
> Counsels & Decrees, in & Work of Creation, & in His Works of Providence
> also Man, as he is a Creature of GOD, capable of Celestial Blessedness, &
> a Subject in His Kingdom: in his fourfold Estate of Innocency, Misery,
> Grace & Glory. In & Estate of Innocency we are to Contemplate the
> Nature & Maner of His Happiness, & Laws under which He was governed,
> & Joys of Paradice, & & Immaculat powers of His Immortal Soul. In &
> Estate of Misery we have his fall, & Nature of Sin Original & Actual,
> His manifold punishment Death Such Calamity Sickness Death &c.
> For & Estate of Grace; & Tenor of & New Covent, & maner of its
> Exhibition under & various Dispensations of & Old & New Testam
> & Mediator of & Covent, & Conditions of it faith & Repentance, &
> Sacraments or Seals of it, & Scriptures Ministers & Sabbaths, &
> Nature & Government of & Church, its Histories & Successions from &
> Beginning to & End of & World. &c. In & State of Glory; & Nature
> of Seperat Souls, their advantages Excellencies & Priviledges, & Re-
> surrection of & Body & Day of Judgment & Life Everlasting. wherin
> further we are to see & understand & Comunion of Saints, Heavenl
> Joys, & our Society with Angels. To all which I was naturaly Born
> to & fruition of all which I was by Grace redeemed, & in & Enjoyment
> of all which I am to live Eternaly.

III Century 43

According to Traherne, that there is a God is known by nature, that
there is one God is known by reason, but only the Scriptures reveal God's
perfection, excellence, attributes, essence, subsistence, and the trinity of
persons. Thus "Divinity" seems to be Traherne's category for revealed or
supernatural theology (as distinct from "Humanity" which is natural
theology based on reason). Scholasticism, however, holds that the essence
and attributes of God can also be discovered by reason without the help of
revelation.[1] Traherne approximates this approach in an extended section
on natural and revealed doctrines in his *Christian Ethicks* (pp. 118-119).

A. "the Unity of His Essence"

Most of the dogmatics texts of the time include a section on the essence, existence, and attributes of God, though not always at the beginning or in the same order.[2] Although Traherne's doctrine of God is within the tradition of the church, his emphases and terminology reflect his peculiar personal outlook. For example, he reiterates that God's essence is "to be" and that He is not "a Being compounded of Body and Soul,"[3] substance and accident, power and act, but Traherne also stresses that God is "All Act" (III *C* 63), which for Traherne is the foundation for the "Generation of His son, the Perfection of His Lov, and the Immutability of God" (III *C* 64). The essence of God, according to Traherne, is to be active, everywhere perfecting and completing the felicity of man (V *C* 10). It is noteworthy how Traherne relates the essence of God to activity and to the felicity of man. Significantly, this particular passage can be seen to be the culmination of the *Centuries* since it is the concluding line of the work.

Traherne does not, however, view God solely with regard to his activity. He also stresses God's immanence, infinity, eternity, and immensity, although he often relates these attributes to activity as well. It is a matter of stress not of exclusion. Moreover, Traherne equates God's essence with eternity (SM IV 27), his perfection (*CE*, p. 89), and his will (*CE*, p. 67). God alone loves by his essence in contrast to men and angels who love by inclination, which is accidental to their nature.

1.   See Mark Curtis, *Oxford and Cambridge in Transition: 1558-1640* (Oxford, 1959), pp. 79ff; and Traherne's notes on "Atheism" (EN, pp. 133-134); "Deitie" (CB 33ff); and "Divinity" in the CB.

2.   Thomas Adams discussed the essence, decrees, creation, and providence of God (1675); Lewis Bayly's *Practice of Piety* (1640) includes similar topics in the same order under the doctrine of God. Henry More in his *Divine Dialogues* includes sections on the existence of God but none on the essence of God.

3.   The term "Being" as a designation for God occurs seldom in Traherne, except for a passage in the CYB (24) in which the word is repeated a number of times. Aquinas begins his *Compendium* with a discussion of the existence of God (ch. 3) stating that God is identical with his essence (chs. 10, 11). Calvin combines the "Unity of the Divine Essence" with the doctrine of the Trinity in his *Institutes*, vol. I, ch. xiii. Bayly defines God as "that one spiritual and infinitely perfect Essence, whose being is of himselfe eternally." *Practice*, p. 4.

B. "the Trinity of Persons"

Traherne does not delve into the detailed and complicated traditional arguments on the doctrine of the Trinity. He refers to it, uses it, and evidently does not take issue with it.[4] There is, according to Traherne, one will and essence in the Trinity (SM II 72). There is one God whose actions are so "terminated in each that the others are not excluded" (CYB 18v). Traherne also maintains the traditional distinction between the internal and external works of the Trinity (*opera divina ad intra, ad extra*).[5] Internal works are those which are not common to the three persons but which are ascribed to one or two of the persons such as the "Generation of the Son, the Proceeding of the H. Ghost" (III C 100), and the consultation of the Trinity (*Hex*, p. 72). Traherne illustrates the mystery of the eternal generation of the Son by indicating that God willed creation not only to appear but to be (I C 53).

Traherne also adapts the doctrine of the Trinity to his own message. He illustrates the workings of love by referring to the Trinity: "Loving is the Producer, and that is the father; Lov produced is the Means, and that is the Son. . .The End of these Means is Lov. . .and that is the H. Ghost." If his conclusion were taken literally in relation to the doctrine of the Trinity, it would be doctrinally problematical. "The End and Producer being both the same, by the Means attained" (II C 46; cf. II C 39). In effect he would be saying that the Father and the Holy Spirit are the same, because of what Jesus did.

In addition, Traherne sees the love of God in the understanding as the "influence of the Holy Ghost proceeding from the father by the Son into the Soul of the Spectator" (*CE*, p. 102). Apparently, Traherne sees love in action toward men (external) as the Holy Spirit, but within the Trinity (internal) love is either the Father or the Son (II C 45). Each of the persons of the Trinity is to be enjoyed (CYB 52v).

---

4.   Traherne's statements approximate those of the Thirty-nine Articles: "And in the unity of this Godhead there be three Persons, of one Substance, power, and eternity, the Father, the Son, and the Holy Ghost" (I).

5.   Trelcatius also distinguishes between internal and external works of God, calling them "Causes of Man's Salvation." Bayly describes three internal works: to beget, to be begotten, and to proceed from both. *Practice*, p. 14. See also II C 59.

The Son does not differ from the Father except that he is begotten of him.[6] He is the means and the mediator (II C 44), the express image of the person of the Father, and has the same nature.[7]

In the Church's Year Book there is a prayer for employing time and talent in studying the essence, excellencies, and effects of the Holy Spirit.[8] Traherne treats these issues in an orthodox manner. The Holy Spirit proceeds from the Father and the Son and is one in essence with the Father (SM IV 43). The Holy Spirit has the name of God, the attributes of God (eternal, omnipresent,[9] omniscient), is coequal with God (CYB 52v), and does the works of God. Therefore he is God. The Holy Spirit also calls, sends prophets as well as Christ (CYB 44v), comforts, recreates, enlivens, enlightens (*Hex*, p. 51), purifies, illuminates, clarifies, and strengthens (*Hex*, p. 54). The Holy Spirit is the communicative goodness of God. Traherne has a tendency to speak of the Holy Spirit in anthropomorphisms: he sees, speaks, rules, sends, commands like a man (see CYB 44r).

The Holy Spirit was active in creation imprinting the waters with efficacy to produce other creatures. What is more, the Holy Spirit also came the same day the law was given which indicates for Traherne that the Holy Spirit both imprints the law on men's hearts and enables them to observe it. Traherne adds that man's ability to observe the law is at least in an evangelical and gospel manner (CYB 46r).

The Spirit blew the heathen oracles, priests, and idols from the world and converted men outwardly and visibly to the church. In New Testament times Christ's Ascension caused the Spirit to be conferred. Traherne does not attempt to reconcile the coming of the Holy Spirit at creation, at Mount Sinai, at Pentecost, and at the Ascension, nor does he attempt to explain how the activity of the Spirit differed in these various appearances.

---

6. See SM II 72; II C 35-46.
7. See ch. vii C 3 for a fuller discussion of Christology, and CYB 7r.
8. CYB 42v.
9. Traherne makes a false conundrum of the Holy Spirit's walking on the waters, yet also being immovable (*Hex*, p. 26). The Spirit, according to Traherne, is also not capable of local motion because he fills all things (CYB 50v). Traherne stresses the mysterious nature of the Spirit (*Hex*, p. 11), and he attributes the name Alpha and Omega to him, although these titles are usually used only in connection with the Son. Compare the Thirty-nine Articles: the Holy Ghost "is of one substance, majesty, and glory with the Father and the Son, very and eternal God" (XVI).

Traherne does note that although the apostles were consecrated before Pentecost, they were not yet filled with the Spirit (CYB 48); this, according to Traherne, is similar to a baptism without the Spirit which Traherne calls "John's Element" (CYB 53v).

Traherne is not an Enthusiast in his doctrine of the Holy Spirit. He does not believe in the immediate reception of the Holy Spirit outside the church without the means of Grace. The Holy Spirit is given only to those within the church (CYB 46r) and is conveyed by the means of grace (CYB 53v). The Holy Spirit infuses grace into the soul (*Hex*, p. 23) and cannot be resisted (II *C* 45). Infused grace is a scholastic concept which in the seventeenth century had a neutral or at least not a positively Roman Catholic tone. That the spirit cannot be resisted places Traherne in the Calvinist camp, at least on this point.[10] The Spirit enables men to believe in Christ and to embrace the Gospel (CYB 47v). Traherne also states that men can cooperate with the Spirit (*Hex*, pp. 11ff), which would have been considered Arminian (if not Semipelagian). Blasphemy against the Holy Spirit is a dreadful and unpardonable sin (*RF*, p. 155), but he who has the Spirit has love which causes joy. Joy in turn brings peace (CYB 54v). Traherne thus connects the doctrine of the Holy Spirit to his central motif: felicity.

C. "his Manifold Attributes"

Traherne says he saw the attributes of God even as an infant ("Nature" 60-64). His writings, however, indicate that he also was aware of traditional discussions concerning God's attributes. Like many other theologians of his day and before, Traherne distinguishes between the incommunicable (negative or quiescent) attributes of God and the communicable (positive or operative) attributes,[11] even though he denies the existence of incommunicable attributes in the Select Meditations. In that work

10. See Article IV of the *Five Articles of the Remonstrants*: "grace is not irresistible." Bettenson, *Documents of the Christian Church*, p. 377. Traherne does not raise the issues with which the Thirty-nine Articles are concerned: "After we have received the Holy Ghost, we may depart from grace given and fall again. . . ." ". . . every deadly sin willingly committed after Baptism is a sin against the Holy Ghost" (XVI).

11. Bayly in the *Practice of Piety* calls them nominal and real attributes or absolute and relative attributes. See Curtis, p. 80. The Thirty-nine Articles refer only indirectly to a few negative attributes: eternity ("everlasting"), infinity, and unity (I).

Traherne defends the thesis that God communicates even his incommunicable attributes (infinity, eternity, power) by exhibiting them to man's view and by making them objects of man's enjoyment (IV 8). Moreover, God implants in man the similitude of the incommunicable attributes (SM IV 9; *Hex*, pp. 85-87). The visible world represents the incommunicable as well as the communicable attributes (II *C* 21).

In the fifth *Century* Traherne focuses on the incommunicable attributes: infinity, eternity, omnipresence. Infinity is, perhaps, the one attribute which most influenced Traherne.[12] Not only does he claim to have been aware of infinity as a child ("Felicity" F 90), but he thinks it was the first thing he knew (II *C* 81). Infinity is also a frequent theme in the writings of the Cambridge Platonists. Peter Sterry thinks that awareness of infinity is an evidence of the presence of the Holy Spirit.[13] Traherne includes lengthy quotes from Hermes on the topic in his Commonplace Book.[14] Perhaps his fascination with the concept was heightened by the use of the telescope and microscope in the seventeenth century.

For Traherne, infinity is the "Region and Extent of His Dominion," the limitless context for treasures, joys and thoughts. He connects immensity with infinity (usually a separate attribute) and glories in its amplitude, mystery, and expansion. Without infinity the imagination, desires, and affections of men "would be coopd up, and their Souls imprisoned" (V *C* 1-3). For Traherne infinity is the essence of the Deity. Paradoxically, he also states that "Evry Man is alone the Centre and Circumference of it." Man's understanding is also an "exemplar" of infinity, as it excludes nothing and contains everything (II *C* 24). All things are created infinite not "in Bulk" but in "Profit and Delight" (*CE*, pp. 179-81). Thus for Traherne infinity contributes to felicity.

---

12. R. Colie maintains that infinity may be the "key to Traherne's total devotion" as well as to his art. *Paradoxia*, p. 146. See Traherne's "Treatise on the Soul" where he attempts to prove the infinity of the soul, as well as SM IV 3; "Capacity," and '"Man" in the CB. Henry More does not devote a separate chapter to infinity in his *Divine Dialogues* although the Cambridge Platonists were fascinated by the topic.
13. Quoted in M. Nicholson, The *Breaking of the Circle* (New York, 1960). Sterry asks "Canst thou tell a way to possess all Things in one point, in a Unity of Life? . . . .a Bright Infiniteness in the narrow points of every dark object? Then thou knowest what the Spirit means. . . ."*Rise, Race, and Royality*, p. 24. See C. Marks, "Cambridge Platonism," *Renaissance News*, 529.
14. See under "Man" (CB 65); "Capacity" (CB 23).

Traherne succinctly defines eternity as an "infinite Length of Duration, altogether present in all its parts in a Stable manner."[15] Eternity is an absence of times and ages as well as their presence and perfection (V C 7). God's essence is eternity, and all things and thoughts are present with reference to eternity (SM IV 28). Traherne also joins eternity with felicity. Eternity magnifies the joys of men because it retains individual moments. Men are able to see themselves eternally beloved and blessed all at one time (V C 8; CE, pp. 67ff). Thus for anything to be seen as an infinite treasure, man must see it in relation to eternity and to God's esteem (III C 55).

Traherne frequently uses place nouns to describe God's omnipresence. It is God's throne (IV C 72), a "Field of joys," a temple, a tower, a castle, a bulwark, a palace, a theater, and an ocean. Omnipresence is also, according to Traherne, the life and soul of the universe which makes men present with God and the angels. Omnipresence enables man to sense and to feel all the delight he gives to God, as well as the beauties, powers, pleasures, and glories which God himself enjoys and creates (V C 9). Omnipresence also helps men to enjoy God (*Life of Christ*, p. 240). Thus omnipresence, too, is connected to felicity.

God, for Traherne, is present everywhere, eternally busied with completing and perfecting the bliss and happiness of men, protecting them from danger and enemies (V C 10). Because men participate in God's omnipresence, they are also able to participate in his treasures, both here and in heaven ("Thoughts IV"). Traherne disagrees with Henry More, who implies in his *Divine Dialogues* that God's omnipresence is to be equated with space or vacuity. Omnipresence is "more lively and Sublimer" for Traherne, as well as more personal.[16]

Because the fifth *Century* breaks off at meditation eleven, there are no separate sections devoted to the other negative or quiescent attributes in

---

15. See *CE*, p. 68. Traherne also defines eternity as an "Immovable Duration" (V C 7). C. Marks notes that Traherne probably read Henry More's definition of eternity: "all things and Actions which ever were, are, or shall be were at this very Instant, and so always, really present and existent before him. . . ." *Divine Dialogues*, pp. 58-60. Thomas Jackson surveys a series of definitions. Among those which approximate Traherne's definition are those of Plotinus "Eternitie is infinitie of life"; Ficino "a fixed instant or permanent Center"; Hermes "a circular duration"; see *CE*, pp. 331-332n. E. N. Thompson also surveys traditional definitions of eternity to clarify Traherne's thought including those of Plato, Boethius, Augustine, Aquinas, and Spinoza. He shows that Traherne's definitions approximate those of Culverwel, Smith, and Spinoza. Traherne differs from Spinoza, however, in his "self-centered philosophy of life." "The Philosophy of Thomas Traherne," *PQ,* 104-107.

the *Centuries*. Elsewhere in his writings, however, Traherne does refer to other commonly considered negative attributes. He combines, for example, immensity with infinity and immutability and bases the immortality of the soul on immutability.[17]

While the negative attributes have traditionally had to do only with God, the positive or operative attributes are thought to be found also in man, even though to a lesser extent. Traherne deals with most of the positive attributes in connection with their manifestation as human virtues: knowledge, love, wisdom, righteousness, goodness, holiness, justice, mercy, and faith among others.[18] These are listed primarily in the second *Century* and as chapter headings in *Christian Ethicks*.

Traherne refers most frequently to the positive attributes of power, wisdom, and goodness, which vie with treasure and pleasure as the most frequently used combinations of words of Traherne. Traherne sees God's goodness, wisdom and power in all things (*Hex*, pp. 10, 12ff; II *C* 1). His poem "The Improvement" (30-36) is a contrapuntal fugue on these three attributes of God. Since these three attributes appear in everything God does, they unite everything together for the one who enjoys. Man must first see God's wisdom, goodness, and power before happiness can become evident. Wisdom, power and goodness become even more apparent in recollection for then God's design becomes evident. In effect, for Traherne, wisdom and power and goodness are one and the same thing (*CE*, pp. 178-179). It is significant that this same triad of attributes occurs in the first of the Thirty Nine Articles.

"All Power is not the Godhead," Traherne asserts in his Commonplace Book, nor is unexerted power wise and good (33ff). If God suspended his power, heaven and earth would be destroyed at once (II *C* 87), yet God limits and moderates his power.[19] Divine power could not exist without

---

16. CB 33ff. See C. Marks' discussion of Traherne's disagreement with More in "Cambridge Platonism," *Renaissance News*, 529-530. Traherne cites Gregory the Great as a support for his views on omnipresence, but St. Gregory had a different purpose in mind. See III *C* 98 and note *Life of Christ*, p. 240.

17. *Hex*, p. 80; I *C* 44. The negative attributes, according to Scholasticism, were: existence, unity, infinity, omnipotence, simplicity, eternity, immutability, ubiquity, and omnipresence. See Costello, p. 80.

18. In the second *Century* Traherne includes wisdom, goodness, power, life, righteousness, love, blessedness, and glory among the positive life attributes.

divine wisdom and will (*CE*, p. 178). Without the power to enjoy worlds, the power to create them is nothing (*CE*, p. 222).

Traherne treats the other positive attributes of God in a similar fashion, making them hinge on their conduciveness to felicity.[20] Love, for example, is the force behind God's other attributes (*CE*, pp. 50ff). That God is love can be seen from his works (II *C* 26, 27). Love is also the "Sole Author of all Felicity" (*CE*, p. 47). Holiness is the "infinit intension & Greatness of his Lov" which makes God delightful to men and men to God (SM IV 64). It is also God's infinite love and delight in his own goodness and righteousness. Thus "all the Raptures and Extasies of Heaven" depend upon the holiness of God (*CE*, pp. 87-88).

According to Traherne the world manifests God's infinity, eternity, beauty, wisdom, goodness, power, life, glory, righteousness, love, and blessedness, which should engulf men in a "Multitude of Wonders," "Delights," and "Diversities of Joys and Pleasures." In fact the greatness of man's felicity should convince him that there is a God (III *C* 21).

D. "his Works, Internal and External"

In traditional dogmatics texts the distinction between internal and external usually has reference to God's attributes, but Traherne extends the category. In the last meditation of the third *Century*, Traherne lists God's internal works: "the Generation of His Son, the Proceeding of the H. Ghost, the Eternal Union and Communion of the Blessed Trinity, the Councels of His Bosom." After this list Traherne goes on to describe apparently what he considers external works: creation, angelology, redemption, providence, christology, the Holy Ghost, ecclesiology, and the last things. Although these works are attributed to one person of the Trinity and yet ascribed to all of them, they are common works of the Godhead directed externally. These, then are more or less the subject of the remaining sections of Traherne's section on "Divinity."

---

19. For a discussion of wisdom and goodness see ch. v. Traherne took detailed notes on Thomas Jackson who was also interested in "curbed omnipotency" (CB 47, 71). See *CE*, p. 355n.
20. See, for example, I *C* 64 and III *C* 39, 40.

E. "his Counsels and Decrees"

Traherne's subsection "Counsels and Decrees" seems to be intended to deal with the categories of election and predestination, two of the more important theological issues in seventeenth century England.[21] Traherne's stand on these doctrines, however, resists easy categorization. His most extended discussion of the problems (one page in *Christian Ethicks*) while not avoiding the issues, in effect skirts them. Traherne states that the election of God can be conceived of either "strictly, or Generally." In the strict sense, particular persons are elected from the "Rebellious Mass of Mankind" as ministers to restore the others. This election, a "matter of Grace," is arbitrary and free (*CE*, p. 74). Thus Traherne avoids the charge of universalism, but he does not take up the problems of election to damnation and of predestination.[22]

In a general sense (later defined as "Primitive Election") Traherne describes the way God chose "the fittest and the best of all Possible Things." This, he says, is "wholy Natural" (in contradistinction to election by grace). It is natural because God chose objects by their "Merit," but he had already infused this merit into them when he first created them (*CE*, p. 74). Calvin's doctrine of predestination is neither implied nor refuted but avoided. Likewise, Traherne states that goodness is not imposed on men (irresistible grace) nor is it easy to remain good (perseverance). Instead, it is difficult to attain and maintain virtue (*CE*, p. 25). Traherne thus approximates later Arminianism, although the Remonstrants did not radically reject perseverance.

---

21.   Wollebius in ch. iii of his work entitled "Concerning the Works of God and the Decrees of His in General" defines God's decree as "the internal action of the Divine Will, by which he hath determined from eternity most freely and certainly of those things which in time are to be effected" (p. 33). Furthermore, "The chief end of God's decree is his own glory" (p. 37). Thomas Adams defines the decrees of God as "his eternal purpose according to the counsel of his own will, whereby for his own glory, he hath foreordained whatsoever comes to pass. God executeth his Decrees in the work of Creation and Providence." *Main Principles*, pp. 14ff. See also Polanus, ch. vii and the sections on "Consultation" (29v) and "Election" (39v) in Traherne's CB in which Theolophilus Gale is quoted to the effect that "The main effect of Consultation is Election."

22.   Cf. the Westminster Confession (1643): "God from all eternity did, by the most wise and holy counsel of His own will, freely and unchangeably ordain whatsoever comes to pass." "Neither are any redeemed by Christ. . . but the elect only." Compare Art. I of the Five Articles of the Remonstrants: "That God. . . determined to save. . . those who through the grace of the Holy Spirit shall believe on the same His Son." Reprinted in Bettenson, pp. 347-48; 376.

A number of passages indicate that Traherne conceives of a group of people who are the elect. The meditational voice in the Church's Year Book asks God to be made part of the elect (10v), as well as for divine aid to make his calling and election sure (6v). God is the father of the elect by adoption (CYB 184). The elect are not yet perfected in sanctification (CYB 56v), but God never interrupts the "General order and Course of Nature" to make men virtuous without their own efforts (CE, p. 26). Traherne says that there are an exact number of the elect who are foreordained (CYB 70r); yet Traherne is not a determinist for he states also that God's dominion is not "Arbitrary" (CE, p. 98), nor is man "fettered by an Iron Fate" ("Preparative" 22).

Even in this dark side of theology, Traherne's inherently positive outlook is evident. God loves to govern by laws and delights in distributing rewards and punishments rightly (Thanks, pp. 218ff). God is infinitely pleased with good deeds, but he hates evil and punishes it. Punishment is, however, according to Traherne, an *opus alienum*, a strange work, as it does not at all compensate for the pleasure God loses by man's misdeeds (CE, p. 253). Justice arises out of God's goodness (CE, p. 98), and Traherne goes to great lengths to demonstrate the patience of God (SM I 84ff; CE, pp. 186ff). Yet even God's judgments ("the very destruction of Nations and the laying waste of Cities") are seen by Traherne as "sweet, and Delightful" (III C 78).

F. "the Work of Creation"

Next to felicity, praising, and childhood, perhaps the next most recurrent theme in Traherne's writings is that of creation. There are widespread ramifications of this doctrine in his thought, and it undergirds and underscores much of what Traherne wants to communicate. The *locus classicus* of the doctrine of Creation in Traherne is his *Hexameron*. Traherne's doctrine of creation is traditional, trinitarian, and thorough. Traherne accepts and uses, for example, the Genesis account. He apparently accepts Usher's conclusion that the world was created "some 5000 years ago" (SM I 95). However, along with this biblicism and traditionalism is an awareness of the latest scientific theories.[23]

---

23.   See ch. viii for a fuller discussion of Traherne's views on science.

The opening lines of the *Hexameron* succinctly depict the trinitarian involvement in the creation: "Thou, O eternal Father. . .by thine eternal Son, through the Operation of thine eternal Spirit" (p. 1). Traherne also elaborates on the consultation of the Trinity in the creation of man (p. 72). Almost immediately, however, Traherne turns to angelology.[24] Almost half of the first chapter of the *Hexameron* treats angelology. Ten pages are devoted to celestial matters and six to terrestrial. Traherne moralizes, allegorizes, and emblemizes the various aspects of creation. He attempts to get to the reasons behind the facts: why God created in the best of all possible ways, and how it might have been had God not created in the way he did. For example, Traherne playfully states that if anyone would ask him "What was God doing before the world was created?" He would not answer (as Augustine is said to have done) that God was "making Hell for such busy enquirors." Instead, Traherne would reply that God was studying to do all in the most perfect manner (SM III 80). This does not mean that Traherne has answers for all the problems involved in the doctrine of creation. He thinks, for example, that the reason behind God's making a visible world is "Deep and fathomless" (SM IV 33).

Fully as important as God's action in creation is man's response.[25] Admiration and praise are constant keynotes (see *Hex*, pp. 32ff). Traherne sees God's power, wisdom, and goodness in almost every creative act (see *Hex*, p. 65). Traherne is, moreover, fascinated by the order, art and curiosity of creation.

Traherne is influenced by other hexameral literature,[26] and he alludes to other writers and their views on thorny issues. Phrases like "it being thought" (p. 2) and "supposed by Divines" (p. 13) indicate his dependence. His theologizing extends to the elements, plants, and animals. "God never gave to Nature a Power in vain" (p. 47). The earth (p. 34), waters (p. 57), and air (p. 59) all concur and cooperate in the creative act. Each newly created creature is to use what is previously created, but is in turn created

---

24. See ch. vii D for Traherne's doctrine of angelology, and ch. iii for a methodological analysis of the *Hexameron*.

25. See ch. v for a discussion of Traherne's understanding of praising, prizing, and wanting. E. Thompson notes the similarity of Traherne's views with those of Lactantius who maintained that God created the world for the sake of man. Man was to admire and praise it. *PQ,* 107. Pico also tells of the wish of the "Craftsman" for someone to ponder, to love, and to wonder at the creation. Discussed in Kristeller, *Renaissance Philosophy of Man*, pp. 224ff.

26. See ch. iii B 3 for a fuller discussion.

for the use, the service, and the delight of man (pp. 61, 65). The creatures are given to man on the condition that man serve and fear God. If that happens, then God will make man "plenteous in Goods" (p. 69).

The beasts are not only created for man but are also more obedient than he, subject to him, and conserved for him. They are used to punish, mend, destroy or enable men to glorify God. Thus the reason God calls the animals good after the creation is that they are to "exercise our Virtues," as well as to help man avoid vice. They also awaken the fear of God in man, incite man to confidence, try man's faith, and sometimes with their inclinations admonish man (*Hex*, pp. 66ff). In this connection Traherne points out that God himself uses animals as symbols (*Hex*, p. 60).

Like other writers on the creation, Traherne stresses the creation of man. As he puts it, there is only one chapter on creation in the Bible; the rest of God's book is on man (*Hex*, p. 82). On the other days God speaks to the creatures, but when he creates man he speaks to himself (p. 72). In speaking more of man, according to Traherne, God indicates his respect, and by repeating his words, God indicates his care and exactness on this particular work of creation. Man is created on the same day as the beasts because he is like them in his corporal and sensitive parts. That similarity should make man humble (p. 70). Yet man is created after all the creatures, because God began with the less perfect animals, then went to the more perfect: from being to vegetative life, to sensitive life, and, finally, to rational and intellectual life. Man comprehends all the previous stages (p. 70). He is the end, epitome, metropole, and summit of the creation (pp. 71, 84). In man all creatures are reduced to unity. Man is the "first in the intention, tho last in the Execution" (IV C 79). Part of man's task is to be a spectator, and his thoughts of the world by which he enjoys it are better and more precious to God than the world itself (II C 90).

As is usual in Traherne's theology, the doctrine of creation is Christocentric and felicity centered. The works of God bring men to Jesus Christ (II C 31, 62), and a life of felicity depends upon a due sense of the excellency of the world.[27]

G. "his Works of Providence"

Most of the dogmatic texts of the time stress the governing and preserving aspects of providence.[28] In addition to these influences Traherne may have had a personal experience of divine providence which he sees at work in creation, preservation, and history. After describing what may have been an early mystical experience, Traherne says that he had discovered a concern at work "in all the World" and experienced "a Communion with the Secrets of Divine Providence" (III *C* 23).

For Traherne providence means the way God governs and "distributes" (*Hex*, pp. 18ff), and it also demonstrates God's perfection in the way everything was created at the fittest moment (*CE*, p. 183). In fact, he uses the term as a synonym for the "best of all possible ways" (*Hex*, p. 15). Traherne thinks that providence is irresistible (*CE*, p. 54). He also indicates that particular events of history can demonstrate God's providence. He thinks, for example, that God's providence was illustrated by the falling of libraries into Protestant hands at the Reformation, because they contained the necessary information to distinguish between records and forgeries in the Roman Catholic archives (*RF*, p.37).

Jesus Christ, according to Traherne, is the "main Business of all the Dispensations of GODS Providence" (*CE*, p. 114), and love is its end. In heaven all the "various lines" of God's "manifest Providence" will be seen to center on the soul of man (CYB 27r). God's providence is not only to be trusted (CYB 9v), it is to be enjoyed.[29] Thus God, his essence, attributes, works, councils, laws, ages, angels, men, thoughts, and affections are the "best of all possible things" (SM II 1).

---

27. *CE*, p. 6; I *C* 14. This is a recurrent theme of Traherne's, "Till you see that the World is yours, you cannot weigh the Greatness of Sin, nor the Misery of your fall, nor Prize your Redeemer's Lov" (II *C* 3; I *C* 14). Contrast Traherne's concept of creation with that of Peter Sterry with whom he is sometimes compared. Sterry thinks that creation is a dream of God which will pass away when God awakes. Sterry conceives of God as a dreamer, lover, and artist. See Vivian de Sola Pinta's discussion in *Peter Sterry*, pp. 94ff.

28. See, for example, Wollebius: "God's active Providence is that by which not only he preserveth his creatures, but also according to his great wisdom, goodness, power, justice, and mercy, he governs all things" (p. 56). Thomas Adams writes: "God's works of Providence are his most holy, wise, and powerful preserving and governing all his creatures, and all their actions." *Principles*, p. 19.

29. *Hex*, p. 112. See also the sections on "Providence" (142) and "God's Providence" (157) in Traherne's EN which are based on Bacon, I, 57. Henry More treats two major issues in his *Divine Dialogues* which Traherne read: the "Attributes of God" and the "Providence of God," the objections against it and the possible solutions to the objections.

Chapter VII

"Divinity" (Man)

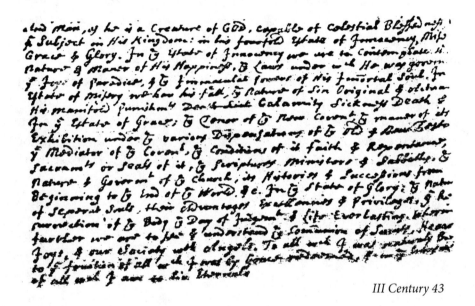

III Century 43

Traherne's doctrine of man is divided into four estates: innocence, misery, grace and glory.

A. "The Estate of Innocency"

Traherne delights in the "Principles of Upright Nature" and is exceptionally interested in the "Estate of Innocency," which he also designates as: Eden, paradise, the "Estate of Legal Righteousness" (SM III 31), and the "estate of Trial" (*CE*, p. 164). Discussion of the Estate of Innocency is part of many dogmatics texts in use in Traherne's time.[1] Traherne, however, is not interested in the Estate of Innocency merely as an historical phenomenon or a subtopic of dogmatics. He describes the estate not only as it probably was, but also as it can be again. For Traherne, childhood approximates, duplicates, and recreates the Estate of Innocency, as do the estates of grace and glory.[2] Like Peter Sterry, Traherne maintains that the grandeur of the estate of innocency is "Muddied," "Blended," "Confounded," "buried," and "drowned," but Jesus Christ restores men to the "Exercise of the same Principles" (V C 53-54). In the *Christian Ethicks*, however, Traherne says the restoration is only partial (p. 145).[3]

In the Estate of Innocence, according to Traherne, everything was from God. This means that there was no sin, sickness, ignorance, calamities, or death, since all of these evils resulted from the fall of man (*CE*, p. 53). There was no need for the apparatus of religion, medicine, education, law, or commerce. There was peace, plenty, prosperity, and equality (*CE*, pp. 33ff).

Integral to Traherne's ethical thought is his theory that certain virtues are necessary in all estates (knowledge, love, righteousness, holiness, goodness, and wisdom), but other virtues are proper to specific estates. Proper to the Estate of Innocency, according to Traherne, are faith, hope, fear, prudence, temperance, humility, and gratitude (*CE*, pp. 30-32; but cf. SM III 53). These virtues were easy to practice, consonant with reason, and necessary for his enjoyment of felicity. They were obeyed and enjoyed without a positive law (*CE*, pp. 30ff).

---

1. Aquinas devotes a section of his *Compendium* to a discussion of the pristine state and original justice. Aquinas theorizes that the body was completely subject to the soul, the lower powers to reason, and reason to God. There was no death, illness, or trouble. The English translations of Trelcatius and Polanus designate this estate: "Integrity." Section one of T. Collier's *Marrow of Divinity* (1646) treats: "Adam's condition before his fall," which he defines as being perfect, upright, in the image of God, having the power to stand or fall, and having everlasting being. Collier was a Quaker. J. Glanville in the *Vanity of Dogmatizing* (1661) begins with "A display of the perfections of Innocence, with a conjecture at the manner of Adam's knowledge." See Thomas Jackson, vol. III and the *Commonplaces* of Musculus, ch. vii. Bacon suggests that a collection of the excellencies and prerogatives of mankind should be made showing the ultimates (as the scholastics put it) or the summits (as Pindar put it) which human nature has attained. IV, i, p. 374. For further references to the Estate of Innocence see *CE*, p. 307n.

2. See ch. ii D and C and D below.

3. Compare Sterry who writes, "the pure Image of God seems to some not to be lost or destroyed, but hid beneath the ruines of the fall. This Knowledge springing in the Soul seems to be a remembrance, the Life of all good, an awakening by reason of the primitive Image of pure Nature raising it self by degrees, and sparkling through the Rubbish, the confusions of his present state. Thus also hath the Soul in her self the measure of all Truth and Good in this pure Image, which hidden in the Center of the Soul, containeth all Forms of Truth and Good in itself." *A Discourse of the Freedom of the Will* (London, 1675), p. 99.

1. "The Nature and Maner of His Happiness"/"The Joys of Paradice"

According to Traherne, Adam knew material and spiritual things naturally (CYB 49v) and saw God in his works (III C 5). Everything he could hope for he had (II C 52). His only task was to admire and enjoy the goodness of God and tend the garden (*CE*, p. 86).

Not only Adam but every man is created in the image of God ("Bible" 106) and being in the image of God is the best thing a man could wish for (I C 67). Precisely because man is in the image of God, he can be assured that God does everything possible in creating him (SM III 91). Traherne criticizes the scholastics and others who, he says, too facily think that the image of God consists only in true righteousness and holiness {SM III 43).[4] Traherne thinks it consists more in doing than in enjoying, more in giving than in receiving, more in being than in having all treasures (SM III 46). However, Traherne also uses the terminology of the traditional definition of the image of God: knowledge, true righteousness, and holiness (*CE*, p. 70).

By giving man a body, God begot in him the divine image which enables man to enjoy the world (*Hex*, p. 74). The image of God, however, is "not seated in the features of your face, but in the Lineaments of your Soul" (I C 19). Thus, for Traherne, the soul resembles the divine image by its invisibility and immortality. In fact the Trinity itself is impressed on the three faculties of the soul: understanding, will, and memory (*Hex*, p. 83). Because man was made in God's image, he is a mirror and representative of God (II C 21). All of God's joys and treasures are also to be the joys and treasures of man (III C 58).

2. "the Laws Under Which He was Governed"

There was no positive law in Eden, just laws of nature.[5] A positive law, according to Traherne, might have made men sluggish. Adam loved, for example, because God first loved him, and he was "avers" to sin because God would be "avers" to him if he sinned (*CE*, p. 145). There was also little

---

4. Thomas Adams maintains that the image of God consists in knowledge, righteousness, and holiness. *Main Principles*, p. 18. T. Collier thinks that it consists in reason, wisdom and understanding in his *Marrow of Divinity*, but in his *Body of Divinity* he says it consists in purity, free will, body, soul, and spirit.

need for law in the Estate of Innocency because man had few enemies and difficulties. Only the laws necessary for man's obedience, gratitude, and fidelity existed (*CE*, p. 167). The judiciary, higher powers, a class system were also unnecessary in Eden, because every man was supreme as well as subject to others by his love (an echo of Luther's idea of the Christian as servant yet free Lord of all). Perhaps because of England's current situation and recent regicide, Traherne adds that a king would also have been necessary (SM III 11). The "holy Ordinance" (by which Traherne apparently means matrimony) was pure in Eden, and it was also lawful and blessed to procreate (*Hex*, p. 73).

3. "The Immaculate Powers of His Immortal Soul"

Traherne includes a section on the powers of the soul under "Humanity" (see chapter five), but evidently he thinks that some of the powers take on added meaning when discussed in connection with "Divinity" or revealed theology. "Reason" is perhaps best discussed in connection with the Estate of Grace, but free will, however, is best discussed here.[6] Traherne seems to agree with Wollebius that the will has different degrees of freedom in the different estates. In the Estate of Innocency Wollebius thinks that the will was free to do good or evil. In the Estate of Misery the will was free only to do evil; it could not but sin. In the Estate of Grace the grace of God freed the will from evil to do the good, even though imperfectly. In the Estate of Glory the will is freed from evil to do the good perfectly; it cannot sin. Traherne does not distinguish so carefully among the estates and tends to imply that man can choose between good and evil equally.[7]

Both angels and men have free will according to Traherne (IV *C* 79). Free will is one of the "Best of all Possible Things" (*CE*, p. 90) and the

---

5. Traherne quotes Pico della Mirandolla to the effect that Adam was loosed from all laws (IV *C* 75). Wollebius defines "The government of man in the state of Innocency" as "that by which God made a Covenant of Works with man, promising him eternal happiness, under the condition of obedience; otherwise eternal death." p. 67. Thus, there is, according to Wollebius, a double Covenant, one of works before the fall and one of grace after the fall. p. 68.

6. See part C below. Wollebius discusses free will under the rubric of original sin, ch. 10. Traherne does not include the topic in his outline. See related issues in ch. v A.

7. See Traherne's extended quotations from Pico on free will (IV *C* 75–76) and his notes from Thomas Jackson's discussion of free will in the CB ("Freedom" 46v and "Libertie" 62v). See also p. Sterry, *Discourse on the Freedom of the Will*, and C. Marks, "Cambridge Platonism," *PMLA* (1966), 525.

greatest excellency, dignity, and exaltation (IV *C* 42 43). Yet it is not easily explained (*CE*, p. 149). Men are not subject to fatal necessity (*CE*, pp. 78, 153) or "fettered by an Iron Fate" ("Preparative" 22). Moreover, man has not only the possibility of sinning, but also of righteous actions (*CE*, pp. 92ff). Man is made free so that he can love, honor, praise, and do good voluntarily (*CE*, p. 85). Without free will man would be like a stone or a tree (*CE*, p. 91), but with it man is made capable of rewards and punishments (*CE*, p. 183), honor, ingenuity, goodness and delight (*CE*, p. 149).

Traherne is, if possible, more enthusiastic about free will than the Cambridge Platonists and departs not only from the spirit but also from the letter of Calvin's theology.[8] However, Traherne is not a Pelagian in his understanding of free will because he distinguishes between a habit and a natural disposition (*CE*, p. 25). His position approximates that of the later Arminians.[9]

B. "the Estate of Misery"

According to Traherne, the Estate of Misery should remind man of his guilt, despair, deformity, and shame, as well as his hatred of God and God's hatred of him. Yet it should also remind him of God's redemptive love (*CE*, p. 214). Although Traherne writes that there are virtues common to all estates (*CE*, p. 4), he also asserts that there are no virtues in this estate (*CE*, p. 185). He does not clarify the problem. Perhaps he means that there are no virtues specifically meant for this estate alone.

1. The "Fall"

Directly impinging on the fall of man, according to Traherne, is the fall of the angels. The devil "was let loose upon men, for the increase of his Honour and Dominion." Satan can try and persuade Adam and Eve "to do

---

8. Calvin asserts that man does not have "an equally free election of good and evil." *Institutes*, I, 15. See Stewart, pp. 60ff.

9. See Stewart, pp. 61ff. The Thirty-nine Articles is more concerned with the state of the will after the fall than during the estate of innocency (X). Even the Remonstrants were careful with regard to free will. Man can think nothing truly good on his own. He must be renewed in the Holy Spirit. See Articles III and IV. Thomas Jackson and the Cambridge Platonists were more positive about the powers of the will.

what was forbidden," but he can not compel them (*CE*, p. 169). The cause of the fall is man's desire to be like God (knowing good and evil) in a forbidden way; that is, he is disobedient, follows his own "Inventions," and resorts to the "creature" (the tree) rather than to God (*CE*, p. 288; II *C* 52). The blame for the fall, according to Traherne lies with Adam's desire to please his wife and with Eve's "Lightness and Credulity" (*CE*, p. 146). In the Church's Year Book Eve is sent by Satan to propagate sin and death (7v). The fall, however, is not the "Whole business of Religion," though there are those who have made religion a "sour thing" by overstressing the fall (*CE*, p. 34).

2. "His Manifold Punishments, Calamity, Sickness, Death"

Traherne states categorically that all the evils which now exist are the fault of man and due to the fall (*CE*, p. 53). Sin changes man more than any physical alteration can (SM IV 31). Everything is fragmented, muddied, confounded. The original innocence is buried, drowned (IV *C* 54), and forgotten (SM IV 31). Everything aggravates man's sin and condemns him. Man knows that he will die, for death is the punishment for sin (*CE*, pp. 101, 102, 119).

The fall makes new ordinances and duties necessary. The apparatus of religion and society are needed (*CE*, pp. 33ff). Sin breeds inequality (SM III 11) and makes men slaves and cowards (*CE*, p. 185). It is not man alone who suffers in the fall; the fall corrupts nature too. The earth is cursed and made barren, making work necessary (IV *C* 23). The order, peace, and beauty of nature are also destroyed (IV *C* 24; *CE*, p. 202). Nature is now perverse and cursed with deformities and diseases. Traherne sees the earth growing old in wickedness. Even the way babies are born (heads downwards) becomes a symbol for Traherne of man's condition (*CE*, p. 238). It is only after the fall that animals can "swerve" from serving man.[10]

The fall has much to do with the resultant loss of man's perception ("Infant Ey" F 86-87), ignorance of his nature, and relationship to God, the world, and the creatures (*CE*, pp. 37-38). Sin also destroys man's happiness (II *C* 47). Man is unable to discern felicity because of his corruption, and more things are necessary for a man to be happy after the fall than before (*CE*, p. 33).

---

10.   SM II 4; *Thanks*, p. 300; *CE*, p. 202.

3. "the Nature of Sin"

a) "Original"

Whereas the fall was general (angels, nature, and man), *original sin* is particular (man). There is a wide divergence of scholarly opinion as to whether Traherne believes in original sin, and, if he does, whether his view is unorthodox or heretical.[11] The passage cited most often in the debate is the eighth meditation of the third *Century*, particularly the statement, "it is not our Parents Loynes, so much as our Parents lives, that. . .Blinds us." A careful reading of the passage indicates that although Traherne does not

---

11. A number of scholars think Traherne denies original sin. Rufus Jones (1914) knows of no other theologian "who has more emphatically denied the fiction of total depravity" (p. 327). James Leishman (1934) thinks that Traherne himself recognizes that he is "being slightly heterodox in the doctrine of original sin" (p. 192). What is more, Traherne never really faces the problem of evil, according to Leishman, even though he is not a Pantheist or a dualist. Leishman states that Traherne attributes the sin of his youth more to ignorance than to evil, and thus asks not for forgiveness but for illumination (pp. 197-204). Hilda Iredale (1935) thinks that Traherne vindicates "children from the charge of original sin" (p. 20). Roy Daniels asserts that the "Christian doctrines of depravity and eternal punishment. . . have no hold upon him" (p. 5). A. L. Clements thinks that Traherne implies that "the infant is born without sin, free from any stain of Original Sin" (500-521). H. Ridlon states that for Traherne "Adam's fall was not inevitable, but the child's fall is" (p. 630). T. Staley (1964) asserts that Traherne does not "take account of a possible fall from grace" (p. 46). R. Uphaus (1968) calls Traherne "heretical from an orthodox point of view in that he happily renounces the possibility of innate depravity, the crux of Calvin's theology" (p. 19). R. Colie in her article, "Traherne and the Infinite," thinks that his "strong Arminian tendencies permitted him to pass more easily over a creation flawed by Adam's fall than. . . Donne" (p. 75).

    There have also been a number of extended articles which have discussed Traherne's doctrine of the fall and original sin, apart from the briefer comments. K. W. Salter in a chapter of his book based on an earlier (1955) article asserts that "Traherne does not believe that the fall was the consequence of a primordial act through which humanity is inevitably infected with sin." Moreover, "Traherne comes close to the Pelagian assertion that we can live the sinless life as Adam did." Salter also thinks Traherne believes it possible to save himself by an aesthetic experience. Traherne is unaware, according to Salter, of the great difference between the natural and spiritual man. *N & Q, N.S.* 2 (1955), 153-156. G. R. Guffey answered Salter's article and subsequent book in 1967 showing that Salter based his argument only on the *Centuries* which are more utilitarian and utopian (i.e. they describe man not as he is but as he could be). Guffey believes Traherne is "more orthodox than is usually thought," believing, as he does in the seriousness of sin, the necessity of grace, and a fall with present effects. *N & Q, N. S.* 14 (March, 1967), 98-111. W. Marshall is even more thorough. He thinks that although Traherne rejects Calvin's doctrine of total corruption, he still does not reject original sin. Traherne, according to Marshall, is not a dualist or a Pelagian since he does not believe that original sin affected only Adam, or that Adam was created mortal. Traherne adheres to the Thirty-nine Articles. *MLN* (1968), 161-165.

deny the doctrine of original sin, he does lay more stress on "Opinion and Custom," "Examples and Inclinations." It seems to be more a question of emphasis than denial. According to Traherne, the present misery of man is due much more to "outward Bondage of Opinion and Custom" than to the "inward corruption or Depravation of Nature." Even this "outward Bondage," however, is derived from Adam, since evil examples and inclinations "arise from his Sin."[12]

What complicates the issue is Traherne's personal experience. He states: "I cannot remember, but that I was ten thousand times more prone to Good and Excellent Things then evil. But I was quickly tainted and fell by others." The "I's" set off this passage from the context, but the subject is the same. Thus the passage as a whole contains the essence of Traherne's position on original sin: (1) He affirms the doctrine of original sin in the tradition of the Thirty-nine Articles; (2) He stresses, however, the influence of bad examples and customs more than the inner depravity of man; (3) Yet he apparently does not feel that original sin applies to his own childhood.

1. Traherne uses the traditional terminology and explanations of the doctrine of original sin. The poem '"Mankind is Sick" (*CE*, pp. 201-204) is a *locus classicus* for Traherne's orthodox approach. The cause of the sickness and insanity of mankind is the "long corrupted Train/of Poyson, drawn from Adam's vein." It has stained "all his Seed, and all

---

12. See EN, pp. 232, 339ff for Traherne's notes on why God cannot be the author of evil. Wollebius thinks that sin is a transgression of the law, and the will of man is the cause of sin (ch. ix). The Cambridge Platonists tend not to stress original sin. Whichcote, for example, asserts that men are "born not with Habits; but born only with Faculties." *Discourses*, I, 364. The nature of man is only "vitiated by the Fall." *Discourses*, III, 128. H. More is somewhat stronger. He calls original sin "that over-proportioned Proneness and almost irresistible Proclivity to what is evil." T. Jackson defines the first sin as "the Desire to be equal with God." vol. II, 782ff. He also thinks that it is "an hereditary disease in all their Posterity." vol. III, p. 28. See P. Grant for Traherne's affinity to Irenaeus. Traherne may even have unconsciously tended toward the Roman Catholic stance, that man's nature is basically uncorrupted, though it is deprived of supernatural and preternatural perfections. See Curtis on the Catholic position on original sin, pp. 114ff. Traherne is unlike Reynolds who defines original sin as "The Privation of that Righteousness, which ought to be in us, and the lust or Habituall concupiscence, which carrieth Nature into Inordinate motions" (p. 397). Nor does Traherne openly espouse the opinion of Robert Barclay, a Quaker, though he seems to tend in that direction: "this seed is not imputed to Infants until by transgression they actually joyn themselves therewith." *An Apology for the Christian Divinity* (1678), ch. iv.

his Kin." Men are in "Chains of Darkness" and "In Bondage and Iniquity" as a result. Other passages in the *Christian Ethicks* undergird this understanding, indicating that his ideas are not to be attributed to poetic license. Traherne writes that men are prone to evil, under God's wrath (*CE*, p. 118), depraved, born sinners (*CE*, p. 38), "contrary to God in almost all things and deformed" (*CE*, p. 230). Original sin is discernible by reason (*CE*, p. 118) making it possible even for the heathen to discover that the miseries of human nature lie in a disease of the will or understanding (*CE*, p. 59).

Though the *Thanksgivings* and *Hexameron* are more dependent on secondary sources, and though his use of more traditional vocabulary in both works may indicate less personal involvement, these works, too, do not depart significantly from the above understanding of original sin. In the *Thanksgivings* Traherne asserts that men "are Desparately bent to grow worse in Wickedness" (p. 323), blind and reprobate (p. 325). In the *Hexameron* the reader is asked to meditate on the kind of person he is: "conceived in Sin, destitute, by the Fall of Adam. . .void of Grace and Virtue, covered allover with Sin and Darkness" (p. 11). The light shows men the errors of their understanding, the deprivation of their wills, the disorder of their affections, and the wickedness of all their ways (p. 14). The meditational voice implies he is inclined to evil (p. 28). Apparently every man has this guilt and blot due to the fall (p. 62).

The *Centuries* and the poetry generally use less traditional terminology and tend not to emphasize original sin. Perhaps this accounts for the common idea that Traherne does not believe in original sin, for most research has been based on these two sources. However, Traherne does not ignore the subject in the *Centuries* and poetry. Corrupted nature, for example, undervalues the divine and heavenly mysteries (III C 81). From this corruption issues labor, contention, discontent, envy, vanity, covetousness, fraud, oppression, and violence (I C 33; II C 4). From that first error, men proceeded to multiply their mistakes (II C 2). This last statement provides, perhaps, the bridge which connects the fall with Traherne's distinctive stress on the evils of custom and example.[13]

---

13. See extended discussion in ch. ii D above and B below.

2.   Without denying eternal depravity, Traherne tends to stress the "outward Bondage of Opinion and Custom." Evil customs and habits, not nature, have made it more difficult for men to think well. By nature, according to Traherne, men think "well" more easily than they think "ill" (I C 8). Custom can actually "beget an evil inclination": evil habits, inclinations, customs, and companions can separate a man from God (CYB 85v). A primary vehicle of sin's inroads into the heart of man is speech (*CE*, p. 277). The infant is dumb so that he might not be "depraved with Tongues" or "Injured by the errors that Mortal Words convey. For Sin and Death are most infused by accursed Breath" ("Dumnesse" 46). What adds weight to this critique of speech is that they are written by a poet in poetry.

3.   Traherne's view of original sin would be less complicated and more orthodox had he not included references to his own childhood. Certain statements in Traherne's writings imply that as a child he was born without sin and was corrupted not by original sin but by the customs and manners of men (III C 7; IV C 2). There are various ways of viewing this problem. Perhaps Traherne was unaware of sin as a child, though it was real (see "Wonder" 8). He may use his childhood as an image or symbol of the Adamic state, meaning to stress the Estate of Innocency not to clarify the Estate of Misery. Traherne may also have forgotten the inclinations to sin in his own childhood. The reader is dependent on what Traherne chooses to report and how he interprets his own life (see III *C* 7). Traherne presents various alternatives, sometimes within the same poem. In "Innocence" (14-19) the persona wonders whether God removed the guilt by a miracle, whether nature was pure and only custom vicious, or whether he found felicity "one Day." Thus, in any discussion of Traherne's concept of sin, one must not only distinguish between original and actual sin, but also between general sin (mankind) and particular sin (Traherne himself).[14]

---

14.   See ch. ii D. Traherne can be contrasted with Peter Sterry who thinks that evil is unreal (in the Neoplatonic tradition). See Pinto, pp. 109ff.

b) "Actual"

Traherne does not define what he means by *actual* sin, but he probably means present, day to day sins in contrast to original sin. Although certain terminology which Traherne uses in his poetry seems to imply that he does not take actual sin seriously, designating it as "contingent," "transient," "aery" ("Instruction" 24-25), Traherne does, however, acknowledge the seriousness of sin. He also distinguishes between sins of omission and commission. Sins of omission, according to Traherne, have "an unknown Guilt and Demerit" (*CE*, p. 91). Men can be condemned for failing to discharge their duty (*CE*, p. 147) or for failing to ascribe constant praise to God (SM III 70). The least sin is of "infinite demerit" because it breaks the union between God and the soul, blasts God's image, and corrupts the nature of the soul (*CE*, p. 99). When a sin is committed, according to Traherne, God himself is alienated from the sinner, and the person is intimately involved. He seems to be saying that God hates sin and the sinner. Yet elsewhere Traherne implies that sin can be separated from the sinner (compare *CE*, p. 90 with II *C* 31). One way to reconcile the difficulty may be to see the sin and the sinner connected for the purpose of judgment but separated for the purpose of salvation.

Once a sin is committed it can never be undone. Thus, for Traherne, a man ought to be more concerned with sins he has committed than those he might commit (*CE*, p. 186). Sin also forces the Holy Spirit and the angels away (*Hex*, p. 26). God is especially concerned about those who hurt others, particularly widows and orphans (*CE*, p. 58). Sins are written down in a "Table Book of God's memory" (*Hex*, p. 22). Sin "breeds a long Parenthesis in the fruition of our joys" (III *C* 51), yet sin (errors, disorders, troubles) can also increase a man's felicity (III *C* 30; cf. Romans 8:28).

The Thirty-nine Articles also distinguish between original guilt and actual sin.[15] Article IX defines original sin as following Adam, as well as being inherently corrupted by nature: "man is very far gone from original righteousness, and of his nature inclined to evil, so that the flesh lusteth always contrary to the spirit." Moreover, "concupiscence and lust hath of itself the nature of sin." Traherne, at least in his general doctrine of the fall

---

15. Wollebius defines actual sin as the breaking of God's law by thoughts, desires, words and deeds, ch. ix. Ursinus, Keckermann, William Perkins all distinguish between original and actual sins, and Thomas Adams differentiates between general and special sin.

and sin, adheres to this view. However, he departs from it when he writes of his own childhood, in that he thinks he was more prone to good than to evil. Traherne, however, would not have agreed with Pelagius that original sin affected Adam alone, nor that Adam was created mortal. Death is a result of sin for Traherne.

Familiarity with the estate of misery, according to Traherne, is necessary if one is to see the manifold mercies of the Estate of Grace, and also if one is to "better understand the Manner of his Recovery" (*CE*, p. 101).

C. "the Estate of Grace"

The broad range of meaning of the term "estate" for Traherne is particularly evident in his understanding of the estate of grace. Traherne uses estate to denote a calling or position; i.e. the estate into which a person is placed is the best, and it is a man's duty to think that it is. Furthermore, the estate of grace can simply mean being in God's favor and being accepted by him (IV C 89). Traherne also uses the term in a narrower sense, as an elect group of people; i.e. some men are in the estate of grace, others in the estate of nature (SM III 77). In addition, the estate of grace can refer to a particular period of time or dispensation, after the fall and before the estate of glory; i.e. the present.[16] The estate of grace is a period of trial, affliction, virtue, and reconciliation (*CE*, p. 185). It is a time of labor not reward or fruition (*CE*, p. 19). Traherne also calls it the "Estate of Evangelical Grace" (SM III 37) or "Evangelical Righteousness" because it is founded on the blood of Christ (*CE*, p. 105). The existence of this estate is revealed not by nature but by revelation (*CE*, p. 101).

According to Traherne, man is placed in this estate to multiply his virtues, and, therefore, not immediately in glory. What have traditionally been labeled theological virtues (faith, patience, righteousness, holiness, humility, meekness, courage, fidelity) are proper to this estate (*CE*, p. 164). Faith is the first and basic virtue of this estate, and patience is proper to it and to no other (*CE*, p. 185). This estate can almost be like a return to Eden, but only a few men have a clear enough vision to see through the darkness

---

16. T. Jackson designates this estate as that of the "Sons of God by Adoption or Baptism." However, Jackson's fourth estate is that of "the Elect or Completely Regenerated" instead of glory.

and customs of this world (SM II 13). Thus right vision is a prerequisite for this estate, and all evil habits, customs, and falsity must be left behind (III C 5). God ordained some of the trials of this estate; God permitted some which men brought on themselves; and God inflicted some to chastise sin or as a medicine for man's soul.[17]

Because of God's grace the world seems to be a paradise or a prison to different people (I C 36). Whereas in Eden Adam had only to enjoy and be grateful for benefits received, in the estate of grace man must be like a "Royal Chemist" turning weeds into flowers or like a god bringing order out of confusion. The world can, however, be better than paradise because miseries, sins, and offences can be the materials of joy, triumph, and glory (IV C 21).

1. "The Tenor of the New Covenant"

The first two subheadings under the estate of grace provide a context in which to discuss Traherne's position on such major issues as nature and grace, the heathen, covenantal theology, law and gospel, and dispensations. Some of these Traherne considers "the principal objects of our knowledge" (*CE*, p. 41).

Traherne has no consistent approach to deal with the tension between nature and grace. In the Select Meditations, for example, Traherne proposes that it is an easy matter for a man to go from the estate of nature to that of grace simply by doing a good work with all his power and might and "to intend God, Angels. and Men." Any man can do this, according to Traherne, because any man is able to use all the power he has (SM III 77). Particularly in the poetry, Traherne sometimes implies that nature alone without grace, without revelation, without the supernatural, is sufficient to teach the truth, to indicate the attributes of God, to make men prone to love. There are also a few sections in *Christian Ethicks* which expand to great lengths on what man can know by natural knowledge or reason alone. In the *Hexameron* he suggests that man can ascend by his own efforts from nature to grace and finally to glory.[18]

Yet Traherne also stresses the more Protestant approach to grace: "all nature without [Christ's] Incarnation, Death, and Passion could never restore a Sinner" (*CE*, p. 195). Grace improves nature (*CE*, p. 52) and

---

17.   *CE*, pp. 189ff; "The Return" F 87-88.

enables men to do far more than they could by nature alone (*CE*, p. 195). Traherne also uses terms like restoration (SM II 3, 7; *CE*, p. 59), mending (III C 6), resurrection (CYB 13v) to describe the change which must be wrought in men before they can belong to the estate of grace. What is more, God's works in the estate of grace are even better than they were in Eden because the death of Jesus Christ and the redemption have been added to creation (SM II 7; I C 31).

Revelation is needed to "unfold" the "Exigency" of men which nature alone cannot do. Thus the grace and mercy of God plus the guilt of men "adapts" men for the reception of the gospel. The incarnation and satisfaction for sin are "above the course of Nature" and need to be revealed; yet, according to Traherne, they are also agreeable to nature (*CE*, p. 119).

Traherne's attitude toward the heathen provides a practical application of his theories about nature, grace, and revelation. The heathen philosophers do not find felicity. Socrates (1 C 39), Seneca and Aristotle (*CE*, p. 58) do not know the fullness of the truth, and there are many errors in the philosophies of the other heathen as well.[19] Heathen morality is defective and falls short of Christian morality (*CE*, p. 58). Traherne makes it clear, however, that he is not criticizing the heathen for doing the best that they can, but rather his purpose is to indicate the superior value of Christianity.[20]

The coming of the Holy Spirit means the demise of the heathen oracles, priests, and idols (*CE*, p. 61). Traherne includes prayers in the

---

18. *Hex*, p. 48; "Nature" 60-64; *CE*, pp. 118ff; and III C 17. T. Jackson, called an Arminian in his day, writes of man's impotency and his "proneness to fall." Men have no "power at all. . . to raise themselves." Moreover, without God's preventing Grace we must still walk in our natural filthiness and uncleanness, that without his Concomitant Grace we can make no eternal Life" (p. 580.) The Five Articles of the Remonstrants are also hesitant in according to man's will too much power and freedom.

19. Traherne does not make any large scale attempt to accommodate "the better sort of heathen." He does criticize the Christian world as barbarous and says: "I am sure those Barbarous People that go naked come nearer to Adam, God, and Angels in the Simplicity of their Wealth, tho not in Knowledge" (II C 12). Culverwel refers to Salmasius who in his Tractate *De Coma* writes that he would "rather search for Natures Law in a Naked Indian, then in a spruce Athenian, in a rude American, rather then in a gallent Roman; in a meer Pagan, rather then in a Jew or Christian." *Light of Nature*, p. 85. That is more pre-Romantic, Rousseauistic than Traherne who quotes with favor Aristotle and Socrates and the other "heathen." See *CE*, pp. 226ff.

20. *CE*, p. 63. Traherne classifies the Greek and Roman philosophers with the heathen (see II C 100).

Hexameron calling the heathen and idolators from their worship of the creatures and idols, but he also indicates that it must have been an easy matter for them to have made a God out of the sun (p. 50). He is also not averse to quoting the heathen philosophers to substantiate his own arguments.[21] Traherne's position on grace is not rigidly Calvinistic nor is it deistic. It approximates Arminian Anglicanism of his time.

Excursus: Traherne as Classicist

Traherne seldom refers to mythology or uses mythological metaphors.[22] In fact in his poem "The Author to the Critical Peruser" (F 23) he states that he rejects the use of references to pagan religions and oracles, as well as imitation of classical authors.

Seventeenth century education concentrated on the classics. Traherne's Ficino Notebook indicates that Traherne continued his study of the classics after he left the university. However, usually the references in his writings to classical authors were mediated to him through secondary sources: Ficino's commentaries on Plato, Gale's comments on Plato and Aristotle.[23] The Ficino Notebook contains Traherne's notes and extracts from Marsilio Ficino's epitomes and summaries of Plato's life and works (10-45). There are also a few notes from Ficino's translations of Plato (especially from the second, third, and fourth books of the *Republic*). C. Marks demonstrates that Traherne increasingly paraphrases and skips around as he proceeds through Ficino's epitomes,[24] and C. Owen shows that Traherne simplifies Ficino's epitomes, omitting obscure comparisons and noting primarily things which appealed to him. Significantly, he omits a passage which limits Socrates praise of beauty to the mind alone which would have deemphasized the beauty of the body.[25] This notebook is closely connected to the other references to Plato in Traherne's writings. In

---

21. See below, "Traherne as Classicist."
22. There are references to Ganimede, Danae, and Jove in his poem "Love" (see also "Fullnesse"), as well as to Homer's description of the travels of Odysseus and Diomedes which Traherne sees as precedents for the travels of the apostle Paul.
23. See chs. iii and iv above. Traherne copies Bacon's comments on the uses of ancient authors into his Early Notebook (93 and 99) from Bacon I, 449-50; see I 458-59.
24. See C. Marks, "Ficino Notebook," *Papers* (1969), 80 and *passim*.
25. See C. Owen, "The Thought and Art of Traherne," Univ. of London Masters' thesis (1957), pp. 29-30, quoted in C. Marks, "FN," *Papers*, p. 81.

one reference he places Plato, Cato, and the "Apostle" (John) on an equal footing (II *C* 84).[26]

In the Ficino Notebook there is also a lengthy section (twenty pages) devoted to a life of Socrates which treats the will, the soul, and the appetites. Sometimes Traherne comments in his notes in the margins of his notebook. There are also references to Socrates in the *Centuries* (see I *C* 40 where he deletes the ascription "that Glorious Philosopher") and perhaps in *Christian Ethicks* (p. 201). Traherne disagrees with Socrates' idea that "They are most Happy and neerest the Gods that needed Nothing." Traherne implies that Socrates was reproached for his stand by "Nature," but Traherne excuses him because perhaps "being an Heathen," he does not know that everything comes from God to man and is returned by man to God.[27]

Traherne also took notes on Theophilus Gale's chapter on Stoicism (CB, 88-89). Traherne disagreed with Stoicism. In the second *Century* Traherne asserts that the philosophers are blind and give offense by their idea that felicity consists in negatives, self-sufficiency, and contentment without indicating what felicity is, or distinguishing between true and false riches, pleasure and honors.[28]

The works of Aristotle formed the basis of seventeenth century education in almost every field and especially in ethics. Traherne calls the Peripatetics wise in so far as they are concerned with the "Nature and Estate of Man in this World. . .defining the Goods of the Body, Soul and Fortune to concur to Man's perfect Happiness" (*CE*, p. 18). He agrees with Aristotle's definition of felicity, although he condenses it. Traherne calls Aristotle "lucky" because he discovered the "Nature of Blessedness" without having heard of man's "Ascension into Heaven, nor of sitting down on the Throne of God" (*CE*, pp. 19, 59), and the "Wisest of Philosophers" because he thought the world was eternal (II *C* 21). Yet Aristotle, according to Traherne, believed only in a finite and terrestrial

---

26. See also FN 37, 3B and III *C* 60, II *C* 20. A reference to Plato in the *CE* (p. 95) is duplicated in SM III 16. Traherne copies some of T. Gale's paraphrases of Plato into his CB (see "Virtue" 96). See Marks, "FN," *Papers*, and E. Thompson's discussion of Traherne's philosophy in *PQ*, (1929), 97-112.

27. I *C* 40.

28. See *CE*, pp. 14, 17, 71, 231 for other references to Stoicism. For a discussion of *"Stoicismus Christianus"* see Marks, "Ficino Notebook," *Papers*, p. 800

happiness, and Traherne is amazed that he missed the truth (*CE*, p. 59). At least some of Aristotle's thought is mediated to Traherne by other sources (Gale and Eustache).[29]

Traherne agrees with Plutarch's definition of superstition (I C 17) and relates Plutarch's report that the "Great God Pan is dead" and the cessation of oracles as evidences of the truth of Christianity (CYB 64ff; 102vff). These may not be direct quotations.[30] Traherne also refers briefly to other Greek philosophers (Hippocrates, Galen), usually, but not always, from secondary sources.

There are fewer references to the Roman philosophers. There is a reference to Horace in the Early Notebook (p. 198), and at least one scholar has seen Traherne as an example of the Hortulan saint: a man who combines love of rural retirement and contemplation with the concepts of "the Earthly Paradise" and nature "as a divine heiroglyph." Horace and Virgil had created this combination of Stoic and Epicurean ideas. There are echoes of these themes in Traherne, but K. Røstvig rightly notes that Traherne's "was the more disembodied voice."[31]

Other scholars have seen parallels between the thought of Seneca and that of Traherne; however, there are few direct references to Seneca in his writings. Traherne attributes the statement "GOD gave me alone to all the World, and all the World to me alone" to Seneca both in his *Christian Ethics* (p. 51) and in his *Centuries* (I 15). This idea is basic to Traherne's thought. T. Harrison notes a number of parallels in ideas yet great differences in spirit and letter. Both Traherne and Seneca stress the beauty of the earth, the personal possession of the creation, service to others, yet Traherne has different bases for these affirmations.[32]

---

29. Traherne copied all of T. Gale's description of Aristotle's *Ethica* into his CB (21ff) and Eustache's comments on Aristotle into his EN (9).

30. For other references to Plutarch see IV C 33, 34; I C 22; II C 21. Traherne quotes him inaccurately in II C 21 saying that the *world* instead of the *light* was the most beautiful thing, another indication that Traherne reads his own ideas into his sources.

31. See *CE*, pp 198. Traherne cites Varro's idea that there are 288 "Opinions of Philosophers concerning Happiness." Traherne calls them blind and disagreeing (II C 99). Traherne uses a quote of Terence to illustrate the effect of penitence (III C 83; *CE*, p. 133). K. Røstvig, *The Happy Man* (Oslo, 1962), p. 314, 323 and *passim*.

32. Traherne bases a poem "Yee that Towers" (Marg, II, 210) on Seneca's *Thyestes*, parts of which he copied into his EN. There is also a reference to learning from Seneca's *Epistles* in the EN (140). See T. Harrison, "Seneca and Traherne," *Arion* 6 (1967), 403-405, and R. Ellrodt, *L'Inspiration*, Part I, vol. II (1960), pp. 276-277.

Traherne also refers to Cicero, Lully, Sallust, Tacitus, Ovid, and Epictetus on minor issues, but evidently Traherne is not significantly influenced by them. He uses their ideas to substantiate or provide contrast with his own ideas. In fact he criticizes the heathen poets (Greek and Roman) for their vanities, dreams, and fables (SM III 30; II *C* 100).

2. "the maner of its Exhibition under the various Dispensations of the Old and New Testament"

Like many other theologians of his day, Traherne recognizes two different covenants: that of works and that of grace.[33] The covenant of grace, the New Covenant, is arbitrary, free, and merciful (*CE*, p. 74), but men can not possibly keep the "Legal Rigour" of the covenant of works (CYB 47v).

According to Traherne, the Jewish people hold a special place in God's dispensation as custodians of the law. The salvation of man would be endangered by the "Extinction of that Nation." Yet the Jews broke their covenant and were punished by dispersion. Traherne prays that they be restored (*Thanks*, pp. 291ff).

The laws are commentaries on God's works (I *C* 20) and are more excellent than the works themselves (III *C* 72). Traherne calls the laws "Articles of Marriage," "Ordinances of God's house," the "Copy of thy Bosom," and they are fulfilled when men "prize all things according to their value" (*Thanks*, pp. 277ff). According to Traherne, the law shows man his need of a Savior, but it cannot bring him "one step nearer heaven."[34] The Holy Spirit imprints the law on man's soul and helps him keep the law in "an evangelical manner" (CYB 46r). In heaven man will be enabled to keep the law perfectly (CYB 47v).

3. "the Mediator of the Covenant"

Although Christology plays a dominant role in most dogmatics of the time, Traherne allots it only a minor position under the doctrine of man in the Estate of Grace. Moreover, neither the name Jesus nor the title Christ appear in his outline of theology. In addition, Traherne entitles his

---

33. See Edward Fisher, *Marrow of Modern Divinity* (1645); T. Adams, *Main Principles*; Matthew Scrivener, *A Course in Divinity* (London, 1674) who term them the old and the new covenants. The Westminster Confession uses the terms covenant of works and grace. Zwingli, Crocius, and Federal theology were all covenantal.

Christological section "the Mediator of the Covenant," which seems to place the major emphasis on covenant.[35] Fully half his subtopics in this section deal with covenant, yet in his writings, the concept of covenant is seldom used.

If frequent mention of any particular subject were an indication of its importance, then either anthropology or angelology is more important to Traherne than Christology. Perhaps this is the case not so much because Christology is unimportant, but rather because it is less a problem for Traherne. Traherne's Christology is usually orthodox doctrine restated with his own peculiar emphases.

Traherne uses and refers to specifically creedal statements on the person of Christ: "equal to God touching his Godhead, tho inferior to God touching his Manhood" (CYB 3; 34v), "Express Image of His Father's Person," all things were made by him (IV C 4). Christ's will and essence are one (I C 94). Traherne also reflects on the issues which the creeds raise. He thinks, for example, that although Christ's humanity was a perfect human nature, Christ was not a "person" because his humanity was related to the Deity; just as the soul of man is not a person but a perfect nature because it relates to the human body (SM III 95).

Traherne relates Christ's Incarnation to the entire scheme of salvation. Christ is not a common or adopted son, but a natural, infinite, immense, eternal, and only Son of God (CYB 76r; *Hex*, p. 6). The Incarnation,

---

34. EN, pp. 165ff. The Thirty-nine Articles confess that although the ceremonial and civil laws are not binding on a Christian, "no Christian man whatsoever is free from the obedience of the Commandments which are called moral" (VII). There is also a section in the *Life of Christ* which distinguishes among ceremonial, moral, civil, and ecclesiastical laws (p. 100). Wollebius provides helpful background information. He thinks that "The Law of God given by Moses, differs not really, but in some respect from the Law of Nature planted in Adam, the remainders of which are as yet to be found among the Gentiles" (p. 90). "The Law and the Gospel agree in the chief efficient cause, to wit God, and in the instrumental causes: both because the Law was delivered by Moses, and the Gospel by Christ fully; and also because the Law is by nature known to man, but the Gospel is not, except by God's gracious revelation. They agree in their common matter, because on both sides obedience is required. . . but they differ in their past matter; for the Law principally teacheth what we must do, and the Gospel, what we must believe" (p. 109). Calvin writes that "Christ, though known to the Jews under the Law, yet only manifested under the Gospel" (ch. 9). Chapters 10 and 11 of the *Institutes* treat the similarities and differences between the Old and New Testaments. *Institutes*, vol. III, chs. 9-11. See CYB 69v and *CE*, p. 61 for other references to "dispensations."

35. Calvin simply describes the office and person of the Mediator. *Institutes*, vol. II, chs. 12, 14, as did Wollebius, chs. 16 and 17.

according to Traherne, is a difficult but necessary doctrine. God uses prophecies, miracles, types, figures, ceremonies, and revelation to confirm it. And, as is usual with Traherne, he relates the Incarnation to anthropology. Man's sins make the Incarnation necessary (*CE*, p. 185), but the Incarnation also infinitely exalts human nature (*CE*, p. 195). "God never shewd Himselfe more a God, then when He appeared Man" (I C 90; *CE*, p. 225). There are some problematical statements, perhaps due to poetical and liturgical language, as well as to Traherne's love of paradox and parallels. For example, he states that Christ's human form is on earth while his divinity is in heaven (CYB 18r).

The Incarnation also provides Traherne with a vehicle for enunciating his own favorite themes. Mary, for example, received the grace to become the "Happy Mother of God's own Son" by her thoughts ("Inference" F 142). He asks rhetorically, who "Contracted this vast Immensity. . .into the narrow Compass of a Manger?" (*Life of Christ*, p. 99). Traherne also says that if he had not seen the goodness of God in the gift of his Son, he would never have understood that God gives all things to men (*Thanks*, p. 264). He reverses this doctrine in the *Centuries*: when once he saw heaven and earth given to him, *then* he could also believe that the Son was given to him (II 6). Of course Traherne rejoices in the incarnation (CYB 37v).

In the *Life of Christ*, there is a chronological treatment of Christ's life (pp. 92-308), although much of the material may not have been written by Traherne. That work ends with the Resurrection, although Traherne seems to be more fascinated with the topic of the Ascension (see CYB). In his writings Traherne alludes to some historical details of Christ's life, but often schematizes them. In the Church's Year Book, for example, he notes that Christ died when he was thirty three, had a three year ministry, was three days in the tomb (thirty six hours) which was three parts of three days (CYB 3).

The overwhelming majority of Traherne's references to the life and work of Christ center on his crucifixion: the root and center of Traherne's joy (*CE*, p. 219; I C 55-56); the mirror in which all things appear in their proper colors (I C 59); and the "chair of his profession" (*Thanks*, p. 267).

Traherne surveys the crucifixion from the point of view of God the Father, Christ himself and man. The crucifixion demonstrates God's hatred of sin (*CE*, p. 135); displays God's attributes of goodness, wisdom, power, mercy, and anger (I C 59); and delineates God's "secret Reservation," since he had told Adam that his recovery was impossible (*CE*, p. 101). Since God can not be reconciled to an ugly object, he found a way to sever sin from the sinner by punishing the transgression rather than the transgressor (II *C* 30).

According to Traherne, Christ voluntarily undertook the task of redeeming man (II *C* 33), partly from self-love (IV *C* 63), and was recompensed with a crown of majesty and a company of angels (CYB 34r; IV *C* 60). Nature (*CE*, pp. 102,195), angels (II *C* 33), or men (II *C* 32) could not have redeemed mankind, so Christ became a curse for man (*CE*, p. 261). By his own merit Christ's divine essence overcame the infinite punishments (II *C* 36). Christ thus pacified God's wrath and satisfied God's justice (*CE*, p. 100). He took the place of the guilty sinner (I *C* 77), paid the ransom, made satisfaction (CYB 34r), and subdued the powers of hell (*CE*, p. 169). Traherne does not accept the Calvinist theory of a limited atonement, for he believes that Christ shed his blood for all (CYB 49v). Moreover, Christ's blood is sprinkled on the heathen, the earth, and man's enjoyments (*CE*, p. 103). All of this is done by God's grace and love without any merit on man's part (CYB 44r). Christ's death is thus "the most delightful thing that can be imagined" (I *C* 80).

The result and effect of the crucifixion is manifold. Primary for Traherne is the restorative nature of the redemption. Men are restored to the end for which they were created, to the exercise of the powers they lost by sin, and to a greater glory than before.[36] However, in the *Christian Ethicks*, Traherne admits that the restoration is only partial (p. 45). Because of the crucifixion, Traherne thinks the soul is infinitely more beloved and precious, man's reason is more exalted (*CE*, p. 196), and man has new strengths (*CE*, p. 101). Traherne uses other related terminology to describe the redemptive process, such as restitution (SM IV 67), improvement, second love (*CE*, p. 61), recovery (SM II 140), and a return to infancy ("Infant Ey").

Traherne is particularly concerned about proving the authenticity of Christ's resurrection and with the post-resurrection appearances. He summarizes the various problems involved in the resurrection accounts and takes great pains to deal with them in detail. A recurrent refrain is "the truth of his resurrection." Christ appeared, for example, five times in one

---

36.   SM II 14, III 95; II *C* 5; and *CE*, p. 102.

day: to both sexes, to the clergy, to the laity, at home, away, at various times, and to all the senses "so that his Truth might be known" (CYB 8v, 11v). The doubts of the disciples and their subsequent belief also confirms for Traherne the truth of Christ's resurrection (CYB 2r).

Traherne devotes a number of pages to the post-resurrection appearances in the Church's Year Book, delving into why Christ appeared as he did, how he could eat, what happened to the food, why he entered the closed room (CYB 10vff). Though Traherne states repeatedly that the issue is the truth of the resurrection, not the nature of the celestial or glorified body, he, nevertheless, concludes that Christ's post-resurrection appearances demonstrate the subtilty, omnipotence, and impassibility of the glorified body (CYB 11vff, 32v).

In the *Thanksgivings* Traherne states that "our human body" is seated at God's right hand (pp. 366-367), yet elsewhere he states that Christ's body is "wholly spiritual" (pp. 384ff). That is a paradox which has exercised theologians for centuries, but Traherne seems unaware of the problem, even though he states that "The Truth is sometimes more Eminent in being vindicated, then when only affirmed" (CYB 2r).

Traherne sees Christ as central: the "end of the Law, the centre of time, the main Business of all the Dispensations of God's Providence," and the focus of the law and the gospel (*CE*, p. 114). At the same time, Traherne's theology does not have Christology as its center in the usual sense of that term. Felicity is more a central motif or anthropology.

4. "the Conditions of the Covenant"

According to Traherne faith and repentance are the principle virtues in the kingdom of grace and, apparently, conditions of the covenant. By them the sinner is restored to his capacity and power of living in the similitude of God (*CE*, p. 106). Faith and repentance also "secure" man's redemption, since Christ's death is sufficient but not efficient until applied subjectively by faith and repentance (*Hex*, p. 34). They are revealed not by nature but by revelation (*CE*, p. 101) and are "Great and necessary Duties" in this estate (CYB 2v).

There seems to have been some disagreement in the seventeenth century as to whether faith and repentance are conditions of the covenant. R. Baxter poses the question;[37] Thomas Collier says they are not conditions of the covenant but a branch and an evidence;[38] and Henry More defines saving faith as covenant.[39] Thomas Adams calls them simply "Graces;"[40] and Calvin discusses faith and repentance in the *Institutes*, but not as conditions of the covenant. [41]

a) "Faith"

Reflecting the disagreement of his age and the conflicting confessions, Traherne has no single definition of faith, nor does he follow any one theologian or school. He thinks that faith is a faculty to believe residing in the intellect and not in the will (*CE*, pp. 106-107); that faith is a virtue by which men acknowledge the credibility of the testimonies they believe to be true with regard to the past, present, and future (*CE*, p. 117); that faith is infused by the Holy Spirit.[42]

The objects of faith are doctrine, history, and prophesy, which parallel the parts of Scripture (*CE*, pp. 117ff). However, in a listing of what constitutes the objects of faith, Traherne mixes spiritual and secular history. Traherne thinks that it is faith which leads men to believe that there were such men as Julius Caesar, Abraham, and Moses stating that neither reason nor nature alone could demonstrate their existence (*CE*, pp. 107ff). Faith can also be propped up by "External Circumstances and inward Properties" by which true and infallible testimonies are distinguished from false (*CE*, p. 100), but the Christian religion is the only religion where all the "Causes of Faith perfectly concur" (*CE*, p. 110).

According to Traherne, faith is suspect only by the lazy, the profane, the half-witted, and the enemies of felicity and virtue (*CE*, p. 111). Atheists exist, Traherne admits, but they must be blind and ignorant because God and the objects of faith are so evident. The consideration of one soul should be sufficient to convince all the atheists in the world of the existence of God (IV *C* 81). The atheist is, according to Traherne, a kind of "miracle" for he is a "walking carcas in the Land of the Living," a prisoner in his bondage to

---

37. *Catholic Theology*, Part II, ch. xii.
38. *Marrow of Christianity* (London, 1646), ch. 5.
39. *Grand Mysterie of Godliness*, p. 325.
40. *Main Principles*, pp. 6ff.
41. *Institutes*, vol. III, chs. 2-3.
42. CYB 88r. Aquinas defines faith as an assent of the intellect. Faith for Aquinas was also a virtue, infused, and inhering in the soul. See Costello, pp. 117ff. T. Jackson defines faith as assent (p. 604), thinks that the will and understanding are identical (p. 623) and that faith is infused. *Works*, p. 873.

what is visible. That God assumed the world for his "Body" should have outdone all the possible wishes or desires of an atheist (SM IV 34).[43] Traherne thus turns the materialism of the atheist against him.

With regard to the relationship of faith and reason, it is necessary to distinguish among Traherne's four estates. Reason has different powers and limitations in each of the four. In the estate of innocence nature instructs man, and man could trust his reason (*CE*, p. 33). After the fall, man was "still a reasonable Creature," but his reason was corrupted and vitiated (*CE*, p. 102). Since men "tumbled out of Eden," they "are almost in all things contrary to GOD" (*CE*, p. 238). Although Adam and Eve, who experienced the estate of innocence and misery, could compare both estates and remember some of the things corrupted reason had taught them, their descendents could not. Thus it is now possible for men to be totally ignorant of God, their own nature, the glory of the world, and their relationship to the creatures (*CE*, pp. 37ff). In the estate of grace Christ restores man to the power he lost by sin, but without Christ he can do nothing (*CE*, p. 102). Reason is, thus, not totally operative in the estate of grace, and man can trust only enlightened reason. In the estate of glory man's reason will be fully restored.

Traherne distinguishes between natural and sanctified reason. The knowledge of the heathen is imperfect, but reason is more exalted since Christ's death (*CE*, p. 196). Although it is not clear whether Traherne thinks it theoretically possible to know God or come to felicity by unaided reason alone, he does state that no one has actually attained this grace (*CE*, pp. 59ff).

Education aids reason in its task of guiding and leading the soul by a life of virtue to felicity (*CE*, p. 60). Traherne cites St. Paul who commands Christians to be mature in their understanding. He deduces from this that a Christian with only a little understanding is a child, a shell, an apparition. Thus, though a weak Christian can "believe great things by an implicit faith," it is desirable that his faith be changed into assurance which requires both knowledge and understanding (IV *C* 6). Traherne, therefore, divides Christians into perfect and imperfect, as well as intelligent and mature, or weak and inexperienced Christians. He does not use the term "ignorant" for he says that that is a contradiction in terms. He deduces that every

---

43.   See T. Jackson, *Works*, vol. V for a discussion of atheism.

Christian will hate the imperfect, and a perfect Christian is a "Divine Philosopher." According to Traherne, a philosopher is a "Lover of Wisdom," and a Christian also is "a Lover of Wisdom," thus the Christian and the Philosopher are united in their love of wisdom (IV *C* 5). This point of view is in tension with his exalted view of childhood. Evidently his view of childhood had been qualified by insights gained from the Cambridge Platonists who placed a high value on education and reason.[44]

Faith and reason are not completely separate, though they are formally distinct. The object that is discoverable by reason, may also be believed by faith. Thus reason does not destroy but confirms, perfects (*CE*, p. 112), assists (*CE*, p. 109), augments, and fortifies faith (CYB 84). Reason and the senses, however, are to be subdued when they oppose God, and the understanding is to be held captive (CYB 2r).

Traherne's handling of the relationship between faith and works is similar to his handling of the relationship between faith and reason.[45] For Traherne faith is a prerequisite for works and is itself a work which God accepts in place of all other works. This is not to say that good works are unnecessary, but rather to stress that man is justified by faith alone. By faith man is given a power and an inclination to do works of love and piety (*CE*, pp. 100, 106ff, 223). Man makes his calling sure with good works (*Hex*, p. 34), and he can purify his nature with a "little industry" (*CE*, p. 16). God infinitely desires that men do good works, for in this way men can be "Activ and Reign in Glory." In all else man is "passiv and Receptiv" (SM III 40-41).

No one can save himself with good works. The works of the heathen, according to Traherne, lack the excellency that should be in human actions, are void of "Life from Heaven," of the "Light of the Understanding," of the "vigor of the Will," of knowledge, and of "GOD'S infinite Love" (*CE*, p. 61).

---

44. Richard Hooker, Lancelot Andrewes, John Donne, and Laud carefully distinguish between grace and nature, faith and reason. See H. Baker's discussion in *Wars of Truth*, pp. 117. Lord Herbert of Cherbury is far more positive on the place of natural reason. See Baker, pp. 121ff. The Cambridge Platonists also stress the power of man's reason. Culverwel asserts that reason can grasp the natural law, but T. Gale thinks that the natural law is "in a great measure obliterated." (Traherne copied this passage into his CB, 64.) Many took offence at the Cambridge Platonist's stress on reason. See C. Marks, "Cambridge Platonism," *Renaissance News*, pp. 526ff.

45. The Thirty-nine Articles state that good works are the fruits of faith and follow justification. They may make known a "lively faith" (XII; cf. XIII, XIV). T. Jackson states that "Faith is the soul of good works." *Works*, ch. v; see also ch. vii.

Faith, however, "being alone" is dead. Man should not "depend upon a meer Historical Faith, which even the Devils have." Men are taught to do good works by faith, and good works reveal and justify faith. Faith must be put into practice (CYB 2lr). In fact in the Select Meditations Traherne implies that a man can know he is in the estate of grace by the doing of good works (SM III 77).

Closely related to the issue of faith and works is the problem of synergism.[46] Some statements of Traherne at first reading are apparently synergistic, but in the context of his writings he is not a synergist. Traherne states, for example, that God implants a principle of goodness in man making him prone to be good, inclined to love, and desirous of being a joy, a blessing, and a treasure (*Hex*, p. 86). According to Traherne, it is impossible for man "to love Evil and to abhor Good" when he sees with open eyes. Traherne does admit, however, that there is the possibility of deception by false appearances, but he hopes for perfection in the life to come (*Hex*, p. 87). He also believes in the possibility of relapsing and repentance.[47]

Traherne exhorts his soul to "be very solicitous to cooperate with Him [the Holy Spirit] in his Holy Motions, that he may assist thee with Perseverance to thy Salvation." He adds, almost as an afterthought: "From thee is all my Good to take Beginning" (*Hex*, p. 12). A more systematic theologian might have reversed the order of the paragraph and paid more attention to details and word usage, and by consistently doing so have been exempted from the suspicion of Pelagianism, semi-Pelagianism, or synergism. At the same time, a more systematic theologian might not also have been a poet and a mystic.

Traherne writes that while God wants man to be perfect, he wants man to participate in the task rather than to receive perfection by divine fiat. In this way, man cooperates with divine grace. Good works can make God's calling sure, but faith and repentance secure redemption. Man's

---

46. The Thirty-nine Articles confess that after the fall man "cannot turn and prepare himself, by his own natural strength and good works, to faith and calling upon God." Man has "no power to do good works. . .without the grace of God by Christ" (X). Wollebius writes that those "who ascribe to an unregenerate man free will, or other faculties by which he may do well, or prepare himself to his own conversion" look for a "house in the ashes" (p. 89). T. Jackson states that "The natural man left to himself. . .will always in one point or other conceive amiss of the Deity" (p. 873).

47. *Hex*, p. 22; and see note 48 below.

cooperation is necessary for his sanctification and perfection (*Hex*, pp. 34-35; CYB 2lv). The whole passage in the *Hexameron* strains at the limits of orthodoxy, but it stays within the pale by slight emphases and word choice: "after it," "Sufficient," "efficient," "applied." At issue is the difference between justification and sanctification. Cooperation is allowable in the latter but suspect in the former. Traherne has opted for the Arminian position. In any event without faith full felicity cannot be enjoyed (*CE*, p. 112).

b) "Repentance"

Traherne's understanding of *repentance* separates him from the Enthusiasts of his day who usually believed in entire sanctification and perseverance.[48] Although the longest section devoted to the issue reads like a textbook definition, related passages indicate that Traherne personally affirms the doctrine of repentance. Traherne states that the remote efficient cause of repentance is God; its immediate efficient cause is the inclination or will of the penitent. Sorrow is its material cause and "the Equity and Piety where with it is attended" is the formal cause. This makes repentance a virtue. The immediate final cause of repentance is amendment of life, and its ultimate final cause is eternal salvation (*CE*, p. 126). Contrasting with this scholastic terminology is a devotion on St. Peter's Day based on personal repentance (CYB 76vff) and a poetic section on tears in the *Hexameron* (pp. 21ff).

Repentance would not be necessary if the Christian were perfect (as some perfectionist sects of the time believed). Although a man can cooperate with God to prevent relapsing, according to Traherne, the possibility of sinning still exists (*Hex*, p. 23). Because every sin after pardon is an infinite disaster and blemish (*CE*, p. 259), repentance is necessary as a remedy for sin (CYB 76v). Without repentance the sinner cannot be

---

48. The Thirty-nine Articles state that "repentance is not to be denied to such as fall into sin after Baptism." Moreover, "they are to be condemned which say, they can no more sin as long as they live here" (XVI). A number of passages in Traherne's writings, if not personal confessions, at least indicate Traherne's theological acceptance of the need for repentance. "And since my Baptisme, and since my Repentance, I have Grieviously sinned. Let this Confession stand here as a Token how I loathe and abhor myselfe" (SM II 34). ". . . the Horrible sin of my Backsliding afterwards. The many Inspirations and Holy Motions which from my Childhood upwards he inspired into me. All which I have Layd wast and neglected wholly" (SM IV 67). See also *Thanks*, pp. 226-227; IV C 30; SM III 98; CYB 57v; 79r.

cleansed. Traherne sees repentance as a result of sin, and thus it cannot exist in the estate of innocence (*CE*, p. 125). It is a grace, a Christian virtue, and the only purgative virtue, but it is not a moral virtue, because God concurs in it (see *CE*, p. 346n). Repentance involves confession, hatred, and forsaking of sin, as well as the intention to amend one's life.[49] Even the heathen have a "Conscience of Sin" and use the name *Poenitentia*, but they mean something else by it. Heathen ordinances, according to Traherne, are "Emblematical" signifying something more. Real repentance is unknown among the heathen (*CE*, pp. 126ff).

Repentance is not only a remedy for sin, it also enables man to recover the divine image.[50] After repentance, the Christian's godliness is divine (*CE*, p. 257). Traherne thinks that repentance should result in a desire not to sin again (*Hex*, p. 20), as well as in a "torrent of joys" (III C 48).

5. "the Sacraments or Seals of" the Covenant

Traherne discusses the sacraments only briefly. He does this chiefly in the *Hexameron* and the Church's Year Book. Designating the means of grace as "Sacraments or Seals" of the covenant is uncommon in dogmatics texts of the seventeenth century. Thomas Adams (perhaps a teacher of Traherne) uses precisely the same terminology as Traherne,[51] and Wollebius uses approximately the same.[52] Perhaps Traherne borrows his terminology from Adams who in turn was influenced by Wollebius. Traherne also uses the terms: means of salvation (CYB 14r), means of grace (*Hex*, p. 38), and ordinances. However, for Traherne, ordinances are not synonymous with sacraments. In the Church's Year Book the ordinances include prayer, the word, and sacraments (53v). Thomas Adams has the same listing. In *Christian Ethicks* Traherne lists "Prayer, Meditation, hearing his Word. . . receiving the Sacrament" as ordinances (p. 142). Traherne also refers to the New Testament practice of anointing with oil and states that it ought to be

---

49.   *CE*, p. 128; III C 48; CYB 74r.
50.   *CE*, pp. 127ff; "Infant Ey" F 86-87.
51.   *Main Principals*, pp. 6ff. Adams defines a sacrament as "an holy Ordinance, instituted of Christ, wherein by sensible signs, Christ and the benefits of the new Covenant are represented, sealed, and applied to believers" (p. 157). By faith men are "made partakers of his body and blood" (p. 165).
52.   Wollebius defines a sacrament as a "Sacred action instituted by God, in which that grace which Christ hath promised to the Covenanters is sealed by visible signes on God's part, and they are tyed on their part to obedience" (p. 175).

symbolically maintained. When someone is sick, the elders should be called to pray over the sick person with "the oil of thy mercies in the name of the Lord" (CYB 22v). Apparently Traherne means that prayer alone was effective without oil. He does not call this practice either an ordinance or a sacrament.

There are no sacraments in the estate of innocency, according to Traherne, because there were no supernatural mysteries to be typified (*CE*, p. 34). In the Old Testament God reveals himself under the elements of oil, water, and fire (CYB 49v; 108r). Apparently Traherne considers only baptism and the Lord's Supper as sacraments, although he once states that God calls men by baptism and "all" the means of grace, implying that there were more than two. Calvin, Wollebius, the Thirty Nine Articles, and Thomas Adams recognize only baptism and the Lord's Supper as sacraments.

Traherne sees the sacraments as "Arteries which convey the Holy Spirit to men" (CYB 53V), as "ordinary Means of Salvation to the chosen" (CYB 14r), as consolations and refreshers of men in distress, as ways of conversing with God, and as means of approaching him. They are also intended to bring men into a closer "Intimacy and familiarity with God" (*CE*, p. 142). Without the presence of the Holy Spirit, the sacraments are not fully effectual (see CYB 53v). Not to use them is to be unprofitable and is "severely punishable" (*Hex*, p. 38).

From the few statements Traherne makes about Baptism, it is difficult to categorize him confessionally. He does not reflect any of the terminology of the Thirty-nine Articles or their concerns,[53] nor is he explicit about the effect of infant baptism which might have clarified his understanding of childhood innocence. Water is used in Baptism, according to Traherne, to signify that spiritual pollution is washed away (CYB 49v). Without the Holy Spirit, baptism is similar to that performed by John the Baptist (CYB 53v). There are two types of Christians "engendred by the Waters of Baptism," the active and the contemplative (*Hex*, pp. 61ff).

---

53. In the *Life of Christ* (of uncertain authorship) baptism is called a "Laver of Regeneration and Baptismal Grace" (p. 114). The Thirty-nine Articles define baptism as "not only a sign of profession and mark of difference. . . it is also a sign of regeneration or new birth." "It is like an instrument which grafts men on to the church. It visibly signs and seals the forgiveness of sins and adoption as sons of God. It confirms faith and increases grace. Children are also to be baptized" (XXVII).

When discussing the Lord's Supper Traherne's choice of words implies a Calvinist and Anglican stance. The efficacy of the Lord's Supper "figures in the Bread," and it is not Christ's "Bodily, but Divine Presence that Benefiteth our Souls." He cites the John six passage in two different ways in the Church's Year Book. In one section, "The flesh profiteth nothing, it is the Spirit that quickeneth," implies that the Spirit is the only efficacious agent in the sacrament (19vff); while elsewhere he writes that without the Holy Spirit in the sacrament "the flesh profiteth nothing" (CYB 53v) implying that the flesh is of some value when the Spirit is present. Traherne also states that the bread and wine used in the Lord's Supper "signify the divine and eternal Feast" which makes men joyous partakers of the body and blood of Christ (CYB 49v).

Traherne uses the sacraments as explanations of how men are united to God. God gives himself to be food, uniting himself with men and is "incorporated" with them. Just as "Bread and Wine are mingled with our flesh and is. . . Diffused through all our members so he is Lov mingling with our Lov" (SM II 66). The traditional controversies center on the relationship of Christ and the elements of bread and wine,[54] but Traherne is more concerned with God's relationship to man and with the benefits of union, joy, and love.

6. "the Scriptures"

The Bible consists of history, prophesy, and doctrine according to Traherne (*CE*, p. 117). Some aspects of Scripture are already known by reason or nature, but Scripture brings them to light again, to sanctify, to approve, and to confirm nature, or to make it easier to understand celestial mysteries (*CE*, p. 119). Traherne includes Scripture along with prayer and the sacraments as the means of salvation to the chosen (CYB 14r). Scripture is infallible (III *C* 45). Turks, Jews, Infidels and especially the church (which is to be believed more than all the others) testify and confess the

---

54.   The Thirty-nine Articles assert that "The Bread. . . is a partaking of the Body of Christ; only after an heavenly and spiritual manner" (XXVIII). The "wicked. . . in no wise are. . . partakers of Christ" (XXXI). Article XXX defends communion in both kinds and XXXI the one oblation on the cross. Cudworth was concerned with relating the Lord's Supper to heathen and Jewish sacrificial rites. See Wade, p. 230. T. Jackson defends "Christ's virtual Presence" or Real Presence against transubstantiation and Consubstantiation (which he considers to be the Lutheran view). pp. 301ff.

"History of the Bible" (*CE*, p. 120).[55] He lists eight reasons why God gave the Bible to man the way he did, which Traherne thinks was in the "best of all possible Manners" (III C 28, 33). There is a variety yet unity in Scripture, and any contradictions are due to the "obscurity" of man's understanding.

Traherne delights in giving the "Reason of Scripture," why things are phrased the way they are, rather than a proof text method (IV C 31). Scripture makes men joyful and exhibits Christ by describing his glory (CYB 64), and it confirms, seals, and witnesses to bliss ("The Evidence" F 126-127).

Although his position is not consistent or neatly categorized, generally in autobiographical passages Traherne seems to stress the place of immediate experience over nature and reason. Elsewhere in his writings he tends to stress the place of revelation (or Scripture).[56] Traherne implies that many things are or seem to be revealed to him alone without the mediation of either Scripture or the church ("Dumnesse" 40-44). He says he had a "pulpit, teacher, and temple in his mind" with a large text (God's works) to comment upon. The heavens and the earth communicate with him, and even as an adult, childhood continues to be his teacher (III C 4). He says he discovered on his own what Scriptures reveal (III C 66), even though elsewhere he says he desired a book from heaven (III C 27). His own senses and nature teach him the truth ("Nature" 60-64).

There is a lack of precision in what Traherne thinks can be discovered by natural and supernatural reason. In one place he states that natural knowledge can discover such things as: that there is a God, that man is

---

55. Thomas Adams calls Scripture the "Means or Rule," and states that it primarily teaches "what man is to believe concerning God and what duty God requireth of man" (p. 7). T. Jackson asserts that Scripture is the "sole, Entire, and Compleat Rule of Faith" (Sect. III; and vol. II, ch. xxii). Jackson is concerned about the "Historical Characters of the Sacred Writings" and the harmony, affections, and dispositions of the sacred writers.

56. See ch. ii D above, but in an "F" poem Traherne states that the restored adult is superior to the child because reason improves his view. Reality rather than novelty teaches the adult. Sense, reason, and intelligence all confirm Traherne's childhood experiences ("Right Apprehension" F 123-126). Compare Calvin "The need of Scripture as a Guide and Teacher in coming to God as a Creator." *Institutes*, ch. 6; "All the principles of piety subverted by fanatics, who substitute revelations for Scripture." *Institutes*, ch. 9. Wollebius also acknowledges "no other principle of Divinity than the written Word of God" (pp. 4ff). T. Jackson devotes a chapter to "the Right use of Reason. . . for determining Controversies in Divinity, whereof the Sacred Scripture is the Sole Rule" (vol. III), ch. 5. Robert Barclay (a Quaker) devotes a chapter to immediate revelation (ch. 2) and another to the "Saving and Spiritual Light, wherewith evry man is enlightened" (chs. 5, 6) in his *An Apology for the True Christian Divinity* (London, 1678).

created in God's image, that death is a punishment for sin, that the soul is immortal, that there are immortal rewards and punishments. These things can be discovered by reason and experience, and, as he puts it, are "therefore taught by the Word of GOD." Scripture seems almost a stamp of approval on reason and experience in such passages (*CE*, p. 119).

Most of his positive statements on reason and nature as well as on immediate or direct revelation occur in the poetry and *Centuries*, but there are also evidences of a similar position in *Christian Ethicks*. He designates coming immediately to God as a "right and safe way" (p. 228). Perhaps imprecise word usage rather than a reference to immediate revelation is at fault. He may be countering the papacy in the passage. During the seventeenth century, however, George Fox uses the term inner light to describe his own illumination, and some of the Cambridge Platonists hold that the Bible is not the sole source of revelation. Reason, which they call a "seed of deiform nature," is also a form of natural revelation. Some comparison might be made with Descartes' "clear and distinct ideas" and Lord Herbert of Cherbury's "common notions."[57] Traherne does state that the church does not bind anyone to believe anything not in Scripture (CYB 98r).

Traherne has another side, one more in accord with the Thirty-nine Articles and the Protestant tradition. Generally (but not always) when he speaks of mankind, he implies that Scripture is necessary. In the *Centuries* he rhetorically asks, "Who would hav believed this had not that Book told me?" Unfortunately, it is not so easy to link Traherne's own stance with that of mankind in general. In *Christian Ethicks* he states that nature alone cannot divulge the way to restoration and recovery. The way must be taught by revelation, miracles, and oracles from heaven (p. 100). Moreover, Christ's incarnation, death, and satisfaction are "above" the course of nature (*CE*, p. 119). In the Church's Year Book (in a section heavily dependent on other sources) Traherne neatly categorizes what can be known by nature, reason and the Bible. By nature men can know there is a God; reason shows that this God is one; but his "Perfections and Excellencies," attributes, essence, subsistence, "the Trinity and the Distribution of Persons" are revealed by the Scriptures illumined and interpreted by the Holy Ghost (57r-58v). There is another section on the

---

57.　See B. Willey's discussion in *Seventeenth*, pp. 78ff; and Art. VI of the Thirty-nine Articles.

topic of how Scripture is superior to reason which has been deleted but is still legible (58vff). Theorizing as to why it was deleted or using it to delineate Traherne's thought would serve no purpose.

Excursus: Traherne as Exegete

Traherne usually uses the King James Version of the Bible, though at times he resorts to the Prayer Book version of the Psalms (1662) or mixes the two (see III *C* 71). Since he quotes them more than other books, the Psalms are apparently his favorite book of the Bible. The historical and prophetic books of the Old Testament and the pastoral letters of Paul seem to be the least frequently quoted. He refers often to Job, Jeremiah, Isaiah, Song of Solomon, Luke, John, Romans, Ephesians, Hebrews and Revelation, especially in his meditational writings. He also quotes the Apocrypha (see *CE*, p. 76).

His poetic style is influenced by the Psalms, and there are times one is not sure where the Psalmist leaves off and Traherne begins (see III *C* 7lff). There are long paraphrases of the Psalms in the *Thanksgivings*. The *Hexameron* includes more material from the Psalms than from Genesis; and the *Centuries* include long sections on the Psalms (see III *C* 69-96). Traherne identifies with the Psalmist David, finding in the Psalms substantiation for his own ideas. He tends also to read his own ideas into the Psalms. He calls David a "Divine Philosopher" and a "Royal Psalmist" (*CE*, p. 41), and rejoices that one and the same Spirit led both David and him (III *C* 20). David was a prophet, according to Traherne, but enjoyed being a poet (III *C* 69). Perhaps Traherne's favorite Scripture verse is Psalm 8:5. For no apparent reason Traherne skips a number of Psalms in a section which is more or less consecutive paraphrase (see III *C* 69ff which omits Psalms 34, 37-44, 52-57, 60-62, 64, 75-83). Traherne does refer to the imprecatory Psalms in this section. The Psalms may have influenced Traherne in part because of the high regard in which they were held in Restoration liturgical life, as well as because of their constant use in Puritan worship. They may also have appealed to his poetic nature.[58]

Sometimes Traherne cites Scripture verses which are not meaningful, coherent, or relevant.[59] Traherne also often quotes verses which make different points from the one he makes or stress other things.[60] Moreover, he mistakenly refers to one verse or book when he means another.[61] At times Traherne's paraphrasing diverges significantly from the text.[62] He sometimes mixes the order of a passage changing its meaning.[63] He alters punctuation and grammar.[64] His usual mistake, however, is faulty quotation since he apparently usually relies on memory.[65] Traherne also commits the unforgivable exegetical sin: altering the text to make his point. In the second *Century* (35) Traherne devotes a section to the question why angels cannot redeem man. However, as Margoliouth notes, the Bible does not treat that question. The verse to which Traherne refers has to do with man's inability to save another man (see Psalm 49:7-8).[66]

An explicit example of Traherne as exegete occurs in *Christian Ethicks* (p. 198). He writes, "Were I for my life to interpret that Text of our Saviour, 'The Meek shall inherit the Earth. . . .'" First, Traherne says that "every knowing man may enjoy the beauty and glory of the whole World. . . delight in all the abundance of Treasures. . .especially since by the Ordinances of Nature all men are to be his peculiar Treasures." Traherne then qualifies this by saying that he might do this if all other men loved

---

58. H. Fisch thinks that "Traherne was perhaps of all the religious writers of the seventeenth century the most deeply conscious of the Psalms as a model for writing and as a model for the good life." *Jerusalem and Albion* (London, 1964), p. 53. E. Christ thinks that the Old Testament may have appealed to Traherne because of its plural and collective concepts (p. 55). However, C. Marks notes that Traherne was probably not a "proficient Hebraist." CB, *Papers* (1964), 462. Stewart attributes Traherne's use of the Psalms to his "high church sympathies." p. 99. However, the Puritans probably held the Psalms in even higher esteem than the Anglicans.

59. Traherne cites, for example, Psalm 103: 1-5 as the keynote for the "Thanksgiving for the Body," but it is not as relevant as verse 20 of the same chapter to which he does not refer. Perhaps the words "Benefits," "healeth," "life," and "youth" suggest the body for Traherne.

60. See *CE*, p. 252, for example, which is paralleled in "Thoughts" II 173.

61. See, for example, *CE*, p. 257 where he refers to Psalm 183 when he means Psalm 139, and *CE*, p. 103 where the reference is to Ezekiel and Malachi and not Matthew.

62. See *CE*, p. 77 on I Cor. 13:12; and IV *C* 92.

63. See I *C* 32 and *Hex*, p. 18, for example.

64. In the *Hex*, for example, he changes questions into answers (p. 18) and pronouns into the third person in the *CE* (p. 175).

65. See *CE*, p. 178 where he quotes from memory and p. 184 where he quotes the same verse correctly.

66. See also *CE*, p. 42 where Traherne quotes "the knowing Man is the friend of God." C. Marks notes that in the book of James, Abraham was called a "Friend of God." There is no passage which states what Traherne does. Also, in the fourth *Century* (92) Traherne substitutes "Glorious Mercy" for "righteous judgments" which is in line with Traherne's positive outlook and in tune with the exultation of the meditation, but it involves an alteration of the text. See Marg II 293. H. Fairchild states that Traherne interprets the Gospels in the light of his own personal temperament (p. 568). R. Ellrodt thinks that he does not falsify the Scriptures, he merely changes their perspective and uses them to confirm his own gospel of felicity. *L'Inspiration*, pp. 289ff.

him, but they do not due to "their perverseness and disorder." Unless "by the vertue of Meekness" he forgives them and maintains "the quiet of his own Soul in the midst of their distempers" he will lose "his Fruitions." Traherne concludes that the meek man may continue to enjoy all things because he is not disturbed by the disorder around him. What is more, the meek man can pacify, rule, heal, and love his enemies and sinners, thus recovering "his Right, and ancient Fruitions." His interpretation not only diverges significantly from traditional exegesis of the text, but he has read into the text (*eisegesis*) his own themes of enjoyment, delight, and treasures.[67]

Traherne uses various types of scriptural interpretation, including literal, moral, mystical, and allegorical methods. There is an example of the allegorical method in the third *Century* (77) where Traherne interprets the marriage described in Psalm 45. The bridegroom is Jesus Christ; the bride is the church; every child (member of the church) is a prince if male or a bride to the king of heaven if female.[68] Like many other seventeenth century theologians Traherne depends upon typology, emblemology, and analogy, particularly in his Old Testament exegesis. There are, for example, a number of extended passages on the law and the ceremonies of the temple and what they typify. St. Paul (especially in Hebrews 9-11), the Medieval commentators, and Calvin are a few of those who provide a precedent for this type of exegesis.[69] Traherne is also fascinated by analogies between the Old and New Testaments: i.e. man was created and redeemed on the sixth day (CYB 3v). However, typology and analogy are more than a tool for biblical exegesis; this type of interpretation is a mind-set as well. Traherne prays, for example, that every day's eating and drinking might be a "Type of our Supping with the Lamb, every days rising a type of our joyful Resurrection" (CYB 46r).

---

67. Traherne also sees the men of the Old Testament (such as Adam, Jacob, Moses, and David) as interested, as he was, with the creation, the heavens, the glory of the world. See, for example, III C 67, 77, 78, 86, 93. There are also biblical commentaries in the Early Notebook. See pp. 215, 217, 222-26, 228-29, 231.

68. Traherne thinks that the departure from Emmaus shows "how the Passion of Fear, many times, make a Timorous Soul Depart not only from the Church, but from Spiritual Comforts, to find Eas in corporal Recreations" (CYB 9vff).

69. For typology, see, for example, CE, pp. 63, 110, 129, 139; CYB 49v-50, SM III 60; and C. Marks notes in the CE, pp. 346-347. T. Jackson's works have long sections on the typology and prefigurations of the Old Testament.

For Traherne exegesis is not merely an intellectual exercise. Illumination is needed to understand the mysteries hidden in Scripture (CYB 10v). Particularly revealing is Traherne's very early poem found in his Early Notebook "On the Bible." There he states that the person who thinks he understands the Bible lacks intelligence. He can be deceived for "The way is intricate/that leads into a Maze." Instead, the Bible should be approached with reverence while "Sence stands By" (205).

His description of the evangelists indicates his use of sources. Mark is, according to Traherne, a "Faithful Scribe," a "Comprehensive Historian," and a "Secretary" of the Holy Ghost. Mark omits nothing important even though his Gospel is shorter than the others. Matthew has the most material on Christ's humanity (i.e. his genealogy); however, Matthew does not slight Christ's divinity. Luke has the most material on Christ's priestly office. Apparently, some of Traherne's generalizations derive from the emblems assigned the evangelists: Luke is emblemized by an ox, for example, evidencing for Traherne the strong labors and sacrifices Christ made (CYB 17vff).

His general attitude toward Scripture reflects the orthodoxy of his time. He never questions or criticizes what he reads in Scripture. Scripture informs his theology and his thought, often providing the images, metaphors, and structure of his ideas. However, to some extent the Bible confirms what he thinks he already knows by experience.[70] Scripture, for Traherne, also encompasses "the best of Tidings, the wisest Counsels, the newest Revelations, Heavenly Discoveries. . . Depths. . . Wonders. . . Promises, the joys of God, Divine Affections, the greatest Encouragements, Hallelujahs, Raptures" (*Thanks*, p. 304). What Traherne finds in Scripture, approximates what he says St. Matthew's Gospel evidences: wonder, effects, and benefits (CYB 17vff).

7. "Ministers"

Traherne's understanding of ministry can be seen historically, doctrinally, pastorally, and personally. Historically, Jesus had twelve disciples, and, according to Traherne, the Holy Spirit had two: Paul and Barnabas (CYB 70r). The apostles were consecrated before the coming of the Holy Spirit at Pentecost but did not have the fullness of the Spirit until afterwards (CYB

---

70.   See III *C* 66, but compare III *C* 28.

48r). Therein may lie Traherne's distinction between consecration and ordination. The apostles have the highest dignity under Christ (CYB 83v). At least in the Church's Year Book Traherne does not intend to discuss the priority, person, place or power of Peter (CYB 77v).

Doctrinally, Traherne recognizes a distinction between the estate of the clergy and the estate of the laity (CYB 8r). The apostles "constituted bishops, priests, deacons for the Government of the Church and left those orders among us" (CYB 3v). The offices of archbishop and patriarch, however, are of human origin for the better government of the church when it grew larger (*RF*, pp. 8ff). The bishops are of equal rank, and the pope of Rome is not superior. Traherne praises God for the ordaining of priests and bishops (CYB 99v), and he thinks that God instituted the laying on of hands from the beginning of the church. Laying on of hands demonstrates the "authority and Comfort" of the church, insures that no "unsound, schismatical or Heretical Person" enters the ministry, indicates that the mission of the church is not invisible, and evidences the order and government of the church (CYB 59/69). He does not mention apostolic succession, but he does say that the Roman Catholic church believes that the episcopacy is of human origin (issues from the Pope alone). Traherne counters by stating that the episcopacy has diverse origins, human and divine (*RF*, p. 196). Ministers have an "orderly" call by the Holy Ghost not immediate but in and through the church (CYB 59v). Traherne thinks it permissible that priests marry, although he was not married and probably preferred celibacy.[71]

Traherne's understanding of the efficacy or necessity of priestly absolution is vague. There are only two helpful references to it. The keys of the kingdom which Peter was given consisted in the power to remit and retain sins (CYB 78r). There is also an aside, "even of Remission of Sins both from thy Church and from those in thy Church."[72] The "and" enables Traherne to avoid completely problems such as: who has the power to forgive sins, how this power is transmitted, when this power is effectual. Evidently he believes that the power to forgive and retain sins resides in the

---

71. Compare Art. XXVI of the Thirty-nine Articles on the consecration of archbishops, bishops, priests and deacons, and Art. XXIII on the lawful calling of ministers. On Traherne's attitude toward celibacy see CYB 71r.
72. See CYB 12r; 78r, 83v.

called ministry. For Traherne the essential points are that sins are remitted, that there is a ministry, that there is decency and order in the church.

Pastorally, Traherne prays for learned, pious, and able ministers (CYB 28v). Their calling is lawful and their task is to teach, preach, convert, divide the word (Law and Gospel), and "Confute all errors."[73] Candidates are to be modest (CYB 69v).

Traherne's distinctive themes are also expressed under the rubric of ministry. Since nature is clouded, the ministry of man is needed to reveal its glory again (*CE*, p. 60). Ministers are "golden pipes, they convey the golden Dye into this world" (CYB 194). Moreover, God needs holy men to call others to the enjoyment of God, to their inheritance of the world, to the recovery of their blessedness, and to the similitude of God (SM II 15).

Personally, Traherne apparently refers to his own parish in Credenhill to which, he says, he was sent by God "to teach immortal Souls the way to Heaven, to sanctify his Sabbaths, to instruct them in his laws. . .to shew them the love of a glorious Saviour. . . to lead them by his Merrits to Eternal joys" (SM III 83). All of his labors would be recompensed, Traherne asserts, if his congregation could be called back to the "fruition of Heaven and Earth" (SM II 21).

8. "Sabbaths"

The Sabbath itself is no longer to be observed, at least in its Old Testament sense, according to Traherne, for where "Moses is kept alive, Christ is dead" (CYB 3v). Now the Sabbath is a day of rest "like a day of heaven observed on earth" (CYB 3r; see *CE*, p. 284).

A discussion of the Sabbath also provides a context in which to portray Traherne's attitude toward public worship, the church year, meditation, and prayer.

The "capacity" of man's soul, according to Traherne, enables him to unite with "the Saints of all ages, past, present and to come" in worship, praise and adoration.[74] Traherne evidences differing attitudes toward public worship. In the poem "Solitude" Traherne states that unless people move his soul with divine love, he finds no "relief" in public worship. The external rite can not "sate" his appetite for felicity (F 100). However, in his

---

73. See note 71 above, and CYB 19v, 18r, 51v.
74. See the discussions of prizing and praising in ch. v above, and *Daily Devotions*, p. 378.

poem "Churches" Traherne states that sacred temples, when they are filled with people worshipping God, delight his soul more than precious metals or fields of corn. Even church architecture evidences God's magnificence and majesty (F 116). (Both poems may have been altered by Philip Traherne.)

Connecting the Sabbath with the church year, Traherne says that "God gave us some Sabbaths, but hath not forbidden us to return to him others."[75] The observance of saint's days, festivals, or fasts, according to Traherne, is neither commanded nor forbidden (CYB 104v); in other words, they are what the Reformers would have called *adiaphora*. The Church Year is the "common fountain of our joy and salvation" (CYB 98r). The entire year, however, is not to be filled with feasts and festivals for that would be resisting the "ordinances of God," but to have no festivals would mean banishing salvation from the world (CYB 100r). There are no set number of feast days, according to Traherne. Even the Jews were able to add others, indicating that some are of human institution; i.e. based upon reason and nature (CYB 23rff). There are obviously, then, such things as holy times, places and things. Festivals are "relics of Eden," "Market Days of Heaven," and "Landskips of Glory" (CYB 100vff). They sweeten the year, enrich men's lives, beautify time, methodize devotions, bring the earth closer to heaven, and make the church more orderly (CYB 46r).

Traherne not only defends feasts and festivals, he also condemns their abuse. Although there is no fast or festival between Easter and Ascension Day, this should not be a time of "excess." "Balls, Revelings, Morris Dances" all abuse this holy period (CYB 16v).

Traherne feels a tension between the active and contemplative life.[76] The active life is founded on faith, the contemplative on love (CYB 84). Contemplation is not to be carried so far as to forget the neighbor, nor is activity to be carried so far as to forget "Divine Speculation." In solitude there may be less opportunity for vice but also less opportunity for virtue (CYB 74v). Activity feeds and strengthens meditation (*CE*, p. 246). "Prayer without industry is meer mockery," but "Industry without Prayer is loose

---

75. CYB 102v. See also *Daily Devotions*: "For the miraculous Preservation of the King and thy wonderful Restauration of thy Church to some degree of its wonted Glory. . . . For the glory of our Festivals. . . . For our weekly, monthly, quarterly and yearly Fasts; in our Fridays Eves Embers and Lent; I praise thee for our excellent Liturgy" (pp. 371-72).

76. See Aquinas on the "Active and Contemplative Life," *Summa Theologiae* II. ii, ch. CLXXIXff.

Presumption" (*CE*, p. 223). Prayer is often a means of asking God to fulfill his decrees (CYB 71v). Traherne advises praying early in the morning, and he may have prayed seven times a day himself (IV *C* 92).

Traherne evidences a sympathy with Laudian worship practices. He thinks it a pity that there are those who neglect primitive and excellent devotions abolishing "Order and Beauty" merely from fear of superstition. These devotions are beautiful in themselves and are taught by reason and by nature, and thus "need not be written in a law."[77] He seems to agree with the stand of the Thirty-nine Articles, that although the ceremonial law is not binding on Christian men (Art. VII), the "Church hath power to decree Rites or Ceremonies" (Art. XX). Traherne wants Christians to avoid both superstition on the one hand and "Profaneness, Ingratitude or Forgetfulness" of God on the other. Thus he prays that men follow "Holy Antiquity," and asks to be saved from novelty.[78] Yet Traherne is also critical of dead, dull, and unnecessary ceremonies (CYB 16r).

Traherne cites, adapts, borrows, and writes much liturgical material.[79] His devotion on the Resurrection in the Church's Year Book seems to be a complete worship service in itself. It includes Scripture readings, commentary, homilies, prayers, litanies, ascriptions of praise, and even hymns (CYB 8vff). Similarly, there is a section in the *Hexameron* which seems to be an original canticle (pp. 14ff). The primary purpose, in fact, for which Traherne writes the Church's Year Book, the *Hexameron*, and the *Thanksgivings* is to encourage men to praise God, which is also one purpose of the liturgy. It can be demonstrated that these writings approximate to a great extent the nature, function, and purpose of liturgical worship.

9. "the Nature and Government of the Church"

Traherne interprets the nature and government of the church historically, doctrinally, communally, and personally. Historically, he sees Christ as the head of the church which is holy and catholic (I *C* 79). The church results from Christ's death and is established and grows from his resurrection

---

77. "It is not necessary that Traditions and Ceremonies be in all places one, or utterly like; for at all times they have been diverse, and may be changed according to the diversity of countries, times, and men's manners. . ." (Thirty-nine Articles, XXXIV).

78. CYB 16r, 24v, 46v.

79. See the excursus on Traherne as Church Historian below.

(CYB 1). In Christ's prophetic office he instructs it, in his priestly office he sacrifices himself for it, and in his kingly office he governs and provides for it (CYB 1v). Men are first brought into the church and from there into glory (CYB 9v). The Holy Ghost is given only to those who are in the church (CYB 46r).

The order and government of the church, according to Traherne, are necessary for its growth and beauty. Traherne appreciates the discipline of the church which God protects from "calumnie and Contempt from the very beginning" (CYB 59/69). Traherne thinks that Satan is particularly interested in destroying the government of the church and uses especially the ingratitude of pious persons to achieve this end (SM III 24).

Doctrinally, Traherne asserts that when the church is "Christian, Catholick and Apostolick, the shadow hath yielded to substance" (CYB 3v). Yet he also calls the church invisible, a Calvinist interpretation (*CE*, p. 129). Elsewhere he employs such terms as: holy, mother (CYB 104r), bride of Christ (III *C* 77), bride of men, assembly of the first-born (*CE*, p. 250), the communion of saints (I *C* 92), and the "fullness of Him that filleth all in all" (IV *C* 72). Jews, Turks, heathen, and impenitent Christians are to be converted and united to the church (CYB 28v). Traherne is also concerned about unity in the church and uniformity in the congregation (CYB 43r), and he criticizes wicked, ignorant zealots who despise the church's union (SM I 85).

Traherne usually conceives of the church in a Laudian fashion (high church Anglican), but in the Select Meditations there is a passage which is peculiarly mixed in referents. He asks whether anyone could believe that it is unlawful for kings, parliament, and elders to covenant with God in a national manner (emphasis added). Since the passage is directed against the sectarians, there is no question as to where Traherne's sympathies lie, but what is significant is that at times his word usage reflects a Puritan training and milieu without the accompanying Puritan commitment.[80]

Traherne feels personally aided by the communal character of the church: the thousands of others in the world who also enjoy felicity, communion with God, and fellowship with the angels (III *C* 28). The way to heaven is by delighting in these saints of God. By esteeming them a man can inherit all things (I *C* 81). The people of God, Traherne thinks, are necessary as "Spurs, Wings, Enflamers" to keep a man from becoming lax in his duties (*Thanks*, p. 327). Yet, he states, it is often difficult to live in a community or be a member of a congregation, for men are seldom innocent and even less so in a congregation (SM IV 52).

10. "Its Histories and Successions from the Beginning to the End of the World"

Traherne's view of history is providential and apologetic.[81] Faith, hope, and reason, according to Traherne, are needed to view historical events. Faith divulges all the aspects of the history of salvation: creation, the fall, redemption, exodus; the life, death, resurrection, and ascension of Christ; the conversion of the Gentiles, the founding of the church, and "above all other Things. . . Jesus Christ." Much of the basis for his point of view can be found in Hebrews 11. History (including Pentecost, prophecies, church fathers, the canons and decrees of the councils, and "all the Transactions of

---

80.   Angela Russell asserts that: "Characteristically, there are no references to church services. . . in Traherne's writings." Although there are comparatively few, the intent of the CYB, *Thanks*, and *Hex* must be taken into account. They were intended as public or private devotional writings. A. Russell also notes that all Church of England clergymen were to say Matins and Evensong daily, but the church of Traherne's time, even after the Restoration, was fairly simple both in furnishings and vestments (pp. 40ff). See also J. H. Overton, *Life in the English Church* (London, 1885). Wollebius in his chapter "On the Nature of the visible Church" defines the visible church as a "visible society of men called to the state of grace by the word and sacraments." It is one, Catholic, and holy. Wollebius also devotes a chapter to the "outward Administration of the Church" (ch. 26). His definition reflects the Thirty-nine Articles: "The visible Church of Christ is a congregation of faithful men, in the which the pure Word of God is preached, and the Sacraments be duly ministered according to Christ's ordinance in all those things that of necessity are requisite to the same" (XX). Traherne has other concerns and does not reflect to any great extent these issues.

81.   See subsections 1 and 2 above on "the tenor of the New Covenant" and "The Manner of its Exhibition." Calvin's *Institutes* include discussions of "the Mode of Government in use before the Papacy," a history of its corruption and development, of councils and their authority, the jurisdiction, and discipline of the church (IV, chs. iv-xii). His last chapter (xx) deals with "Civil Government." T. Jackson devotes a number of chapters to the history of the church. Polanus discusses civil magistrates (ch. 61) and the false church (ch. 63). H. More treats the kingdom of God, its history, progress, and possible future successes in the *Divine Dialogues* (pp. 14–15). For Traherne's providential view of history see ch. vi G above and compare T. Jackson "Of the manifestation of Divine Providence in the remarkable Erections, Declinations and Periods of Kingdoms in over-ruling Policy, and disposing the success of Humane Undertakings" (vol. vi, ii, section iii). General rather than special providence apparently is meant here. See Calvin, *Institutes*, chs. 16–18. Traherne makes comparatively little reference to prophecy and fulfillment, in contrast to Polanus (ch. 29) and Jackson (vol. I, section iii; ch. 29). Traherne does note Bacon's admonition to those who study prophecy, that they have been fulfilled in all eras. Bacon, I, 515 quoted in Traherne's EN (P. 125). Traherne also copied some of Bacon's comments on civil history into his EN (pp. 123–124).

the World drawn down to our own Age in a continued series") illustrates and confirms revelation (*CE*, p. 120).

Traherne's interpretation of the Christ event stresses the changes which were wrought. Jesus Christ and his followers were to change the "state and conditions of Kingdoms," to alter public worship, and "to dissettle the secular Interests." Everything has been "improved by the Work of Redemption." Trades and occupations result in cities, temples, and other splendors (IV *C* 24), and men are meant to "Restore the world to the Beauty of Paradice" by their labor (SM III 31). Because of Christ's love toward the church, it has increased in size and glory in spite of its problems and persecutions (CYB 1v).

Traherne is also concerned with demonstrating the veracity of salvation history (apologetics).[82] That these prophecies and doctrines are true, according to Traherne, is witnessed to by the "Universal Tradition of all the world." The Catholic Church is only a small part of this tradition in Traherne's opinion. It is also attested to by a "stream of Effects and clear Monuments" which are all in harmony. The Bible is yet another witness to its truth (*CE*, p. 110). Moreover, all the ways of God (promise, prophecy, miracles, types, figures, ceremonies, and revelation) are meant to confirm that Jesus Christ is the Savior, the redeemer, and the Son of God (SM III 21).

Roman Forgeries treats church history in the first five centuries and indirectly the Reformation period and after. It is Traherne's attempt to prove that Rome has forged ancient documents to support the power and primacy of the pope. Traherne accuses Rome of simony, lying, sacrilege, and even blasphemy in her attempt to support her supremacy (p. 4). Traherne also accuses Rome of imposture and counterfeit in the subtitle, of usurpation, ambition, forgery, and cruelty in the Premonition (preface), and of heresy in the Introduction.

God allows men some freedom in ecclesiastical affairs in Traherne's view. However, this freedom has been misused according to Traherne. When the papacy was in control, there was a secret attempt made to mingle forgeries with genuine records of the church. They were believable in the

---

82. In theology apologetics is concerned with the defense of Christianity, as ethics, for example, is concerned with morals. The term can be used in a narrower sense, as of the defense of a particular denomination. In this sense *Roman Forgeries* is partisan apologetics, which is equivalent to polemics. Both senses are referred to in this study.

time of Isadore because it was an age when "Fables. . . Dreams, Visions, Miracles" were rampant (p. 35). Traherne calls this attempt to establish the primacy of the pope a "Conspiracy" and thinks it extended over a long period of time: "it is impossible to debauch all Antiquity and Learning with so much Labour and Art, without some deep Counsel and Design" (p. 81). Traherne criticizes, in this connection, the theory that the end justifies the means (p. 85), commonly thought to be a Jesuit idea.

Traherne documents so many forgeries in the first five centuries that he planned to write a second volume on those of later centuries (p. 35). As it is, Traherne writes very little on the Middle Ages and Reformation periods. The Reformation, he thinks, was caused by "the impiety and excesses of the popes" as well as the "impudence and security of his Followers." It was a happy and providential event (pp. 37, 40).

Like George Hakewill and Joseph Glanville, but quite in contrast to the prevailing mood of theologians of the time,[83] Traherne tends to see the age in which he lives very positively. He sees his land as the "English Zion" (*CE*, p. 213) and states that God spent ages preparing and providing the external blessings which England has (SM II 23). Christianity is more freely and purely professed in England than anywhere else, making it possible for Englishmen, to be as "divine and heavenly as angels" (*CE*, p. 281). At times Traherne is triumphalistic: "Christianity Triumpheth, Religion flourisheth, Jesus Reigneth, Fools are destroyed and Christians are Kings throughout all the world. Ours are the Temples and the Cities, ours are the Laws and the Princes. . . . Shall not all this Grandeur fill us with Delight. The World is turned into the Paradise of God."[84]

---

83. George Hakewill attempts to show the progress made in most areas of endeavor in his *Declaration of the Power and Providence of God in the Government of the World* (London, 1627). See also J. Glanville's *Plus Ultra* (London, 1668). However, compare Sir Thomas Browne, who thinks that the world is "a place not to live, but to dye in." *Religio Medici*, p. 83. Jeremy Taylor admonishes: "Learn to despise the world." *Sermons*, p. 86. See H. Baker's discussion in the *Wars of Truth*, pp. 1-90, 116-134, and C. Marks, *CE*, p. 374n.

84. See CYB 84v; *CE*, pp. 279, 283. Sometimes Traherne is almost overly positive. In the *Thanks* he writes: "Thou givest thy self, by employing all thy wisdom, all thy Goodness, all thy Power, in producing the best of all possible Delights, for the satisfaction, and exaltation of every Soul; And in giving thy self in the best of manners. . . . Thou givest thy self by living the best of all possible lives: Which is by doing the best of all possible things" (pp. 316-317). This raises the problem of theodicy which was not a serious problem for strict Calvinists who believed in the arbitrary will of God. There is a similarity to Leibnitz here. Evidently neither man was familiar with the works of the other. There may be a common source or tradition which influenced each man in his word choice.

Traherne is also aware of the darker side. He writes that men are "Desparately bent to grow worse in wickedness," and he prays that men would not "lay waste the heritage," or "break down our Temples" (perhaps referring to the tumultuous times of the Civil War). He hopes that God will leave a remnant. The differences in outlook may be due to different conditions. The darker view was written earlier. Traherne sees two dangers to the kingdom of God on earth: the blindness of the profane who do not see "celestial joys" and the ingratitude of the "Holy ones" who "kick at Heavenly treasures," probably referring to the sectarians of his time.

Sectarians Traherne calls "Holy Ones" even though he thinks they are a danger to the church and ignorant because they advocate abolishing "Order and Beauty" (SM II 23). He fears that the sectarians will really "Introduce Atheism by Degrees," as well as bring about "Total Oblivion of thy Glorious Wonders" (CYB 46v). His prayers ask for deliverance from "private and fals Interpretation of Scripture, Innovations in Holy Things, and Strange Doctrines" as well as from heresy, schism, and scandal (CYB 31v). The sectarians are tools of Satan in Traherne's view, but he is sure, nevertheless, that holiness will triumph.[85]

The excessive individualism and divisive tendencies of the sectarians, Traherne thinks, will lead to confusion. Traherne seems to prefer an established, national church and to yearn for a return to pre-Commonwealth days when the church was protected by laws, when solemn assemblies met in peace, when there was "Quiet and Ease and Repose and Safety."[86]

After the turmoil of the Civil War, the stringencies of the Commonwealth, and the excesses just before the Restoration, it is not surprising that Traherne has conservative political and religious tendencies. God (and Traherne) has regard for the "external flourishing of settled Kingdoms" (SM I 88). His prayers, like many of the time, ask for deliverance from foreign invasions, from civil insurrection, from the displacing of good magistrates, from anarchy and tyranny, and from all evils of state (CYB 31v).

---

85. SM III 24. Calvin states that "All the principles of piety subverted by fanatics, who substitute revelations for Scripture." *Institutes,* I, ch. 9.

86. See 3M III 25; 3M II 23. The Select Meditations are an earlier work, written perhaps during the Commonwealth. See ch. iii above.

There may be yet another explanation for Traherne's religious and political conservative tendencies (Laudian and royalist). Like St. Paul, who desires "decency and order" in the church, Traherne also has an inherent love of order, of things in their proper places, whether that be in his writing style, in his personal life,[87] in the life of the church, in the state, or in the orders of creation. Friends, magistrates, ministers (*CE*, p. 255), kings, priests, bishops, angels, time and eternity, all have their proper place, according to Traherne.[88] That's why his is a "mind in frame."

Traherne's understanding of law and justice is integral to his political philosophy. The basis of a nation is its laws which keep it from barbarism (*Thanks*, p. 296). Laws are to be maintained both on earth and in heaven (*CE*, p. 97), and thus Traherne delights in the king's "Regiment of the World," and pays kings due respect and honor. However, kings are not to be "loose and careless" because "licence and profaneness are of a spreading Nature" and may also infect the people. The king's "glory and true repose" consists of a "Catholick and eternal Kingdom" (*CE*, p. 233). It is justice which upholds thrones, kingdoms and laws. Justice, law, guardian angels, kings, counselors, priests, soldiers, tradesman all have their respective duties in a kingdom, and where those duties are properly observed, the nation is blessed with order and beauty.[89]

His religious and political attitudes intertwine. He compares conscience with the duties of a priest, right reason with the duties of a king, and the rightful workings of the mind with that of a kingdom (*CE*, p. 96). His fear of anarchy even leads him to defend the pope against deposition (which he compares to a parliament trying their king). "If this be admitted, all must be Disorder and Confusion in the Kingdom" (*RF*, p. 232). Those who oppose established religion are to be detested and despised, and this detesting and despising, according to Traherne, is also a "part of felicity" (SM III 25). He compares the interconnections between government and religion to "two Pillars of the Earth" which strengthen one another,

---

87. There is a prayer in which the speaking voice asks not to be "irregular" in his passions, nor to allow the passions to draw him "from those Bounds of Reason, and Bonds of Religion and Sobriety which thou hast assigned them, and commanded me to keep within the compass of" (*Hex*, p. 28).

88. *Thanks*, p. 223; SM IV 48; I C 38; V C 8.

89. On justice see ch. vi E above and EN pp. 17-18; "Banishment," "Fury," "Passion," and "Punishment" in the CB; and C. Marks, *CE*, pp. 338-339nn.

"Religion rooting Justice within, Justice fencing Religion without" (*Thanks*, pp. 329ff).

In his poem "Christendom," which his brother may have revised, Traherne writes a short description of what might be considered his utopia. The word "Christendom" for the child Traherne draws forth the image of a city "wherin there reigned sweet content." There is no commerce, nothing useless, no boundaries, gates or walls. The city is filled with plain, simple, and inexpensive things, but his "chiefest Joys/Were Girls and Boys." In Traherne's vision, the town seems to be in "constant Holiday" and summer. The streets are not paved but are of grass and red clay; in fact much of the vision is a pastoral description of streams, springs, sun, and trees. Joy, beauty, and happiness are words frequently used in the poem to describe the place and its inhabitants. It reminds him of the New Jerusalem. His utopia is reminiscent of his description of childhood. He implies in the last stanza of the poem that this "Bliss and Glory" is not only past or to come, it is also present: "for Children, Maids, and Men/Make up the King of Glory's Diadem." They are, of course, always with us (F 106-110).

Excursus: Traherne as Church Historian

Anthony à Wood's seventeenth century biography states that Traherne "was well read in primitive antiquity as in the councils, fathers, etc."[90] *Roman Forgeries*, his first published work of uncontested authorship, which deals with the records of the first 420 years of church history indicates as much. In addition, his other writings contain frequent references to church history, and he made extensive notes on Francis Bacon's "Of Ecclesiastical History" in his Early Notebook (122-223). Traherne's interest in history apparently resulted from his seventeenth century English education, from the Restoration church's concern for "Antiquity,"[91] and from the nature of his writings which are often of necessity based on traditional materials (Church's Year Book, *Roman Forgeries*, Hexameron).

In *Roman Forgeries* Traherne states that he does "not trust other mens information but, mine own eyes" (Sig. B6v). However, it seems that many of Traherne's references to the records and to the church fathers really are

---

90. Marg, I, xxiii.
91. *RF,* p. 89; CYB 16.

from secondary sources, not only in *Roman Forgeries*, but in his other writings as well.[92] At times he acknowledges his debts to other scholars, particularly to Jewel, James, and Barlow.[93] Furthermore, Traherne states that to be objective, he examined various collections of the "Apostles Canons, decretal Epistles, and Ancient Councils," some of which, he says, are also recognized by the church of Rome (p. 39). Among them are those of James Merlin, Peter Crabbe, L. Surius, Severinus, Binius, Labbe, Cossartius, Francis Turrian, Baronius, Carranza, and Nicolinus. G. Wade notes that Traherne must have read Cassaubon, even though he does not name him in *Roman Forgeries*.[94] Traherne states that he does not condemn entire collections, but he does think that "a little Poyson spoileth the greatest Mass of the most wholesome Meat" (p. 66). He reviews the value and contents of these collections, noting new forgeries or acceptance of old ones. Traherne attempts to give the impression that he is an objective scholar, but the task and effect is polemical. He also says he will not discuss doctrinal matters, but the doctrinal issues surrounding the power and primacy of the papacy loom large in every attack Traherne makes. Strangely, these collections are seldom referred to again in Traherne's later writings.

Traherne uses various methods of uncovering and demonstrating the existence of forgeries: contradictions (pp. 105ff), "absurdities, Errours, Tautologies, and Barbarismes" (p. 113), arguments from particulars to universals (pp. 166ff), obscure language meant to "blind the reader" (p. 167), and lack of harmony with the Scriptures (p. 230). The true records, however, are "clear and pure, and well-advised, full of uniformity, Sense, Gravity, Majesty, Smoothness, order, Perspecuity, Brevity, Eloquence, and Verity" (p. 112).

A chronological survey of Traherne's citations indicates his sources, influences, and methodology. Next to biography most Traherne scholarship is in the area of sources and influences. One of the more interesting recent theories relating to Traherne's sources is P. Grant's attempt to link Traherne with Irenaeus. There was a revival of interest in the early Church Fathers in the seventeenth century, and Origen and

---

92.   See C. Marks, "CYB," *Papers* (1966), 31-72.

93.   See full discussion in ch. iii above, and *RF*, pp. 66, 96.

94.   Wade, pp. 123ff.

Clement are frequently quoted by the Cambridge Platonists. P. Grant sees similarities in Traherne's and Irenaeus' understanding of the fall, evaluation of creation, optimism, understanding of redemption as a return to innocence, and style. Grant proceeds more on the basis of parallels in their thought than by direct quotation and reference.[95] In many ways the comparison to Irenaeus is more helpful than other attempts to compare Traherne with Pelagius or contrast him with Augustine. Traherne mentions Irenaeus once in his *Roman Forgeries*, but affinity rather than influence seems to be a better way of describing the likenesses.

In some ways Traherne's high regard for man resembles the deification or apotheosis of man in Irenaeus, Origen, Gregory of Nyssa, and Athanasius.[96] However, Traherne refers only a few times to these Fathers, and usually his references are meant as support for his argument rather than as sources of it: "As Nazianzen. . . admirably Expresseth it;" "Nazianzen professed him self to be a Lover of right reason."[97]

His quotations from Dorotheus, Ambrose, and Eusebius are often from such secondary sources as Meredith Hanmer's *The Auncient Ecclesiastical Histories* (a 1577 translation of Eusebius), Daniel Featley's *Ancilla Pietatis*, Edward Sparke's *Scintilla-Altaris*, and William Austin's

---

95. P. Grant, moreover, thinks that the structure of *RF* derives from the tract *Adversus Haereses* by St. Irenaeus (p. 45). Grant states that the favorite author of Servatus was Irenaeus, and the doctrine of man of Servatus and Traherne is similar because both have Irenaeus as a source. For Irenaeus original sin is less serious than actual sin (p. 46). Sin includes misvaluing the things of the world (p. 47). Return, recapitulation, unlearning are aspects of Irenaeus and Traherne's theology of redemption, according to Grant. Furthermore, Irenaeus and Traherne use similar terminology: precious metals, jewels, prizing, and praising. Their understanding of God, the natural dignity of man, the similarity of Adam's pristine innocence with that of a child is similar. Salvation for both, according to Grant, consists in rediscovering the vision of childhood (pp. 40-61).

96. Traherne refers to Chrysostom twice in his *CE* (pp. 187-188, 250) and twice in the CYB (20, 71v-72r). Some of the references have not been located, one is a mistake, and one is from Sparkes. See *CE*, pp. 356n, 370n. Patrides summarizes a number of the theories of these Church Fathers: Origen believes that "by fellowship with divinity human nature might become divine"; Athanasius that the "Son of God was made man so that we might become Gods"; St. Gregory that the image of God in man enables him to partake of divinity "both in rank and in name"; Gregory Palamas that "man, by virtue of the body created in the likeness of God, is higher than the angels" (pp. 17ff). See also R. Ellrodt, "Scientific Curiosity and the Seventeenth Century," *MP*, 61 (1964), 180-197. Traherne's reference to Origen in the CYB (52) derives from John Donne's sermon on Pentecost. See C. Marks, "CYB," *Papers* (1966), 59. His reference to Origen in the *CE* (p. 4) derives from T. Jackson. See *CE*, p. 307n.

97. Traherne refers to Nazianzus twice in the *Centuries*, once in connection with goodness (III *C* 65), and once in connection with right reason (IV *C* 81).

Devotionis Augustinianae Flamma. His comparatively frequent references to Eusebius indicate not so much an influence as a source of facts.[98] The "Truth" of the writings of Eusebius and other Church Fathers "being Historical, Obligeth us to a Moral Belief, tho not to a Divine & Infallible Faith" (CYB 98). Historical truth, thus, induces a different kind and quality of belief than biblical truth.

There are surprisingly few direct references to Augustine in Traherne's writings, and most of his references seem to come from secondary sources.[99] G. Wade and L. Martz, however, see affinities with Augustine not so much in the content of his writings as in his meditational style, particularly the style of the *Centuries*. Traherne's use of repetition, memory, and his stress on wants, desires, felicity, happiness are similar to Augustine's *beata vita* which signifies intense happiness, well-being, joyfulness, and blessedness according to L. Martz.[100]

Traherne refers to Gregory the Great (III *C* 98), but as Margoliouth points out, Gregory's point is different from Traherne's. Traherne apparently seldom rechecks his sources.[101] C. Marks asserts that Traherne's reference to Leontius (CYB 51v) may be one of the few examples of original research in the Church's Year Book, perhaps dating from his studies of the councils. This quotation is found only in Gelasius, *Cyzicenus Commentarius Actorum Concilii Nicaeni.*[102] His reference to Anselm in the first *Century* (91) is more natural ("rather to suffer with S. Anselm the Pains of Hell then to Sin against Thee") but scarcely indicates that Anselm is an influence.

In contrast to his other references and quotations of earlier Church Fathers, scholasticism is definitely an influence on Traherne. It influenced the content of his thought as well as his way of expressing his ideas, yet he

---

98. See CYB 59v, 68, 71v, 72r, 88r, 103-104.
99. There is a quote attributed to Augustine in his EN (P. 70), and his notes on the unidentified Latin work on religion include references to Augustine and Bernard (EN, pp. 213-231, 339-341). There is a translated "Hymne of Paradise" which derives from the pseudo-Augustine *Meditations* in the CYB (55r). Some of his other references to Augustine (CYB 22, 57v, 104v) derive from secondary sources (i.e. Sparkes). C. Marks thinks that St. Augustine stands for the "spiritual authority of the early church" for Traherne. See "CYB," *Papers* (1966), 31-72.
100. See G. Wade, p. 190; L. Martz, *Paradise Within*, pp. 50ff. Martz also finds affinities with Bonaventura's stages of meditation. See ch. iii above.
101. Marg, I, 281. See his reference to Isadorus in the CYB (102r).
102. C. Marks, "CYB", *Papers*, 61.

can also disagree with scholasticism (see I C 2).[103] Although Traherne refers to Thomas à Kempis (I C 7), F. Löhrer convincingly shows that he is not influenced by him.[104] Traherne also refers to Luther's *Table Talk* (IV C 34), Oecolampadius (EN 226), and Melanchthon (EN, 214) but these are neither major sources nor influences. Apparently, he does not refer to Calvin by name. Traherne calls the Socinians "Blind" and "Enemies" of Christ's deity (II C 33).

D. "the State of Glory"

According to Traherne, the estate of glory and eschatology are concerns of the "Magnanimous Soul" (*CE*, p. 230). Traherne devotes frequent and extended discussions to questions of eschatology in his writings, and both sets of poems[105] and his *Hexameron* conclude with references to heaven.

In the estate of glory the virtues of faith, hope, repentance (*CE*, p. 177) and patience shall cease (*CE*, p. 185). The virtues of the estate of glory (knowledge, love, righteousness, holiness, goodness, charity, wisdom, humility, gratitude, godliness, and contentment) are exercised there by the continual infusion of God's grace. They will also be enjoyed.[106] No one, according to Traherne, can "willingly and Wittingly" fall from the kingdom ·of glory. A man who sees the beatific vision, God's face, cannot sin because he would be sinning against his own happiness (II C 97).

---

103. See ch. iv above. G. Wade thinks that the psychology, terminology and scientific framework of the *CE*, as well as Traherne's classification of the virtues derive from Aquinas and only indirectly from Aristotle and Augustine. She also asserts, perhaps too enthusiastically, that Traherne was "thoroughly master of that mass of material" (referring to the *Summa Theologiae*). She admits that there are few quotations or references to Aquinas in Traherne's writings (see CYB 12v) and "philosophically their difference outweighs their resemblance." She concludes that Traherne is "perhaps a follower of St. Francis rather than St. Thomas." "St. Thomas Aquinas and Thomas Traherne," *Blackfriars*, 12 (1931), 666- 673; and see her book *Traherne*, p. 141.

104. F. Löhrer, *Die Mystik*, pp. 24ff.

105. The Dobell folio ends with the poem "Goodness," which awaits the "Blest Sight/Of his Eternal Goodness" (40-41). The Burney manuscript ends with the poem "The Review II" which sees "Thoughts" as "An Earnest that the Actions of the Just/Shall still revive, and flourish in the Dust" (11-12). See Stewart, pp. 94ff, 211. In the last line of the *Hex*, the speaking voice asks that he might "Enjoy thee in an everlasting Day" (p. 91).

106. See *CE*, pp. 30, 177, 214.

1. "the Nature of Seperat Souls, their Advantages, Excellencies and Privileges"

The only other reference to "Seperat Souls" besides this one (III C 43) in Traherne's writings refers to them as "Single Angels" who relate both to the Godhead and to earthly bodies. They are able to enjoy heaven and "to see and Delight in Spiritual Things as Angels do" (SM II 95). The terminology may echo metaphysical usage.[107] Joseph Hall in the second book "Of the souls of blessed men" of *The Great Mysterie of Godliness* (1652) devotes his first chapter to "their Separation and Immortality." In chapter eight Hall treats "The re-union of the body to the soul, and both glorified." Apparently, the reference, then, is to that time between death and the resurrection, when, according to the theological thought of the time, the soul is separated from the body. The term seldom occurs in traditional systematic theologies.

2. "the Resurrection of the Body"

"The Doctrine of the Resurrection is the proper faith of Christians" according to Traherne. He defines resurrection as a return to the estate from which one has fallen. "Without the Body of Man the world would be in vain, without the Resurrection, the Body of man" would be in vain. Traherne maintains that the resurrection can be demonstrated by reason and by simile. Nature, for example, demonstrates the truth of the resurrection by "the new Birth of Stars, Days, Seasons, Planets. . . the setting Sun riseth in the morning. . . Spring" (CYB 12r, 13v). In Christ's resurrection man is to see his own immortality, eternal life and glory (CYB 2r). It is furthermore, an easy matter for God to raise and "remake" the body he made from nothing (CYB 131).

In the Church's Year Book Traherne writes that it is sufficient for man to know that in heaven his glorified body will be subject to his command and that nothing will be an obstacle to it. Traherne is not sure whether that means that glorified bodies are penetrable or that other bodies will give "Place" (11r). However, elsewhere, Traherne goes into more detail on the

---

107. Burgersdicius entitles a section of his *Metaphysica*, "*De Anima Humana separati*," and Eustache uses the phrase "*De statu amimae Separate*" in his *De rebus Naturalibus*. Richard Baxter also discusses *Quoad Animae* in *Gloriam Introitum, Quoad Animae separatae Statum,* and *Quoad Continuationes illus status* (1681).

nature of the glorified body. In *Christian Ethicks* he states that the body will enjoy health, agility, beauty, vivacity, strength, and liberty in heaven. These are part and parcel of happiness. [108]

3. "the Day of Judgment and the Life Everlasting"

The Cambridge Platonists tend to minimize eschatology,[109] Traherne does not, nor does he maximize it. Traherne thinks that man's "greatness of Spirit" brings him to wonder "Whether the world shall end? If it shall, after what manner; whether by Design or Accident? Whether all Ages and Nations shall rise from the Dead? Whether there shall be a general Doom, or a day of Judgment? Whether I am concerned in all the transactions and passages at that day?" (*CE*, p. 229). Traherne does not discuss in detail the majority of these questions elsewhere in his writings. He does state that the second coming will be attended with signs of justice and fury, that the elements and the worlds will be on fire (CYB 34r), that the evil servants will weep and gnash their teeth (*CE*, p. 97), and that the day of judgment will be a day of terror (CYB 38v). All of men's deeds will then be seen in "relation to the Recompenses" which Christ will give when he comes. On the last day, furthermore, there will be no other test of man but whether they have been generous (*CE*, p. 241). Thus, to a great extent, Traherne reflects the traditional understanding of the Day of Judgment: its justice, weeping, terror, and testing. He brings little of his own distinctive comment.

4. "Communion of Saints"

There seems to be no precedent for including a discussion of the communion of saints under the rubric of eschatology. It usually is a

---

108. *CE*, p. 18. See also CYB 11r, 35r. Aquinas lists as characteristics of the resurrected body: impassibility, subtilty, agility, and clarity in his "Treatise on the Resurrection," *Summa Theologiae*, Part II, ch. LXXV as well as in his *Compendium*, ch. 168, p. 190. Richard Seldon in his *Mans Last End* (London, 1634) and Joseph Hall (1659) list the same four. C. A. Patrides surveys seventeenth century eschatology in "Renaissance and Modern Thought on the Last Things," *Harvard Theological Review*, vol. LI (July, 1958), n. 3, pp. 169-185.

109. According to Patrides, only H. More believes that "the Last Judgment was imminent." *Intro.*, p. 23. See *CE*, p. 339. There are no articles on eschatology proper in the Thirty-nine Articles. There is only a brief statement that Christ will "return to judge all men at the last day" (IV) and the article against purgatory and the invocation of the saints (XXII). See Martin Schmidt, *Eigenart und Bedeutung der Eschatologie im Englischen Puritanismus* (Arthur Dent, Lewis Bayly, John Bunyan). *Sonderausgabe* of the *Theologia Viatorum* (1952).

subsection of ecclesiology or perhaps of the Lord's Supper after an ancient interpretation of the Apostle's Creed. However, it does provide an opportunity to discuss departed saints which Traherne does not discuss elsewhere in his outline.

Article XXII of the Thirty-nine Articles calls the invocation of saints "a fond thing vainly invented, and grounded upon no warrenty of Scripture, but rather repugnant to the word of God." Traherne tends to agree that the saints are not to be invoked or prayed for, because they are already happy (CYB 104; *RF*, p. 212). He holds that while the commemoration of the saints in the church's year is neither commanded nor forbidden in Scripture, the church commemorates them by imitating their virtues (CYB 20v, 104r). A defense of the Roman practice of the veneration of relics seems to be implied by his statement that the "very Bodies of the Saints are held Sacred by us, and used venerably by us." However, Traherne implicitly criticizes the Roman Catholic practice by explaining that the saints are "honorably Disposed in quiet graves" (CYB 104r). Traherne praises God for the "order of Infants" who "never passed the test of any Trial" (CYB 109r), meaning perhaps the slaughtered innocents, but he does not clarify whether these infants are baptized or not or whether they are in a *limbus infantum*. Traherne calls Mary, the mother of God, a virgin, "Highest of the Saints," "Most Glorious" of the creatures, the most perfect of God's works, the dearest, and the "Tabernacle of the Most Glorious Trinity" (CYB 107r), which may reflect more his sources than his own enthusiasm for Marian devotion. Traherne is not concerned with the kind of knowledge the saints have, how they are employed and other such questions with which Joseph Hall among others concerned himself.[110]

Traherne's position is like that of the Thirty-nine Articles, except for some unclarity. He does mention the happiness of the saints which for him means they need no prayer.

5. "Heavenly Joys"

Traherne thinks it also important to enquire "What shall be after the end of the World? Whether we shall live forever? Whether we shall see God, and know one another? Whether we shall reign in eternal Glory" (*CE*, p. 229).

---

110. See *The Great Mysterie of Godliness* (London, 1652), vol. II, chs. 4-7. Perhaps Traherne had in mind something like Wollebius' "blessed society of the Saints" (p. 168).

Men's trials on earth are meant to make men long to be with Christ, for eternal rest, and for the liberty of the sons of God (*CE*, p. 19). According to Traherne, men's treasures and joys will be the same in heaven as on earth, but will differ in glory (*CE*, p. 245). Heaven will be a happy and joyful place (CYB 6v; *Hex*, p. 91). Sins which are conquered will be roots of bliss, and each tear will be a pearl (III *C* 47). There will be no sin, death, sorrow, darkness, work, or satiety in heaven (*Hex*, p. 15). On the basis of the youth of the angel at the tomb, Traherne theorizes that there will also be no aging, sickness, or infirmities in heaven (CYB 5v). The blessed, according to Traherne, will fly with angel's wings and walk on spices, flowers, jewels and gold (*CE*, p. 260). Heaven is filled with glory, love, light, space, joys, beauty, and variety ("Vision" 26-29). In heaven the directions of God's providence will be seen to center on the soul of man, and the soul will be all act (CYB 27r; II *C* 73). All actions, thoughts, mysteries, and secrets will be known by everyone forever (*CE*, p. 254; SM III 31).

Traherne seems to work with a realized eschatology. Heaven is here and now, if men were able to see it (SM IV 15; "Thoughts" IV). Those who live as poor men in the midst of riches, who enjoy God, paradise, and christendom, who see the value of men's souls, who prize all things rightly, are in the estate of immortality on earth (IV *C* 27). To possess and to prize blessings, for Traherne, is to be in heaven, but having blessings and not prizing them is to be in hell on earth. "To prize them and not to hav them, is to be in Hell" (I *C* 47). Thus heaven for Traherne is not so much a change of position as a change of condition: practicing glorious principles. Angels are happy anywhere and devils miserable (IV *C* 37). It is not so much God's love to man, as man's love to God which makes heaven (*CE*, p. 131). Traherne labels it a mystery that in this life some should be living in "hell, Golgotha or Prison" while others are in Eden, heaven and paradise (I *C* 36).

Traherne thinks that a magnanimous soul also wonders "Whether in the Confusions of Hell there be any Beauty, and whether in the Torments of the Damned we shall find any joy or satisfaction" (*CE*, p. 229). Traherne does not mention hell in his outline, yet he treats the topic in some detail in his writings. He brings to his discussion his particular point of view. In this passage, or example, Traherne wonders about beauty, joy, and satisfaction in hell.

Hell is a necessity for Traherne, because the way God "guards and fortifies his Law" is by the fear of infinite punishment, and he encourages men by offering infinite rewards. [111] Rewards and punishments are necessary, because sin is more terrible than hell (*CE*, p. 97; III *C* 49). If men do not see "their wants from all eternity" on earth, they will see "their Treasures to all Eternity" in hell. According to Traherne, considering hell while on earth, may help to avoid it in the hereafter, but to refuse to consider the torments of the damned in this life will mean being forced to remember the felicities enjoyed while on earth. Although hell is a prison, it is to be enjoyed because it is part of God's creation and loved because it is an evidence of God's justice (I *C* 48; IV *C* 67).

Traherne is rather explicit as to how hell is merited. Hell is reserved for those who "despise" God's creation, who "follow the Prince of Darkness," who offend God's justice, who injure orphans, widows, and saints, who fail to live in God's image, who do not love others as they love themselves, who are not grateful.[112] Traherne calls hell the "fire" (SM III 49), "eternal Darkness" (I *C* 32), and prison (I *C* 48). It will be, Traherne thinks, just to be excluded from heaven and reasonable to be eternally punished (*Thanks*, p. 227; *CE*, p. 98).

Traherne sees love as the key to understanding the torments of hell. Angels are to love men, as they love themselves, "upon pain of eternal Damnation" (*Thanks*, p. 272). A major aspect of the "Misery of Devils" is their repentance without its necessary accompaniment: love. The torments in hell are caused by the absence of love. In fact, no other fire is necessary in hell, but for the damned to know how much they are hated by God and how evil their actions were (*CE*, p. 98). Softening, somewhat, this harsh description of hell is Traherne's note in his Commonplace Book under the topic "Banishment:" "the damned are not banished from God's essential presence, only from his 'joyful presence.'"

Thus heaven and hell for Traherne are both physical realities and states of mind both here and hereafter. Although his central theme of felicity pervades his discussion of heaven and hell, his view of hell as a reality, a necessity, a possibility, tempers his usual optimism.[113]

---

111. Wollebius asserts that "eternal happiness consisteth in our freedom from all evil, in the variety, magnitude, and eternity of joyes. The variety of joyes is considered in the glorification of man, in the delights of Heavenly Mansions, in the blessed society of the Saints; but chiefly in the union with God" (p. 306). See "Beatifick" in Traherne's CB which quotes Hermes on the beatific vision.

112. I *C* 31, 32; CYB 112v; *Thanks*, pp. 272, 311; *CE*, p. 9.

6. "Society of Angels"

Finally, according to Traherne, the magnanimous man will wonder "What kind of Communion and fellowship Angels and Men shall have with each other" (*CE*, p. 230). This passage in the *Christian Ethicks* is surprisingly parallel to the section on the estate of glory in the *Centuries*, although different terminology and emphases are evident. Traherne ends his section on divinity and the estate of glory with a subsection devoted to angelology. Most traditional dogmatics do not conclude with angelology. Traherne does not seem to place angelology last because he thinks it least important of the doctrines. Perhaps he means angelology to be a culmination and climax of his section on divinity. There is some evidence that this is the case. Feuerbach may make all theology anthropology, but Traherne has a tendency to relate angelology to much of his theology.

Traherne, like others of his time, thinks that the angels were created on the first day simultaneously with the light.[114] Scripture is not specific on the matter. Traherne states that their nature is unknown (*CE*, p. 145), and if men are ever to understand their nature, they must esteem and delight in the angel's powers of loving, adoring, praising, obeying, admiring, rejoicing, and pleasing. Evidently Traherne did just that, for in his "Meditations and Devotions on St. Michael's Day," he elaborates upon the nature of angels in detail, listing their appearances and indicating their relationship to Jesus Christ. The devotion is almost a textbook on angelology. His information about what angels do, why, when, and how is drawn from the Scriptures and other sources.[115] Traherne does not merely restate what he reads, however. He adapts the theories of others to his own needs, making theories more practical and transforming dry dogma into lively literature. Traherne is also critical of what he reads. In a section devoted to the orders and tasks of angels, he questions: "How much exercise here is of Phancy, and by consequence, how little of certainty?" In

---

113. Traherne deletes a reference to hell in I *C* 47. See the discussion of "Justice" above in ch. vi C. Willett states that Traherne does not believe in a "material hell" but rather that hell and heaven are within us, but she does think he believes in eternal punishment (p. 46). Peter Sterry does not believe in eternal damnation, nor does he believe in the reality of evil, according to V. Pinto, p. 109. John Smith writes that "Hell is rather a Nature then a Place: and Heaven cannot be so truly defined by anything without us, as by something that is within us." *Discourses*, pp. 446-447. See D. P. Walter, *The Decline of Hell,* and C. Marks, "Cambridge Platonism," *PMLA*, 530ff, and *CE*, p. 339.
114. See, for example, Wollebius, ch. v.

fact, he says he uses the material "more. . . for agreement sake. . . than for any real or well Grounded Certainty" (CYB 93r-95v). Traherne points out, for example, that the illumination ascribed to archangels and the knowledge ascribed to cherubim are basically the same thing, which indicates for Traherne that the distinctions are perhaps not accurate. Moreover, Traherne wonders whether it is possible to distinguish among the various orders of angels. He does agree that angels and archangels seem to be sent abroad on missions, that cherubim and seraphim tend to stay around the throne of God, but virtues, thrones, dominions, principalities and powers seem to be more of this world (CYB 93r-94v). In any event, Traherne praises God for the glorious orders of angels, and thinks it impossible to be an atheist if one considers their nature (CYB 90v).

His description of angels is quite detailed. Angels are pure and simple beings, endless in extent, instant in motion, all sight and love, free agents, and courageous.[116] What constitutes an angel is not the lack of a body but spiritual intelligence. (IV *C* 77). That fact may illuminate Traherne's dedicatory poem for the *Centuries*. Traherne states that the one who receives the *Centuries* "may write my Makers prais therein/And make her self therby a Cherubim." Evidently Traherne implies that the receiver can make herself spiritually intelligent. Angels are as "small as indivisible Atoms" or "Intelligible Spheres" (CYB 90r).

The fall of the angels was caused by pride, ingratitude, and discontent. As a result of the fall, the evil angels are in darkness forever (*Hex*, p. 3). Because Christ did not assume the nature of angels, the devils cannot be saved.[117] Traherne lists a number of theories about the angel's fall: to show

---

115. Austin, John Gerard's *Meditations*, 2nd ed. (Cambridge, 1631), and Puente are Traherne's chief sources. See C. Marks discussion in "CYB" *Papers*, pp. 50ff, and Lynn Sauls, "Puente." Traherne states that his listing is indebted to the Schoolmen and Bishop Andrewes, but apparently it is mediated to him via Austin. Traherne's listing attributes tuition to the angels, illumination to the archangels, miracles to the virtues, judgment to the thrones and so on for the nine ranks of angels (dominions, principalities, powers, cherubim, and seraphim). Aquinas in his *Compendium* (ch. 126) reverses the order and stresses other aspects of each order. Joseph Hall is also sceptical about delineating their ranks, offices, and employments. *The Great Mysterie*, p. 145. Traherne also lists seven reasons why the archangel Michael is to be identified with Christ.

116. CYB 90vff; IV *C* 79, 91.

117. Both Smith and Cudworth imply that God will forgive Satan; George Rust and Peter Sterry defend the idea explicitly. See Patrides' discussion and *CE*, p. 339n. There are references to Satan in the EN, pp. 215-217, 234ff.

God's dominion, to declare his justice, to demonstrate that God alone is perfect, to instruct men in their frailties, and to teach men to honor and fear God. However, Traherne concludes that they fell "not so much to teach us, as to honour thee" (CYB 3ff). The fall of the angels was more shameful than the fall of man, but if the angels had withstood the temptation, it still would have been with less glory than man's withstanding temptation, because they are not subject to all the human frailties (*CE*, p. 104). The "Prince of the Power of the Air" continues to work in the "Children of Disobedience" (*Thanks*, p. 300), but Traherne seldom refers to the present activity of Satan.

Traherne is particularly interested in the interactions of angels with men. Although in their first estate angels had a higher prerogative than man and were nearer to God (SM IV 37), man is now superior and more beloved of God (*CE*, p. 195; II *C* 33). In fact an angel cannot redeem man in part because of man's dignity (II *C* 34). Every man has a guardian angel, who "suggests what is needful for his salvation." Traherne praises God for this guardian angel (*Hex*, p. 7). Angels are not to be adored or invoked (CYB 91v), but men are to rejoice in their being, imitate them in serving all mankind, pray for the conversion of men, obey, and do God's will (*Hex*, p. 8). The tasks of angels on behalf of men are: to reveal, teach, direct, protect, comfort, help, destroy enemies, pray for them, rejoice at their conversion, gather their bodies at the resurrection (*Hex*, pp. 7ff), to love, honor, praise, and adore God; to love, serve, and minister to men; and to admire and rejoice in God's treasures (CYB 89r). Good angels can suggest good thoughts and evil angels evil thoughts. Angels can heal diseases "By conveying the virtues of herbs or by forming the air into sanitive Spirits" or by "expelling the noxious and redundant humors." They can also make man rich by bringing him gold and silver or by letting him know where it can be found. Traherne admits, however, that these latter tasks are "little and mean things."[118] Angels are also dependent to some extent on man. They smell, taste, hear, touch, feel, and sing by means of man's senses, because they do not have the physical faculties for sensing (*Thanks*, p. 225).

Traherne devotes a section of the *Thanksgivings* to speculating about life without the angels. Without angels he would fear being devoured and

118. CYB 90v, 91v. In the *Daily Devotions* there is a section which attributes to angels the ability to keep men "from Falls, Fractures of Bones, Dislocations, epidemical and noisom Diseases and from the Hands of the violent and wicked Men" (p. 342).

annoyed by briars and beasts, terrified by guilt. The world would be a desert and a wilderness, and he would be "Naked and hungry,/Blind and brutish,/Without house or harbour;/Subject unto storms;/. . .Feeding upon roots;/But more upon melancholy,/Because void of thee." The angels build, procure, provide (bread, drink, clothes, bed, household wares), and teach (the use of meats and fire).[119]

Angels experience joy and contentment beholding one another and God. However, angels please men most when they stand with him "before the Throne of God, praising and magnifying him for ever." In fact, it should be men's desire that the angels sing and praise, according to Traherne (*Hex*, pp. 2ff, 8ff). Thus the angels participate with man in his felicity and worship, the keynote and endnote of the theological thought of Thomas Traherne.

---

119. *Thanks*, p. 222.

Chapter VIII

"Natural Philosophy"

Natural philosophy teacheth us ye Causes & Effects of all Bodies simply & in ye selves. But if you extend it a little further, to ye midired wch its Name imports, & signifying ye Lov of Nature, it leads us into a Diligent inquisition into all Natures, their Qualities, Affections, Relations, Causes & Ends, So far forth as by Nature & Reason they may be known. And this Noble Science, as such is Sublime & perfect, it includes all Humanity & Divinity together GOD, Angels, Men, Affections, Habits, Elections, Virtues. Every Thing as it is a Solid intire Object singly proposed, being a Subject if it, as well as Material & visible things But taking it as it is usualy Bounded in its Terms, it treateth only of Corporeal things, as Heaven, Earth Air Water, Fire, & Sun & Stars, Trees Herbs, flowers, Influences, Winds, fowles Beasts fishes Minerals & precious Stones; wth all other Beings of ye Kind. And as they it is taken it is nobly Subservient to ye High ost Ends; for it openeth ye Riches of Gods Kingdom, & ye Nature of His Territories Works & Creatures in a Wonderfull Maner, Clearing & preparing ye Ey of ye Enjoyer.

III Century 44

Thomas Traherne includes "Natural Philosophy" among the "Materials of Religion," and he labels it a "Noble Science" which "includes all Humanity and Divinity together" (III *C* 44). The seventeenth century was an age of major scientific advances and of preoccupation with the sciences and with such pseudo-sciences as astrology, alchemy, and animism.[1] It was an age in which clergymen were scientists and scientists dabbled in theology, but few accorded natural philosophy such high praise or included it as an integral part of divinity as Traherne did. Major contributions were made in medicine, biology, chemistry, astronomy, and mathematics,[2] but science proved to be not only a boon but a bane. It called into question many

---

1. See Bush, pp. 273ff.
2. In England Thomas Harriot (1560-1621) was active in mathematics and astronomy; William Harvey (1578-1657) in anatomy; Thomas Hobbes (1588-1679) in psychology and science; Robert Burton (1577-1649), John Wilkins (1614-72) in astronomy. Descartes, Huygens, Leibniz, Merseene, and Gassendi were active on the Continent. See Willey, *Seventeenth*, pp. 32-64 and Bush, pp. 273ff.

theological and philosophical assumptions, and in so doing, threatened a world-view which had dominated Western thought for more than a millennium.

Oxford became a center of scientific study after 1648, but following the Restoration the center moved to Gresham College and London. Traherne's career roughly parallels this movement,[3] and although his writings evidence little direct influence, they do reflect the scientific concerns of the age. There are a variety of stances on science in the seventeenth century. Puritanism, for example, can be seen both to have fostered an interest in natural science by its orientation to reform, utilitarianism, empiricism, and action, as well as to have hindered the advance of science by its emphasis on revelation rather than reason and its stress on the religious significance of nature rather than its significance *per se*. At the same time, it should be noted, that a number of important mid-seventeenth century scientists were Puritans.[4]

The approach of the Cambridge Platonists to scientific study is less ambiguous. In the words of G. R. Cragg they "apprehended God in and through nature, not in spite of or beyond it" like the Puritans.[5] Moreover, according to Joseph Glanville, the Cambridge Platonists studied "all sorts of *late* Improvements in *Anatomy, Mathematicks, Natural History,* and *Mechanicks*."[6] Henry More thinks, for example, that the world is a "picture, shadow, or footstep of the Divinity," and God is immanent in the creation.[7] This affirmation of the physical universe exists side by side with their Neoplatonism, but there is some basis for their viewpoint even in Plotinus and the Church Fathers.[8]

There were also widely divergent opinions about the relationship between science and religion. They ranged from Bacon's absolute

---

3.   Traherne was in Oxford approximately from 1653 to 1661 and in London after 1669. Some of the men who formed this important scientific nucleus were: Thomas Willis, Lawrence Rooke, John Wilkins, John Wallis, Jonathan Goddard, Robert Boyle, Seth Ward, Robert Hooke and others. See Bush, pp. 283ff. William Petty, a renowned lecturer and scientist in anatomy and mathematics and Elias Ashmole, founder of the Ashmolean museum, were both Brasenose men.

4.   See Cragg, *From Puritanism*, pp. 53ff, and compare Bush, pp. 283ff.

5.   Cragg, *From Puritanism*, p. 53.

6.   "Anti-fanatical Religion and Free Philosophy," Essay 7 in *Essays on Several Important Subjects in Philosophy and Religion* (London, 1676), p. 9.

7.   H. More, *Divine Dialogues*, Dialogue Two, p. 279. For a fuller discussion of the scientific views of the Cambridge Platonists, see C. Marks, "Cambridge Platonism," *PMLA* (1966).

separation and Hobbes' materialism to Sir Thomas Browne's belief that they are inseparable.[9] Although Traherne read Francis Bacon, he differs in his approach to the relationship between science and religion. While Bacon separates the two, stating that there is a truth of religion and a truth of science and that these truths are not to be mixed, Traherne, like Sir Thomas Browne, thinks the truths are inseparable.[10] Similar to Traherne in his high evaluation of natural science is Robert Boyle, a contemporary of Traherne, who was not a theologian but a scientist. To Boyle natural philosophy, if not a "Handmaid to Divinity," is a "Lady of lower rank." Although Boyle insists that he is an "assiduous Courter of Nature," he, nevertheless, maintains that the study of nature is inferior to the study of theology.[11] Traherne, in contrast, includes "all Humanity and Divinity" under the rubric of Natural Philosophy, "this Noble Science" (III *C* 44).

Traherne is fascinated by scientific facts and theories.[12] Even as a child he thought about scientific questions, he says, and when he learned the answers to these questions, he "knew by the Perfection of the Work there was a GOD, and was satisfied, and Rejoyced" (III *C* 17). His early notebooks have numerous references to such scientific subjects as: "Astonomie" and "Physiognomie" in the Early Notebook,[13] "Cold" and "Co-haesion" in the Commonplace Book, and excerpts from Timaeus' *De Mundi Natura* in the Ficino Notebook. There are references in his writings

---

8. Plotinus writes, "Do not suppose that a man becomes good by despising the world and all the beauties that are in it. Those who despise what is so nearly akin to the world yonder prove that they know nothing of the world yonder, except in name." Quoted in Inge, *Mysticism in Religion*, p. 116. *Explicatio Dei* is a concept of Nicholas of Cusa and *liber creaturarum* is a concept of Raymond de Sabunde.

9. See Willey, *Seventeenth*, p. 35.

10. See Willey, *Seventeenth*, pp. 35ff, and Bush, pp. 288ff.

11. R. Boyle, *Excellency of Theology compar'd with Natural Philosophy (as both are Objects of Men's Study)* was published in London in 1665. Levinus Lemnius in *Secret Miracles of Nature* (London, 1658) writes that "but for arts that are necessary and profitable for our lives, as Natural Philosophy, Physick, Law, wherein chiefly the mind of man rests, and receives comfort, I mean, not humane, but heavenly Philosophy, whereby Christ leading us, we attain the knowledge of God, and to love and trust in him" (p. 329). A copy of this book in the Baltimore Medical Library bears Traherne's signature indicating that he possessed the book.

12. See R. Ellrodt, "Scientific Curiosity," *MP*, 61 (1964), 180-197.

13. Traherne did not take notes, however, on Bacon's discussion of the nature, use, and divisions of natural philosophy. See C. Marks, "Early Studies," *Papers*, 1968. Marjorie Nicholson thinks that "training, science, and philosophy served only to heighten youthful intuition." *The Breaking of the Circle*, rev. ed. (New York, 1960), p. 197.

to the workings of gravity and magnetism (I C 2), the antipodes,[14] the effects of the sun, the levitation of the earth, and the mechanics of rain (*Hex*, pp. 41ff). He also reflects the fascination of the age with dissection and anatomy. His "Thanksgivings for the Body" focus on the "Limbs, Arteries, Veins, Sinews" and marvel at how the body is so "fit. . .for Dissections. . .for Draughts in Anatomy" (p. 215). Even the Means of Grace are described as "Arteries to convey the Spirit to us" (CYB 53r; *Thanks*, p. 215). Traherne's understanding of infinity, eternity, and the plurality of worlds also evidences his interest in and understanding of the scientific theories of his day.

His writings also evidence a love and appreciation of nature.[15] Traherne is impressed with the order, art, curiosity, and beauty of nature (*Hex*, p. 33), and he tends to see a spiritual significance in natural phenomena: "Shall they then be Signs, and signify Nothing?" Nature is intended to teach man as well as to be for his use and benefit. Even God himself uses the natural world as a source of metaphors, symbols, and similes according to Traherne (*Hex*, pp. 47, 60). The heavens and earth not

---

14. See *CE*, pp. 120, 210; "Shadows in the Water."
15. There are interesting parallels in continental seventeenth century art. Jacob van Ruysdael (1628-82), Rembrandt van Rijn (1606-69), Jan Vermeer (1632-75), Peter Paul Rubens (1577-1640) among others evidenced an interest in landscape, still life, and scientific scenes.
      Critics have had varying interpretations of Traherne's attitude toward nature. F. Towers (1920) states that Traherne is "as far removed from the intimate spirit of nature as he is from the beating heart of humanity," and nature appeals to Traherne "intellectually or spiritually rather than sensually." She continues by saying that Traherne "notes her manifestations and draws conclusions from them as if she were a wonderful work of art, a picture painted by the Master Hand, or a poem hiding a heavenly secret" (p. 1026). W. K. Fleming (1913) says that there "is no one in the whole range of mystics who looks on Nature just as Traherne does" (p. 193). Q. Iredale (1935) sees "The love of nature" as the "Central theme in Traherne's life" (p. 1). G. Wade states that Traherne believes that nature "infallibly brought those who followed it into the presence of God" in her article on "Traherne and the Spiritual Value of Nature Study," *London Quarterly* (1934), p. 243. M. Williams thinks Traherne believes "in the immanence of God in Nature and at the same time that all creation emanates from God." *Cithara*, III (1963), p. 38. T. Staley states that "Traherne cannot be looked at in the light of romantic ideas of beauty and nature, for he shows in his poetry the certainty that in nature outward beauty is the proof of inward beauty, and outward good of inward good." *Cithara*, IV (1964), p. 44. R. Uphaus asserts that Traherne thinks that "God can only be known through the creation." Moreover, "God's presence is both immanent and transcendent." *U. of Windsor Review*, (1969), p. 20. W. Barnstone indicates that Traherne is not a romantic, for he thinks that "Nature is not a mirror in which he sees himself. Nature is a part of God's creation, as he is himself." *Books Abroad* (1968), p. 16. See also M. Bottrall, "Traherne's Praise of the Creation," *Critical Quarterly*, I (Summer, 1959), 126-133.

only exhibit the wisdom, power, and glory of God, they also magnify, beautify, and illuminate the soul. The "visible World is the Body of God."[16] Traherne does not set the spiritual against the natural, but he does see a difference between the world which was created by God and the world which was corrupted by men. His affirmation of the physical world is perhaps nowhere more evident than in his raptures on the human body.[17]

Traherne is, nevertheless, a man of his age who accepts uncritically many mistaken scientific notions. He copies sections on magic (119-120), astrology (135-138), and natural divination (150) into his Early Notebook. He seems to prefer the Ptolemaic to the Copernican theories (*CE*, p. 195) and to accept Usher's dating of the age of the earth (*Thanks*, p. 289). He states often that the sun "operates upon, refineth, and prepareth minerals in the rocks" (*Hex*, pp. 41ff). Salt, he thinks, is strained from the waters through the pores of the earth (*Hex*, p. 31). All stars are seen by everyone at the same time (*CE*, p. 254). Yet, he also corrects his sources. While Puente, for example, states that the sun is "a hundred tymes bigger" than the earth, Traherne writes "several thousand times larger." L. Sauls notes that no other hexameral works of the time contained the new calculations of Kepler, Vendelinus or Riccioli which Traherne reflects.[18]

There are a number of scientific contradictions, errors, or paradoxes in Traherne's writings, sometimes within the same paragraph. They often involve a juxtaposition of the biblical worldview or pre-modern scientific theory with an emerging modern scientific stance. In one paragraph, for example, he states with regard to the earth: "How great is thy Power in making a Bulk of this immense weight, to stand up in an empty Space all about it, without any Prop or corporal Support? and yet hast thou laid the Foundations of this Earth so fast, that it cannot be moved" (*Hex*, pp. 9-10). Traherne does not note or resolve the problem of how the world could be without "Support" yet have "Foundations."

Elsewhere, he explains how the rain in heaven rises from the vapors of the earth and salty, bitter seawater. These then are converted into clouds and "afterwards distilled down in sweet and refreshing Showers." Immediately afterward he describes how God divided the waters on the

---

16. I *C* 27; II *C* 21, 78.
17. See "Thanksgivings for the Body;" *Hex*, pp. 73-80; and the poems "Salutation," "The Estate," "The Enquirie," and "The Person."
18. See L. Sauls', "Puente," *PQ*, L, 2 (April, 1971), 168-169.

second day of creation "because he would leave the more gross and terrestrial Waters upon the Earth; and lift up those which are more subtil and delicate, into the Regions of the Air, which are the Clouds we see, which water and refresh the dry Earth" (*Hex*, p. 17). Thus he describes the scientific explanation of the connection between clouds, water vapor, and rain together with the Genesis account. His method seems to be to cite first the current theory about the levitation of the earth or the formation of the rain, and then to cite the biblical view. Perhaps he intends to let the reader decide between, ignore, or live with the contradictions or paradoxes. Traherne seldom provides any help in the matter, not even defining his own position or resolution of the problem. It does not seem to be a problem for him.

Traherne is not uncritical of science. When bodies are dissected, Traherne states, man as "A living Inhabitant/Of the great World/And the Centre of it!/A Sphere of Sense,/And a Mine of Riches" flies away and is lost (*Thanks*, p. 216). Scientific analysis or dissection is unable to discover the essence of man or the fullness that lies within and may even destroy these qualities of man.

Traherne's love and high regard for nature leads some scholars to consider him a pantheist. Yet, as J. Leishman notes, Traherne not only avoids both pantheism and dualism, but he also preserves God's immanence and transcendence. Nature gives no final solution.[19]

Traherne imbues even his discussion of natural philosophy with his central concerns. He tends to see only the positive aspects of nature. Fire, for example, "is a universal Instrument of Good" and is "admirably beneficial to us in all its Uses" (*Hex*, p. 51). He lists its various uses but ignores the fact that it can also maim and destroy. He restates the law of the jungle in such a way that he avoids its negative effects. God "gave them defensive and offensive weapons" that they might defend themselves from others and "get that of others which they should desire and seek" (*Hex*, p. 66). Moreover, anyone who sees God's works cannot help but admire them and praise God for them (*Hex*, p. 22). The workings of the sea alone, according to Traherne, are enough to lose all philosophy "in that Tomb of

---

19. See the poems "Right Apprehension" and "Solitude." J. Leishman writes that Traherne "insists that God can only be known through the creation." However, Traherne recognizes revelation through the Scriptures and personal experience. See also ch. vii above and the discussions of nature and grace, reason and faith in ch. viii.

Curiosity" (*Hex*, p. 29). This is, for Traherne, truly the best of all possible worlds (see II *C* 8ff).

His suggested outline for natural philosophy is a mixture of metaphysics, physics, and theology.

A. "Natural Philosophy. . .leads us into a Diligent inquisition into all Natures, Qualities, Affections, Relations, Causes, Ends"

Basically Traherne thinks that the purpose of Natural Philosophy is to teach the "Causes and Effects of all Bodies simply and in themselves." However, he does extend this basic definition to include the love of nature "which its Name imports." W. T. Costello's description of the curriculum in seventeenth century Cambridge, especially the areas of metaphysics, physics and theology, illuminates Traherne's concerns. Metaphysics, according to Costello, focuses on being as such, its principles (the one, the true, the good) and its attributes. It was considered the primary and the loftiest of the sciences because all others depended upon it. Physics focuses on changeable being (time, motion, matter, extension) and the natural sciences. Both were considered to be based on reason and not on revelation. Thus, when Traherne in his outline elaborates on natural philosophy stating that "it leads us into a Diligent inquisition into all Natures Qualities Affections Relations Causes Ends," he is probably referring in part to metaphysics and physics.[20]

All *natures* may refer to "essence." (Essence, form and substance are basically the same thing according to Costello.) In metaphysics essence is the basic element and root of the properties of being. Potency and act are being's first principles (see *CE*, p. 36). *Qualities* may refer to the nine accidents or qualities (modifications, states, and relations) of being or to one of the accidents. Costello defines quality, one of the accidents of being, as "being as affecting substance in its essence or its operation, like a warm night, a happy child." Relations may refer to another accident which is "being" in logical or real connection with another "being" by way of equality, similarity, identity. The other accidents are quantity, action, passion, position, place (where located), time (before or after), and habit.

---

20.   Costello, pp. 70ff.

These nine accidents plus substance are equivalent to Aristotle's ten categories. Only quantity and quality are physical accidents, and all are primarily ways of cataloguing and describing things.

Causes may refer to the four causes which are matter, form, efficient cause and *end* (also in Traherne's outline). Matter in metaphysical theory according to Costello, is either primary (potentiality) or secondary (which is the subject of physics because it exists in natural bodies). Form is a principle of determination and unites with matter to form an individual being. Matter and form uniting and dissolving are the efficient cause. Everything that exists also has a final cause or purpose: "That on account of which a thing is made or something done." It is identical with form.[21]

B. "And this Noble Science, as such is most Sublime and Perfect, it includes all Humanity and Divinity together"

Traherne elaborates on this assertion by stating that "GOD, angels, Men, Affections, Habits, Actions, Virtues" are included in the purview of natural philosophy (III C 44). *Affections*, listed twice in his outline, may refer to a "contingent, alterable, and accidental state or quality of being" from the Latin *affectio* which can be active (an influence) or passive (a state of mind). *Habit* is one of the nine accidents, which describes "being modified by an adjacent substance" (clothed in wool). *Action* (another of the nine accidents) describes "being that is productive of change" like opening or carrying, in contrast to passion which describes being changed or suffering change (being opened, being carried).

Moreover, Traherne also includes "Evry Thing as it is a Solid intire Object singly proposed, being a subject of it, as well as Material and visible Things" which approximates the scholastic definition of Physics.[22] Material substance was the object of physics whereas immaterial substance was the object of metaphysics. Angelology, for example, according to the tradition was not normally considered a part of metaphysics but the doctrine of God was, since God's existence can be proved by reason. Traherne lists both as objects of Natural Philosophy. Aquinas equates

---

21. Ibid.
22. Costello, pp. 83ff.

physics with natural philosophy and thinks that it should be studied before metaphysics.[23] Traherne in contrast evidently thinks it should be studied after metaphysics. Traherne's terms "Philosophy" and "Natural Philosophy" are often equivalent to what is meant by natural sciences today (see *Hex,* p. 40).

C. "But taking it as it is usualy Bounded in its Terms, it treateth only of Corporeal Things"

This rubric is a further elaboration on the subject of physics or, as in Eustache's system, *De rebus Naturalibus.*[24] Traherne expands on what he means by "Corporeal Things": "Heaven, Earth Air Water, Fire, the Sun and Stars, Trees Herbs, flowers, Influences, Winds, Fowles Beasts Fishes Minerals, and Precious Stones; with all other Beings of that Kind" (III *C* 44). Earth, air, fire, and water are the four elements, and the nature, form, and perfection of all bodies depends upon the proper mixture and proportion of these elements (see *CE,* pp. 171, 227). Traherne also refers to the four humors, "Choler, Melancholy, Flegm, and Blood," but he states that many other things are also necessary in proper proportion (*CE,* p. 171). The four humors are subject to the will of men and can be altered enabling man to live a life of reason (*CE,* pp. 174ff). Eustache includes discussions of *De Corpore Naturae in genere, De causis, De corpore Naturali Inanimanto, De Mundo, De Caelo, De Igne, De Aero, De Aqua, De Terra* in the section *De rebus Naturalibus* of his *Summa Philosophiae Quadripartite.*

Traherne concludes his section on natural philosophy by asserting that "it is Nobly Subservient to the Highest Ends: for it Openeth the Riches of Gods Kingdom and the Natures of his Territories Works and Creatures in a Wonderful Maner, Clearing and preparing the Ey of the Enjoyer" (III *C* 44). Thus Traherne seemingly qualifies his assertion that natural philosophy includes humanity and divinity, by saying that it too is "Subservient to the Highest Ends." Moreover, natural philosophy for Traherne seems to be something like a *preparatio Evangelii* in that it opens, clears, and prepares the "Ey of the Enjoyer" (III *C* 44). Traherne often stresses the importance of apprehension and vision. In "An Infant-Ey" and

---

23.   See Copleston, *Aquinas,* pp. 71ff.
24.   *Summa Philosophy Quadripartite,* part III. Compare Burgersdicius, *Inst. Meta.*

"Sight" Traherne postulates the existence of an inward eye or a third eye which provides insight.[25] The objects of "Natural Philosophy" like "Divinity" and "Humanity" are to be enjoyed (III *C* 44).

While the Royal Society's program assumes that *"The Natural Philosopher is to begin, where the Moral ends,"* Traherne reverses this suggested order and ends his outline of the "Materials of Religion" with a section devoted to "Ethicks."[26]

---

25. See *CE*, pp. 64, 155, 329; II *C* 84. Montaigne writes that "Whoever contemplates our mother Nature in her full majesty and lustre is alone able to value things in their true estimate" in his essay "Of the Education of Children." Quoted in Willey, *Seventeenth*, p. 41.

26. Sprat, *History of the Royal Society*, ed. and intro. Jackson Cope and H. Jones (St. Louis, Missouri, and London, 1959), p. 33.

Chapter IX

"Ethicks"

45.

Ethicks teach us ỹ Mysteries of Moralitie, & ỹ Nature of all Affections vertues & Maners, as by ỹᵐ we may be Guided to our Highest Happines. The former for Speculation, this for Practice. Ỹ former furnisheth us wᵗʰ Riches, this wᵗʰ Honors & Delights, Ỹ former feasteth us, & this instructeth us. for by this we are taught to liv Honorably among men; & to make our selvs Noble & usefull among ỹᵐ. It teacheth us how to Manage our Passions, to Exercise vertues, & to form our Maners, so as to liv Happily in this World. And all these put together Discover ỹ Materials of Religion to be so Great, ỹ it plainly manifesteth ỹ Revelation of GOD to be Deep & Infinit. for it is impossible for Languages, Miracles, observations or appearances to teach us ỹ Infallibility of GODs Word or to Shew us ỹ Certainty of true Religion; without a Clear Sight into Truth it self ỹ is into ỹ Truth of Things. Wᶜʰ will them selvs wᵉⁿ truly seen, by ỹ very Beauty & Glory of ỹᵐ, best Discover, & prov Religion.

III Century 45

In their second and third years at Oxford, undergraduates were required to attend Francis Howell's lectures on moral philosophy twice a week. The text used was Aristotle's *Ethica*, but evidently later commentaries were taken into account. Aquinas, for example, modifies and Christianizes Aristotle, and Traherne in his Early Notebook has lengthy quotations from Eustache de Saint Paul's *Ethica*. Eustache uses both Aristotle and Aquinas as his sources.[1]

Whereas Traherne did not write a systematic theology or a treatise on natural philosophy that we know of, he did write a book on ethics which clarifies and expands, to some extent, his short outline of "Ethicks" in the third *Century* (45). Thus the discussion which follows is two-pronged. His suggested outline of "Ethicks" in the third *Century* is discussed, and the outline is supplemented by a discussion of the *Christian Ethicks*.

A. "Mysteries of Moralitie" (Speculation)

A book on ethics provides an exceptional opportunity for an examination of the author's explicit and implicit psychological, moral, and theological presuppositions. Of first importance among the presuppositions in his *Christian Ethicks* is the intended audience. Traherne explicitly states that he intends his work for the "Curious and Unbelieving Soul" (*CE*, p. 3). His intention, however, is not fully realized. The wealth of scriptural allusion and the frequent reference to Christian tradition and doctrine assume a reader who is not only well-trained in Christianity, but one who is interested in the minutiae of that tradition as well.[2] In addition, Traherne questions the motives, the sanity, the rationality of unbelievers, and he uses predominantly Christian motivations for the virtuous life. These are hardly calculated to appeal to his declared audience (see *CE*, p. 70).

Traherne holds that a man who is virtuous "in the Quality and Capacity of a Son of God" is quite different from one who is virtuous in a mechanical way. Each deed has infinite significance, and although the "Matter of the Act" seems like nothing, the form is "Divine and Blessed" (*CE*, p. 61). The Christian's virtue is founded on the love of Christ. This foundation distinguishes the Christian from the rest of mankind, especially when the Christian loves his enemies, is meek, and is humble (*CE*, p. 25). A Christian and a heathen can do the same act, but their motivations differ. The heathen does good deeds to "satisfie his Conscience and please the Gods." Traherne labels these "limited and finite" considerations and idolatry. In fact, the heathen aspires "to little more than a Glorious name in following Ages." The Christian, however, does good deeds in a way that enables many graces to "concentre in every Action." Thus, the heathen's

---

1. EN, pp. 7-21. For a thorough introduction to Traherne's *CE* and to ethical thought in the seventeenth century see Marks and Guffey edition of *Christian Ethicks* (herein abbreviated *CE*). Eustache de Saint Paul (1573-1640) was a professor at the Sorbonne, a friend of Francis de Sales, and the author of *Summa philosophiae quadripartita* (Paris, 1609). Traherne took notes on Meno's *De Virtue* (FN, 13), Plato's *De Summo Bono, De Amicitia, De Temperantia, De Fortitudine* (FN 18-24). See discussions of S. Stewart, G. Wade, A. Russell, and Martin Schmidt, "*Biblizismus und Natürliche Theologie in der Gewissenslehre des englischen Puritanismus,*" *Archiv für Reformations Geschichte.* T. Gale's *Court of the Gentiles* treats moral philosophy before metaphysics. Wollebius concludes his Abridgement of *Christian Doctrine* with a Second Book devoted to the worship of God, the "Nature of Good Works," "Of Vertues and Works," and the commandments.

2. See Traherne's references to the "Hypostatical Union" in *CE*, pp. 104, 114 for example.

good works are defective, inferior, and works of darkness. Traherne does not want to discourage the heathen from doing the best that they can, but to stress how highly Christianity ennobles man, and to "provoke Christians to a more Intelligent and lofty Practice of Christian Vertues, lest they differ not in their Morals from the better sort of Heathens." Traherne, however, stresses that Christianity is necessary for the perfection of an action not for its acceptance. He is not clear, however, as to the value of this acceptance or who is to accept it (*CE*, pp. 62ff). "The Heathens, who invented the name of Ethicks, were very short on the Knowledge of Mans End: but they are worse than Heathens, that never consider it" (*CE*, p. 14).

Thus the theoretical audience of *Christian Ethicks* and the real audience of *Christian Ethicks* sometimes come into conflict. Entitling a book *Christian Ethicks* and intending it for the skeptic or atheist is almost a contradiction in terms. It would seem almost as if the dedication of the book to the "Curious and Unbelieving" were *pro forma*. Traherne actually addresses himself to a Christian reading public whose faith at times was weak or wavering and needed strengthening.[3] Traherne may be appealing to the Christian skeptic, educated Christians like Dryden and members of the Royal Society who considered themselves skeptics.[4]

Traherne does not treat virtues as "duties enjoined by the law of God" (legalism), nor as "prudential expedients" (pragmatism), because he says that others have approached the subject in these ways (*CE*, p. 3). Instead, Traherne seems to want to educate, purify, and inspire. The humble tone of the closing paragraph rather than its opening remarks indicates the intent of the book. In the closing paragraphs he states that he writes on the virtues so that everyone who reads his book might "be elevated a little higher," "have something more erect and Angelical in their Souls, be brought to the Gates (at least) of GODs Kingdom, and be endued with GODLINESS a little more compleatly... than hitherto they have been" (*CE*, p. 286).

Most of the ethical writings of the seventeenth century were concerned either with the vices or with casuistry.[5] Traherne's *Christian Ethicks* is meant neither to supplant them nor to refute them but to supplement them

---

3. Internal evidence (*CE*, pp. 17, 259, 260) indicates that Traherne also expects his audience to be from the middle or upper classes.
4. See, for example, James William Johnson, *The Foundation of English Neo-Classical Thought* (Princeton, 1967), p. 82.
5. See the discussion in *CE*, xv-xxvi.

with his distinctive attitude toward virtue. Much in contrast to traditional ethical works, Thomas Traherne does not organize his work around the various vices and failings of man, but around his virtues. In fact, Traherne does not "speak much of *Vice*" because he is "intirely taken up with the abundance of Worth and Beauty in *Vertue*" and has so much to say about the "positive and intrinsick Goodness of its Nature" (*CE*, p. 3).

Traherne's stance on certain key issues in seventeenth century ethics is somewhat surprising. For example, Traherne, like Hobbes, acknowledges that by nature men love themselves. Traherne affirms this basic characteristic of man and builds upon it. Self-preservation and self-love, however, are not to be the sole concerns of man, and it is possible, according to Traherne, for a man to love others better than himself. In fact man should love God more than himself, but "Self-love is the first round."[6] Traherne also maintains that God commands what is holy, good, and true, in contrast to Jeremy Taylor, for example, who considers things holy because they are commanded. However, Traherne combines both views in one place and declares that man is to obey God's commands because they are holy, good, and true *and* because God commands them.[7]

Traherne is not mainly a theoretician. In his outline in the third *Century* he stresses that ethics consists of practice as well as speculation, and in *Christian Ethicks* he adds that the "Office of Morality" is "to teach Men the Nature of Virtue, and to encourage them in the Practice of it" (*CE*, p. 13).

B. "the Nature of Affections Virtues Maners, as by them we may be Guided to our Highest Happiness" (Practice)

Speculation, according to Traherne, furnishes man with riches, practice with honors and delights. Speculation is a feast: practice, which teaches man to live honorably, nobly, and usefully, is instruction. In a practical sense, ethics also teaches man to manage his passions, to exercise virtues,

---

6. *CE*, pp. 260ff, and see notes *CE*, pp. 372ff. Aristotle and Spinoza considered self-love to be a virtue. Calvin considers self-love a pest in the *Institutes* (ch. 7, paragraph 4, p. 622) as does T. Gale in vol. I, ch. 4.

7. See SM II 49-52 and *CE*, p. 337n.

and to form his manners so that he may live "Happily in this World" (III C 45).

Affections are apparently another name for passions. Plotinus uses the terms interchangeably.[8] Traherne has two definitions of *virtue* in his *Christian Ethics*: a "habit of Soul by force of which we attain our Happiness," and a "Right and well-ordered Habit of mind, which Facilitates the Soul in all its operations in order to this Blessedness."[9] By defining virtue as a habit, Traherne distinguishes it both from a natural disposition or inbred inclination and from a power of the soul. Traherne thinks habits are acquired by repeated acts, and that virtuous habits are sometimes infused, but the latter he thinks are better labeled graces. Habits are virtues only when a man consents to them by an act of his will (*CE*, p. 25). A habit is a frame of soul (*CE*, p. 285), and once gotten "makes all Virtue exceedingly Easie. . .Happie and delightful" (*CE*, p. 27). Habits are either vicious or virtuous, and Traherne categorizes the virtuous habits as theological, intellectual, moral or divine virtues.[10]

Theological virtues, according to Traherne, have God as their object and are taught by God's word. In *Christian Ethics* he lists them as faith, hope, charity, repentance, obedience, devotion, and godliness (*CE*, p. 123), but in the Select Meditations he lists them as faith, righteousness, holiness, and humility (IV 62)[11] Faith is the first virtue and the basis of all others (SM IV 62), but later Traherne states that humility is the basis of all virtues

8. See ch. viii above. Traherne's *CE* includes very little discussion of the "principles of human actions, human actions themselves, the passions and the vices." See discussion in *CE*, xxxi. Traherne's outline in the third *Century* indicates that he knew these things were important. See *CE*, xxii-xxiii.

9. *CE*, xxxi. Traherne notes Eustache's explanation that the subject of moral philosophy is human action as it may be directed to human behavior (EN, p. 7). See III C 45. Epicurus defines ethics or morals as "that part of Philosophy, which hath for its proper Object the End, or Final and main scope of Mans Life; containing certain Directions and Precepts, for the right information of his Understanding, and (Consequently) the conduct of his Will, in the Election of real Good, and Avoidance of Evil, in order to his attaining the true End of life, the Supreme Good, or Felicity." Epicurus, *Morals*, trans. by Walter Charleton (1659), p. 2 (Quoted in *CE*, p. 310n). Compare H. More who defines ethics as "the Art of Living well and happily," in *An Account of Virtue*, tr. by Edward Southwell, 1960, p. 1. More defines virtue as a power of the soul not a habit. *Account*, p. 11. Aristotle thinks it is a habit, as does Aquinas. See Costello's discussion, pp. 64ff. Compare Robert Crofts, *Paradise Within us* (London, 1640), p. 12.

10. *CE*, p. 23; 316n.

11. Usually only faith, hope, and love are considered to be theological virtues. See *CE*, xxxv.

(IV 66). Perhaps the difference in virtues in the various estates explains this problem. Faith exists only since the fall (SM IV 62).

The intellectual virtues are seated in the understanding and "exercized in Contemplation." Traditionally, Traherne says, the intellectual virtues are considered to be intelligence, wisdom, science, prudence, and art. He says he may reduce this number. Those that are acted upon are practical or moral virtues such as art and prudence (*CE*, pp. 23-24). Intelligence, wisdom and science were traditionally thought of as speculative virtues (*CE*, p. 314n).

Traherne uses various names for the moral virtues. Sometimes he calls them cardinal, sometimes principal. Among them are prudence, justice (which Traherne also lists among the divine virtues), temperance, and fortitude. These enter into all other virtues (SM IV 56-61). The less principal virtues are magnificence, liberality, modesty, magnaminity, gentleness, affability, courteousness, truth, and urbanity. They are of "less avail in the way to Felicity" (*CE*, p. 24).[12]

"Divine" virtues, a term which Traherne prefers to the term '"Heathenish Heroical" virtues, have God as their pattern and example, and consist of wisdom, knowledge, truth, goodness, righteousness, holiness, and divine love.[13] Christian virtues, such as love to one's enemies, meekness, and humility, are taught only in Christianity.[14] Traherne has yet another division of the virtues according to their practice in the various estates.[15]

Traherne uses various persuasive mechanisms in his *Christian Ethicks* to bring men to a life of virtue. These are indicative of his theological stance, as well as of his grasp of human nature. He audaciously uses the power of example, suggesting that man love God and follow his example (*CE*, p. 142). Most chapters in *Christian Ethicks* begin with an examination of a particular virtue as evidenced and practiced by God. His method may appear to be discouraging since such perfection is unattainable, but Traherne may have used this method to show the reality of virtue behind

---

12. See discussion in *CE*, xxxiv-xxxv; p. 314n. See also Traherne's notes on Ficino's commentary on Plato, FN, pp. 12, 42, and his notes on Eustache in EN, p. 17. For his notes on the less cardinal virtues which are not from Eustache, see EN, pp. 20-21.

13. *CE*, pp. 24, 94, 315n.

14. *CE*, pp. 24ff, 315n.

15. See ch. vii for a fuller discussion of this schema.

the appearance, to explain the ways of God to man, or to recall man to the image of God which is capable of being restored. To Traherne the image of God is like a mirror which reflects godly virtues. For example, the consideration of God's patience makes patience acceptable to men (*CE*, p. 185). Since God "acquired all His joys by temperance," men too may "accomplish wonders" (*CE*, p. 183).

Helen White notes that the *imitation of Christ* is seldom evident in the devotional literature of seventeenth century England. Instead Christ is acknowledged as Savior and his human nature is not stressed.[16] Traherne, however, does refer to the humanity of Christ and uses it as a persuasive device. Anything man may do, say, or bear in being virtuous is easy in comparison with the life, sufferings, and death of Jesus Christ. The nature, actions, and merits of Christ compel obedience, as do the commandments (*CE*, pp. 186ff).

Virtue is also a *response* to God's gifts of creation, salvation, and sanctification. Love is "the Motive, and the Incentive to Vertue, the Cause of Obedience. . .the form and the Essence of every Grace, and the fulfilling of the Law." Men obey the commandments for Christ's sake (*CE*, p. 143). That God is concerned for man's welfare is an "infinite encouragement" to virtue (*CE*, p. 242). Man's gratitude to God not only results in a virtuous life that will please him, but it also overflows to others. In fact, man is "in danger of bursting" until he can communicate to a "fit and amiable Recipient" (*CE*, p. 258). Man's gratitude to God is best expressed through service to needy people (*CE*, pp. 244ff).

Virtue is not only an evidence of Christianity, but it is also an encouragement to the practice of it. Virtue is commended in *Scripture*, according to Traherne, as something expected of the Christian. It suggests the Christian way of life (see *CE*, pp. 236ff). For Traherne, the experiential argument seems to be the weightiest (see *CE*, p. 246). Traherne says that the life of virtue is to be lived not only to demonstrate faith but to strengthen it.

The *reasonableness* of virtue is yet another persuasive device. Sometimes Traherne borders on the prudential arguments he intends not to use. "When virtue is rewarded and vice suppressed, the city flourisheth" (*CE*, pp. 95ff). According to Traherne it is also reasonable to live the

---

16. For a fuller discussion see Helen C. White, *English Devotional Literature (Prose) 1600-1640* (Madison, 1931).

virtuous life, because it matches the natural law and God's design (*CE*, pp. 3-6).

Virtue is also a remedy for vice. By sin man forfeits his happiness, but by practicing virtues he may recover it (*CE*, p. 33). Although Traherne's form of argument here ignores the reasons for vice, there is an inherent logic in playing off a virtue against a vice.

Virtue is *glorious* and *desireable*. The glory of virtue, according to Traherne, makes vice look like dirt beside a jewel: "There will need no other Exposition of its Nature, to dehort Men from the love of it, than the Illustration of its Contrary" (*CE*, p. 4). This is, in effect, an aesthetic argument. The very beauty of good works will draw men into the good life. Scripture uses a similar motivation: "whatsoever things are lovely. . .think on these things" (Phil. 4:8). Traherne maintains his positive approach by making good desirable rather than making vice abominable.

The corollary of making virtue desirable is to make vice *abominable*. This is not a primary argument, but it is there even though Traherne vows not to "speak much of Vice." To pass by or neglect the perfection that might be infinite or to be remiss or lazy is "infinitely Base and Dishonourable. . . unclean. . . Odious and Distastful" (*CE*, pp. 88ff). The combination of the beautiful (the aesthetic argument) with honor and duty is an effective method of argumentation.

Traherne also sometimes "poisons the well" (a fallacy of false presumption in logic). He questions the motives, sanity, ability, and worth of the impious. For example, only lazy, profane, halfwitted, empty, self-conceited, rash, wanton men, who are enemies to felicity, virtue, truth, and goodness, according to Traherne, suspect faith (*CE*, p. 111). The virtuous life is enhanced by portraying vice in the ugliest of clothing.

Traherne also uses what might be called the *eschatological* motivation to godliness. On judgment day, according to Traherne, men's lives are seen in their perfection and imperfection, and the only question asked is what men "have done or neglected in Liberality" (*CE*, p. 241). On that last day, sin is punished and virtues rewarded. Because God hates sin, God himself uses the fear of punishment as a deterrent, and the promise of infinite rewards as an encouragement (*CE*, p. 97).

Finally, he uses *felicity* itself as a persuasive device. Felicity has a great influence on virtue, not only because it inspires men to do good works, but also because it enters into their constitution. By their beauty and form, good works influence men (*CE*, pp. 63ff). What is more, felicity feeds the capacity of men, animates their endeavors, encourages their expectations, enables them to subdue lust, supports them in temptation, and assists them in overcoming every obstacle (*CE*, p. 16). Because all men inherently desire happiness, according to Traherne, and because the life of virtue is the only road to happiness, therefore, men will live a virtuous life. Virtue, however, is only a means to that end, not an end in itself. Traherne states that the end (the excellency of bliss) must be described to animate a man to be virtuous (*CE*, p. 13): "to be like God is the way to be Happy" (*CE*, p. 70). The virtuous man is a "celestial Epicurean" in that he knows that the world and heaven are his to be enjoyed (*CE*, p. 285).

Thus as persuasive mechanisms in *Christian Ethicks* Traherne uses the power of example, the imitation of Christ, the response to God's gifts, the commendation of Scripture, the reasonableness of virtue, virtue as a remedy for vice, the gloriousness and desirability of virtue, the abomination of vice, a logical fallacy, eschatological motivations, and felicity itself.

Christian Ethicks, like the outline of ethics in the third *Century*, maintains that virtue leads men to true felicity. In fact Traherne wrote the book to lead men to felicity. His purpose is not "to alter or contradict the Catholic Faith," nor to "stroak and tickle the Fancy," but to elevate, refine, inform, purify, enflame, enrich, and "guide Men. . .in the Way of Vertue; to excite their desire, to encourage them to Travel, to comfort them in the Journey, and so at last to lead them to true Felicity both here, and hereafter" (*CE*, p. 3). In the outline in the third *Century* the concern is with living "Happily in this World." *The Whole Duty of Man*, in contrast, stresses that happiness is only to be attained in the next life (heaven),[17] and Robert Crofts is mainly concerned about this life (earth).[18] Traherne believes happiness is attainable both in this life and the next.

To be a philosopher, according to Traherne, one must not only contemplate happiness, but also practice virtue by subduing vice, living by reason, ordering the desires, ruling the passions, and avoiding the customs of this world. A man is divine if he does these things not only because

---

17. *Whole Duty*, ch. 9: "That by vertue the mind becomes apt, and wel prepared to enjoy the choycest and sweetest felicities on Earth"; ch. 10: "That by vertue, also, the Mind becomes apt and wel disposed. . . ."
18. *Paradise Within* (London, 1610).

"vertue is Amiable and felicity Delightful" but also because there is a God, heaven, and redemption (IV C 8). Morally good actions require both a clear understanding and a free will. Intention is more important than the result, and the principle and manner more important than the deed (*CE*, p. 78). Moderation or the golden mean is a basic principle in Traherne's treatment of the virtues, as it is in Aristotle and Eustache.[19]

The term *Maners* in Traherne's outline may come from the Latin *mores* from which the English word moral is derived. Practical virtues are sometimes called moral because they help men perfect their manners as they relate to other men. Traherne subdivides these virtues further into principal and less principal.[20]

Traherne concludes his suggested outline of the content of "Ethicks" with the assertion that "all these put together Discover the Materials of Religion to be so Great, that it Plainly manifesteth the Revelation of GOD to be Deep and Infinit." Moreover, "Language, Miracles, or Apparitions" cannot teach men the "Infallibility of GODs Word" or show them the "Certainty of true Religion" unless men have a "Clear Sight into Truth it self," i. e. into the "Truth of Things." When this truth is actually seen, its beauty and glory will "best Discover and Prov Religion" (III C 45). In part it is the "Office of Morality" to open the nature of virtue in order to display the beauty of religion (*CE*, p. 13). The practice of virtue is an argument for the truth of religion.[21] Living a virtuous life brings salvation, enjoyment of the world, a beautiful life, the advancement of the neighbor, preservation of one's estate, and felicity. Moreover, religion is "actuated Exprest and promoted. . . Heathens converted, atheists convinced" (IV C 23). Thus in "Ethicks" as in "Humanity," "Divinity," and "Natural Philosophy" felicity is the starting point, the theme, and the end.

---

19.   *CE*, pp. 172, 354n.
20.   III C 45, *CE*, pp. 24, 315n. C. Marks notes that Aquinas thinks that *Mores* was a "natural or quasi natural inclination to do some particular action." The Greek word which is equivalent to *mores* is *ethos* from which the English word ethics is derived. See Aquinas, *Summa* I-II, 58, a. 1.
21.   CYB 73r; *CE*, p. 246. Aristotle also sees happiness as the highest good and the object of morality. See Costello, pp. 65ff.

Chapter X

Concluding Summary

This study has described, defined, and analyzed the theological thought of Thomas Traherne. An examination of all of Traherne's known writings and, where necessary, subsidiary investigations of texts, biography, and influences indicate the following.

A. Traherne *is* a theologian, an issue sometimes disputed.[1]

B. Though his interests are extensive, including doctrine, liturgy, homily, ethics, apologetics, polemics, devotions, and poetry, much of what is known about him from secondary sources, what he reveals of himself, and what he writes is primarily theological in nature. Theology evidently motivates his life and work and inspires his prose and poetry.[2]

C. His theology is comprehensive. He omits only a few major doctrines in his outline of theology in the third *Century* (42-45), and he treats most doctrines of traditional dogmatics at some point in his writings, though not always in depth.[3]

D. His theology has an ordered structure or system.[4]

E. His suggested structuring of the "Materials of Religion" in the third *Century* is a useful guide to understanding his theological thought. Traherne's structure or system combines theology, philosophy, ethics, and metaphysics and is the outline for the exposition of his theological thought in chapters five through nine of this study. The outline shows

---

1. See ch. i and notes 41-44.
2. See the Introduction, and chs. ii B, C, D; iii B.
3. See ch. iv C.
4. *Ibid.*

Traherne's system and is a key to the methodology of Traherne's theology.[5]

F. His outline of theology in the third Century contains Calvinist and Scholastic elements: Calvinist in the use of the four estates theory and covenant in the sections devoted to humanity and divinity; Scholastic in the ordering and terminology used particularly in the subsections of humanity, ethics, and natural philosophy.[6]

G. In addition to the formal structural elements of his outline, felicity is a recurring and unifying theme. Felicity interrelates most aspects of his life and thought. Traherne may not have intentionally related every doctrine of his outline to felicity, but because the concept is so important to him, he sees most doctrines as related to felicity or leading to felicity.[7]

H. There are a number of distinctive or unique elements in Traherne's theological system. For example, there seems to be little or no precedent for Traherne's fourfold division of the "Materials of Religion" into humanity, divinity, ethics, and natural philosophy; his inclusion of natural philosophy as a part of theology; his combination of the estates theory with scholastic terminology; his relegation of Christology to a minor position under the section on man in the estate of grace; his discussion of the "Communion of Saints" as an aspect of eschatology; and his concluding the section on divinity with angelology instead of eschatology.[8]

Certain general directions are evident in the description of Traherne's theological thought in chapters four through eight of this study. Traherne's theology appears to be a distinctive amalgam of Laudian Anglicanism with strands of Arminianism, Platonism, mysticism, Enthusiasm, and Scholasticism. However, this study also indicates that Traherne's

---

5.   *Ibid.,* and see ch. v C.

6.   See ch. iv C, and notes 11 and 17 below.

7.   Traherne relates such doctrines as the end of man, the faculties of the soul, the attributes of God, providence, free will, sin, repentance, Scripture, angels, ethics, and "Natural Philosophy," to felicity.

8.   See ch. iv C, for example.

theological thought is not easily categorized.[9] In his Laudian Anglicanism, for example, there are traces of Puritan influences. His formative years were spent in a Puritan milieu, and he was ordained a Puritan minister.[10] Though he is doctrinally more Arminian than Calvinist in his stress on foreknowledge rather than on predestination, on Christ's death for all rather than on limited atonement, on the possibility of falling from grace rather than on perseverance, he also seems to hold some Calvinist views on grace and the four estates.[11]

Traherne is similar to the Neo- and Cambridge Platonists. His high evaluation of man, for example, approximates that of Ficino, Hermes, Plotinus, and Pica della Mirandola,[12] and his attitude toward infinity, free will, knowledge and the soul, for example, approximates that of many of the Cambridge Platonists.[13] Yet Traherne criticizes aspects of Neo- and Cambridge Platonist thought, such as their tendency to denigrate the body and the physical world.[14]

Traherne's mysticism is in the broader tradition, and he does not dispense with reason, tradition, theology or community. Mysticism is not, however, his major proclamation, even though it is integral to his life and thought.[15] There are also strands of Enthusiasm in Traherne's theological thought: a tendency, for example, toward perfectionism, a positive evaluation of childhood, a stress on internal experience, and word usage. This may be due, in part, to the times, his milieu, and his predilections. However, Traherne does not oppose revelation to reason, or elevate immediate experience over reason or Scripture. He also would not have identified himself as an Enthusiast.[16] Traherne's education and later readings were probably the primary sources of his Scholastic tendencies. Though he disagrees with many tenets of Scholasticism, he uses its definitions and terminology.[17] Other sources which contributed to Traherne's thought include the following: the classics,[18] Scripture,[19] creeds

---

9. See ch. iii A, for example.
10. See ch. ii A, B, C, and chs. vi and vii *passim*.
11. See chs. vi, vii, and ix *passim*; ch. i, n. 21.
12. See chs. iii, v–ix *passim*; and ch. ii notes 82 and 85.
13. See chs. iii, v–ix *passim* and ch. ii notes 50-52.
14. See, for example, ch. ii notes 50, 51, 58, 67.
15. See, for example, ch. ii E.
16. See chs. ii A, D; v–ix *passim*, and ch. ii notes 35-40; ch. iv notes 21, 22.
17. See chs. iv–ix *passim* and the Excursus, "Traherne as Church Historian."

and confessions,[20] the Church Fathers,[21] and his contemporaries, including Eustache de Saint Paul, the Latitudinarians, the Caroline Divines, the Metaphysical Poets, Thomas Adams, Francis Bacon, Thomas Jackson, Isaac Barrow, and Theophilus Gale.[22] Traherne is opposed to Sectarianism[23] and Romanism,[24] believing them a danger to the church. He is not a Pelagian,[25] a Pantheist,[26] a synergist,[27] or a heretic.[28] In part Traherne's writings have occasioned misunderstanding and disagreement because of their imprecision.[29]

Aside from various textual difficulties resulting from missing manuscripts or pages, works of uncertain authorship, the revisions of his brother Philip and an amanuensis,[30] there are also certain problems in the way Traherne uses his sources, whether classical, biblical, historical, or contemporary. Traherne, for example, seldom acknowledges a source, and he usually depends on secondary rather than on primary materials. He seems to select that with which he agrees and in which he is interested. He summarizes, condenses, simplifies, and paraphrases his sources, and omits that with which he does not agree. Sometimes he alters the style, distorts the meaning, changes the voice, modernizes the text to accord with his own distinctive approach. What he quotes tends to corroborate and substantiate what he has apparently come to believe on other grounds. Thus eclecticism or affinity rather than influence is usually a more usable term for Traherne's use of his sources.[31]

The content of Traherne's theological thought, in contradistinction to the form or structure, is also often unique and distinctive, particularly his

18. See ch. iv A and the Excursus, "Traherne as Classicist."
19. See ch. iv A and the Excursus, "Traherne as Exegete."
20. See ch. iv A for example.
21. See ch. iv A, and the Excursus, "Traherne as Church Historian."
22. See ch. ii A, E; ch. iii B 1-5; ch. iv; and chs. v-ix *passim.*
23. See, for example, ch. vi.
24. See, for example, ch. vi.
25. See, for example, ch. vii B.
26. See, for example, ch. vi F and ch. viii.
27. See, for example, ch. vii C 4.
28. See, for example, ch. i.
29. See, for example, ch. ii D and vii B.
30. See ch. iii *passim.*
31. See iii and the Excursuses, "Traherne as Classicist," "Traherne as Exegete," and "Traherne as Church Historian."

positive or optimistic approach to life;[32] his use of felicity as a theme;[33] his attitude toward natural philosophy;[34] his stress on virtues rather than on vices;[35] his doctrines of prizing, and praising,[36] the "Liveliness of Interiour Presence,"[37] childhood,[38] and self-love.[39]

Perhaps the best conclusion to a study of the theological thought of Thomas Traherne is his own conclusion to his structuring of theology in the third *Century*.

> And all these put together Discover the Materials of Religion to be so Great, that it Plainly manifesteth the Revelation of GOD to be Deep and Infinit. For it is impossible for Language, Miracles, or Apparitions to teach us the Infallibility of GODs Word or to shew us the Certainty of true Religion, without a Clear Sight into Truth it self that is into the Truth of Things. Which will them selvs when truly seen, by the very Beauty and Glory of them, best Discover, and Prov Religion (III *C* 45).

32. See, for example, ch. vii D and viii.
33. See note 7 above, and his theological autobiography with its structure of childhood felicity, felicity lost, and felicity regained.
34. See ch. viii *passim.*
35. See ch. ix *passim.*
36. See ch. iv.
37. See ch. iv.
38. See ch. ii D.
39. See other emphases in chs. v-ix *passim.*

Bibliography

I. PRIMARY SOURCES

A. PUBLISHED WORKS (in chronological order of publication)

1. *Roman Forgeries, Or a True Account of False Records Discovering the Impostures and Counterfeit Antiquities of the Church of Rome.* By a Faithful Son of the Church of England. London: Printed by S. and B. Griffin for Jonathan Edwin, 1673.

2. *Daily Devotions, Consisting of Thanksgivings, Confessions, and Prayers by a Humble Penitent.* London: for Jonathan Edwin, 1673 (see item 5).

3. *Christian Ethicks: or divine Morality, opening the Way to Blessedness, by the Rules of Virtue and Reason.* London: for Jonathan Edwin, 1675 (see item 8).

4. *A Serious and Pathetical Contemplation of the Mercies of God, in Several Most Devout and Sublime Thanksgivings for the Same.* Published by the Reverend Doctor Hicks, At the Request of a Friend of the Authors. London: Printed for Samuel Keble, 1699 (see item 6).

5. *A Collection of Meditations and Devotions in Three Parts.* Published by N. Spinckes. London: Printed for D. Midwinter, 1717. Part III was a reprint of *Daily Devotions* (see item 2); Part II. *Meditations and Devotions on the Life of Christ,* was reduced and published by Philip Traherne as *The Soul's Communion with her Saviour* in 1685. Part I, *Meditations on the Six Days of the Creation,* was reprinted in 1966 (see item 7).

6. *Thomas Traherne: Centuries, Poems, and Thanksgivings,* ed. H. M. Margoliouth. 2 vols. Oxford: Clarendon Press, 1958 (see items 4, 9, 11, 12, 13).

7. *Meditations on the Six Days of the Creation.* Introduction by George Robert Guffey. Los Angeles: Clark Memorial Library, U.C.L.A. 1966 (Augustan Reprint Society Publication, no. 119); see item 5.

8. *Christian Ethicks.* eds. Carol L. Marks and George Robert Guffey. Ithaca: Cornell University Press, 1968 (scholarly edition of item 3).

B. MANUSCRIPTS

9. Commonplace Book, Bodleian MS. Eng. Poet. *C. 42* (see item 6).

10. Church's Year Book, Bodleian MS. Eng. th. e. 51.

11. Centuries, Bodleian MS. Eng. th. e. 50 (see item 6).

12. Early Notebook, Bodleian MS. Lat. misc. f. 45 (see item 6).

13. Ficino Notebook, British Museum MS. Burney 126 (see item 6).

14. Select Meditations, James Osborn Collection, Yale University.

See also Appendix, pp 214–215

II. SECONDARY SOURCES

A. PARTICULAR (Studies which refer directly to Traherne, as complete as possible to 1973)

Altick, Richard D. *The Scholar Adventurers*. New York: Macmillan, 1950.

Ames, Kenneth J. "The Religious Language of Thomas Traherne's *Centuries*." *DA* 28 (1967), 3173-A (So. Calif.).

Aubrey, John. *Miscellanies upon various subjects*. 4th ed. London, 1696.

Barnstone, Willis. "Two Poets of Felicity: Thomas Traherne and Jorge Guillen." *Books Abroad*, 42 (1968), 14-19.

Beachcroft, T.O. "Traherne and the Cambridge Platonists." *The Dublin Review*, 186 (April 1930), 278-290.

_____. "Traherne and the Doctrine of Felicity." *Criterion*, 9 (January 1930), 291-307.

Bennett, J. A. W. "Traherne and Brasenose." *N & Q*, 189 (August 25, 1945), 84.

Berry, Lloyd E. *A Bibliography of Studies in Metaphysical Poetry, 1939-1960*. Madison: University of Wisconsin Press, 1964.

Bicket, Zenas Johan. "An Imagery Study in Thomas Traherne's *Centuries of Meditations*." *DA*, 26 (1966), 4624 (Arkansas).

Blyth, Reginald H. *Zen in English Literature and Oriental Classics*. New York: E. P. Dutton, 1960.

Boas, George. *The Cult of Childhood*. Studies of the Warburg Institute, No. 29. London, 1966.

Bottrall, Margaret. "Traherne's Praise of the Creation." *Critical Quarterly*, 1 (Summer 1959), 126-133.

Bradbury, S. *Bertram Dobell: Bookseller and Man of Letters*. London: Bertram Dobell, 1909.

Brewer, L.E. "Studies in the Thought of Thomas Traherne." *Index to Theses Accepted* (in Great Britain and Ireland), 6 (1955-56), p. 10, item 164, Bristol (M.A.).

Brinkley, Roberta F., ed. *English Poetry of the Seventeenth Century*. New York: Norton, 1942..

_____. *English Prose of the Seventeenth Century*. New York: Norton, 1951.

Bullen, A.H. "Bertram Dobell." *The Nation*, 100 (February 11, 1915), 165-166.

Bullett, Gerald. *The English Mystics*. London: Michael Joseph, 1950.

Burton, K. M. P. *Restoration Literature*. London: Hutchinson University Library, 1958.

Bury, R. G. "A Passage in Traherne." *TLS* (June 8, 1940), 279.

Bush, Douglas. *English Literature in the Earlier Seventeenth Century 1600-1660*. Oxford: Clarendon Press, 1945. Rev. ed. 1962.

Christ, Ernst. *Studien zu Thomas Traherne*. Tuebingen: E. Goebel, 1932.

Clements, A. L. *The Mystical Poetry of Thomas Traherne*. Cambridge, Mass: Harvard Univ. Press, 1969.

_____. "Thomas Traherne: A Chronological Bibliography," *The Library Chronicle*. (Winter-Spring 1969), 36-51.

Coffin, Robert P. T., and Alexander M. Witherspoon, eds. *Seventeenth Century Prose and Poetry,* 1963.

Cohen, John M. *The Baroque Lyric*. London: Hutchinson Univ. Library, 1963.

Colby, Frances L. "Thomas Traherne and Henry More," *MLN*, 62 (November, 1947), 490-492.

_____. "Traherne and the Cambridge Platonists: An Analytical Comparison." Doctoral dissertation. Johns Hopkins, 1947.

Colie, Rosalie Littell. "Cosmic Response of Thomas Traherne: A Study of Traherne against the Scientific Background of His Day." Unpublished master's thesis. Columbia University, 1946.

_____. *Paradoxia Epidemica: The Renaissance Tradition of Paradox*. Princeton: Univ. Press, 1966.

_____. "Thomas Traherne and the Infinite: The Ethical Compromise," *HLQ*, 21 (November, 1957), 69-82.

Connolly, Brian W. "Knowledge and Love: Steps Toward Felicity in Thomas Traherne," *DA*, 28 (1967), 1047A.

Cox, Gerald H. "Traherne's *Centuries*: A Platonic Devotion of 'Divine Philosophy.'" *MP*, 69 (Aug., 1971), 10-24.

Daniels, R. Balfour. *Some Seventeenth-Century Worthies in a Twentieth-Century Mirror*. Chapel Hill: Univ. of North Carolina Press, 1940.

Darbishire, Helen. ed. *Wordsworth: Poems in Two Volumes*. Oxford: Clarendon Press, 1914.

Davidson, Anne. "Innocence Regained: George Herbert, Henry Vaughan, Thomas Traherne." Unpublished master's thesis. Columbia Univ., 1952.

Dawson, M. L. "Thomas Treherne," (sic) *TLS,* September 29, 1927, p. 667.

Day, Malcolm M. "Traherne and the Doctrine of Pre-existence," *SP,* 65 (1968), 81-97.

_____. "Thomas Traherne and the Perennial Philosophy." Doctoral dissertation. Western Reserve, 1964.

Denonain, Jean-Jacques. *Thèmes et Formes de la Poésie "Métaphysique."* Paris: *Presses Universitaires de France*, 1956.

Dobell, Bertram. "An Unknown Seventeenth-Century Poet," *Athenaeum*, nos. 3780, 3781 (April 7, 14, 1900), pp. 433-435, 466.

_____. ed. *Centuries of Meditations.* London: Dobell, 1908.

_____. ed. *The Poetical Works of Thomas Traherne.* London: Dobell, 1903.

Dobell, P. J. "A Passage in Traherne," *TLS,* June 15, 1940, p. 291.

Doughty, William L. *Studies in Religious Poetry of the Seventeenth Century.* London: The Epworth Press, 1946.

Durr, Robert A. *Poetic Vision and the Psychedelic Experience.* Syracuse: Syracuse Univ. Press, 1970.

Eliot, T. S. "Mystic and Politician as Poet: Vaughan, Traherne, Marvell, Milton," *Listener,* 3 (1930), 590-591.

Ellrodt, Robert. "*Le Message de Thomas Traherne,*" *Cahiers du Sud,* 31 (1950), 434-456.

_____. *L'inspiration personnelle et l'esprit du temps chez les poètes métaphysiques anglais.* 2 vols. in 3. Paris: Jose Corti, 1960.

_____. "Scientific Curiosity and Metaphysical Poetry in the Seventeenth Century," *MP,* 61 (1964), 180-197.

Fairchild, Hoxie Neale. *Religious Trends in English Poetry.* Vol. I. New York: Columbia Univ. Press, 1939.

Ferry, Anne Davidson, ed. *Religious Prose of Seventeenth-Century England.* Vol. V in *The Borzoi Anthology of Seventeenth-Century English Literature.* New York: Knopf, 1967.

Fisch, Harold. *Jerusalem and Albion: The Hebraic Factor in Seventeenth Century Literature.* New York: Schocken, 1964.

Fitzgerald, W. B. "A Literary Resurrection," *The London Quarterly Review,* 107 (April, 1907), 312-323.

Fleming, W. K. "Post Reformation Mysticism in England—Browne and Traherne," chapter X in *Mysticism in Christianity.* London: R. Scott, 1913.

Gilbert, Allan H. "Thomas Traherne as Artist," *MLQ,* 8 (1947), 319-341 and 435-447.

Grabo, Norman S. *Edward Taylor.* New York: Twayne, 1961.

Grandvoinet, Renee. "Thomas Traherne and the Doctrine of Felicity," *Etudes de lettres,* 13 (1939), 164-177.

Grant, Patrick. "Original Sin and the Fall of Man in Thomas Traherne," *E.L.H.* (March 1971), 40-61.

Grierson, Herbert and J. C. Smith. *A Critical History of English Poetry.* 2nd rev. ed. London: Chattoo and Windus, 1947.

Grigson, Geoffrey. "The Transports of Thomas Traherne," *Bookman,* 82 (August, 1952), 250.

Guffey, George R. "Margoliouth's Emendation of a Line in Traherne's 'For Man to Act,'" *An & Q*, 5 (1967), 162-163.

_____. "Thomas Traherne on Original Sin," *N & Q*, N.S. 14 (March 1967), 98-100.

Hall, William C. "Poetical Works of Thomas Traherne," *Manchester Quarterly*, 30 (October, 1904), 376-382.

_____. *Thomas Traherne: Selected Poems*. Hull: J. R. Tutin, 1904.

Happold, Frederick, C. *Mysticism: A Study and an Anthology*. Middlesex and Baltimore: Penguin, 1963, 1964.

Harrison, Thomas P. "Seneca and Traherne," *Arion, 6* (1967), 403-405.

Harvey, George. "A Precursor of Whitman," *The North American Review*. 185 (June 21, 1907), 463-464.

Hayward, John. Introduction to *Centuries of Meditations*. London: Dobell, 1950.

Hepburn, Ronald W. "Thomas Traherne: The Nature and Dignity of the Imagination," *Cambridge Journal*, 6 (1953), 725-734.

Herman, Emily. *The Meaning and Value of Mysticism*. 3rd ed. New York: Doran, 1925.

Highet, Gilbert. "Heir of the Whole World," *The Powers of Poetry*. Oxford: Univ. Press, 1960.

Hobhours, Stephen. "A Poet's Resurrection," *The Spectator* 157 (November 6, 1936), 804.

Hodgson, Geraldine E. *English Mystics*. London: Mowbray, 1922.

Hollander, John. The *Untuning of the Sky: Ideas of Music in English Poetry, 1500-1700*. Princeton: Univ. Press, 1961.

Holmes, Elizabeth. *Henry Vaughan and the Hermetic Philosophy*. Oxford: Blackwell, 1932.

Hopkins, Kenneth. *English Poetry: A Short History*. London: Phoenix House, 1962.

Hopkinson, Arthur W. *Be Merry: Some Thoughts on Mirth as a Christian Duty*. London: Mowbray, 1925.

_____."Thomas Traherne," *TLS*, October 6, 1927, 694.

Howarth, R. G. "'Felicity' in Traherne," *N & Q*, 193 (1948), 249-250.

Huntington, Virginia E. "Thomas Traherne, Priest, Mystic, Poet," *Living Church*, 109 (December 3, 1944), 13-14.

Husain, Itrat. *The Mystical Element in the Metaphysical Poets of the Seventeenth Century*. London and Edinburgh: Oliver and Boyd, 1948.

Hutchinson, F. E., "The Sacred Poets," and W. H. Hutton, "Caroline Divines," in *The Cambridge History of English Literature*, ed. A. W. Ward and A. R. Waller. Vol. VII Cambridge: Univ. Press, 1911.

Iredale, Hilda Queenie. *Thomas Traherne*. Oxford: Blackwell, 1935.

Huxley, Aldous. *The Perennial Philosophy*. London: Chatto and Windus, 1946.

Jennings, Elizabeth. "The Accessible Art: A Study of Thomas Traherne's *Centuries of Meditations*," *Twentieth-Century*, 167 (February 1960), 140-151.

Jones, Rufus M. "Thomas Traherne and the Spiritual Poets of the Seventeenth Century," chapter XVII in *Spiritual Reformers in the 16th and 17th Centuries.* London: Macmillan, 1914.

Jones, W. Lewis. "Thomas Traherne and the Religious Poetry of the Seventeenth Century," *The Quarterly Review,* 200 (October 1904), 437-464.

Jordan, Richard Douglas. "Thomas Traherne: Eternity-Time and the *Centuries,*" *DA,* 31 (May 1971).

Kenner, Hugh, ed. *Seventeenth-Century Poetry: The Schools of Donne and Jonson.* New York: Holt, Rinehart, and Winston, 1964.

Korte, Donald M. "Thomas Traherne's 'The Estate,'" *Thoth,* 6 (Winter 1965), 13-19.

Lehrs, Ernst L. *Der rosenkreuzerische Impuls im Leben und Werk von Joachim Jungius und Thomas Traherne. Studie und Versuche,* 5. Stuttgart, 1962.

Leishman, James B. The *Metaphysical Poets: Donne, Herbert, Vaughan, Traherne.* Oxford: Clarendon Press, 1934.

Lock, Walter. "An English Mystic," *Constructive Quarterly,* 1 (1913), 826-836.

Loehrer, Frieda. *Die Mystik und ihre Quellen in Thomas Traherne.* Zurich: Buchdruckerei Rheintaler Volksfreund Au, 1930.

Lloyd, M. W. Review of Anne Ridler's *Thomas Traherne. R.E.S.* 18 (1967), 200-201.

Macaulay, Rose. *Some Religious Elements in English Literature.* London: Hogarth Press, 1931.

MacClintock, W. D. "A Re-discovered Poet," *Dial,* 34 (June 16, 1903), 395-398.

Mahood, M.M. *Poetry and Humanism.* London: Jonathan Cape, 1950.

Anon. "Manuscripts of Thomas Traherne," *Bodleian Library Record* III, No. 32 (August, 1951), 179-180.

Margoliouth, H.H. (i.e. H. M.). "Traherne's Ordination and Birth-Date," *N & Q,* N.S. 1 (1954), 408.

Marks, Carol Louise. "Ficino Notebook," *The Papers of the Bibliographical Society of America.* 63 (1969), 73-81.

_____. "Traherne's Church's Year-Book," *The Papers of the Bibliographical Society of America.* 60 (1966), 31-72.

_____. "Thomas Traherne and Cambridge Platonism." *PMLA,* 81 (December 1966), 521-534.

_____. "Thomas Traherne and Hermes Trismegistus," *Renaissance News,* 19 (Summer 1966), 118-131.

_____. "Thomas Traherne's Commonplace Book," *The Papers of the Bibliographical Society of America,* 58 (1964), 458-465.

_____. "Thomas Traherne's Early Studies," *The Papers of the Bibliographical Society of America,* 62 (1968), 511-536.

Marshall, William H. "Thomas Traherne and the Doctrine of Original Sin," *MLN,* 73 (March 1958), 161-165.

Martz, Louis L. *The Paradise Within: Studies in Vaughan, Traherne and Milton.* New Haven and London: Yale Univ. Press. 1964.

_____. *The Poem of the Mind.* New York: Oxford Univ. Press, 1966.

Masefield, John. "Thomas Traherne's Poetry," *The Speaker,* 8 (April 25, 1903), 74.

Massingham, Harold. "A Note on Thomas Traherne," *The New Statesman,* 4 (December 19, 1914), 271-272.

Merton, Thomas. *Mystics and Zen Masters.* New York: Farrar, Straus, and Giroux, 1967.

Meyer, Robert H. "Seventeenth-Century Contemplative Poetry: An Imitation of Mystical Experience," *DA,* 27 (1967), 250. 4 - A (Univ. of California, Davis).

More, Paul Elmer. "Thomas Traherne," *The Nation,* 88 (February 18, 1909), 160-162.

Naylor, Edward W. "Three Seventeenth-Century Poet-Parsons and Music," chapter IV in *The Poets and Music.* London and Toronto: J. M. Dent & Sons, 1928.

Anon. "A Newly-Discovered Poet," *TLS* (March 27, 1903), 94-95.

Anon. "A New Old Poet," *Harper's Weekly,* 50 (November 3, 1906), 1559.

Nicholson, Edward. "Treherne (sic): Curious Rimes to 'Joy,'" *N & Q,* 3 (March 25, 1911), 232.

Nicholson, Marjorie Hope. *The Breaking of the Circle: Studies in the Effect of the "New Science" upon Seventeenth Century Poetry.* New York: Columbia Univ. Press, 1960.

Nomachi, Susumu. "Thomas Traherne," *Studies in English Literature* (Tokyo), 23 (January and July 1943), 1-26, 235-258 and 24 (April and July 1944), 79-90, 154-168.

Osborn, James M. "A New Traherne Manuscript," *TLS* (October 8, 1964), 928.

Osmond, Percy H. *The Mystical Poets of the English Church.* New York: Macmillan, 1919.

Owen, Catherine A. "The Authorship of the *Meditations of the Six Days of Creation* and the *Meditations and Devotions on the Life of Christ,*" *MLR,* 56 (January 1961), 1-12.

_____. "The Thought and Art of Thomas Traherne: A Study of His Works with Some Reference to Their Major Sources," *Index to Theses Accepted* (in Great Britain and Ireland), p. 11, item 193, London, M.A.

Parker, S. T. H. "The Riches of Thomas Traherne." *The Living Age,* 314 (July 22,1922), 223-225.

Payne, Arthur. "A Prose Poet: Thomas Traherne." *The Educational Times,* 4 (August 1922), 347.

Pinto, Vivian de Sola. *Peter Sterry.* Cambridge, Eng.: Univ. Press, 1934.

Price, C. "Thomas Traherne," *TLS,* October 27, 1927, p. 767.

Proud, J. W. "Thomas Traherne: A Divine Philosopher." *Friends Quarterly Examiner* 51 (January 1917), 65-82.

Quiller-Couch, Sir Arthur. "A Great Discovery: Thomas Traherne." *The Daily News,* March 30, 1903, p. 8.

_____. *From a Cornish Window.* New York: E. P. Dutton, 1906.

_____. *Studies in Literature.* First Series, Cambridge: Univ. Press, 1918.

Randolph, Jamesena Chalmers. "Thomas Traherne's Conception of Sin." Unpublished master's thesis. Syracuse University, 1963.

Anon. "A Rediscovered Poet," *The Living Age*, 237 (June 18, 1903), 696-699.

Reed, Edward Bliss. *English Lyrical Poetry*. New Haven: Yale University Press, 1912.

Rickey, Mary Ellen. *Utmost Art: Complexity in the Verse of George Herbert*. Lexington: Univ. of Kentucky Press, 1966.

Ridler, Anne. ed. *Thomas Traherne: Poems, Centuries and Three Thanksgivings*. London: Oxford Univ. Press, 1966.

_____. "Traherne: Some Wrong Attributions," *RES*, 18 (February 1967) 48-49.

Ridlon, Harold G. "The Function of the 'Infant-Ey' in Traherne's Poetry," *SP*, 61 (October 1964), 627-639.

Rostvig, Maren-Sofie. *The Happy Man: Studies in the Metamorphoses of a Classical Ideal, 1600-1700*. Oxford: Basil Blackwell, 1954.

Ross, Malcolm M. *Poetry and Dogma*. New Brunswick: Rutgers, 1954.

Rowley, Victor. "Thomas Traherne's *Centuries* and Aristotle's Theory of Change." Unpublished Master's thesis. Ohio State University, 1967.

Russell. Angela. "A Study of Thomas Traherne's *Christian Ethicks*." Unpublished B. Litt. thesis. Oxford University, 1952.

_____. "The Life of Thomas Traherne," *RES*, N. S. 6 (January, 1955), 34-43.

_____. "The Date of Traherne's Ordination," *N & Q*, N.S. 1 (1954), 282.

Salter, K. W. "The Nature of Traherne's Mysticism," *Index to Theses Accepted* (in Great Britain and Ireland), 4 (1953-54), p. 9, item 155, Bristol (M.A.).

_____. *Thomas Traherne: Mystic and Poet*. London: Edward Arnold, 1964, and New York: Barnes and Noble, 1965.

Sandbank, S. "Thomas Traherne on the Place of Man in the Universe," pp. 121-136 in *Scripta Hierosolymitana: Studies in English Language and Literature*, vol. 17, ed. Alice Shalvi and A.A. Mendilow. Jerusalem: The Magnes Press, 1966.

Sauls, Lynn. "The Careless Composer for *Christian Ethicks*," *Papers of the Bibliographical Society of America* 63 (1969), 123-126.

_____. "Traherne's Debt to Puente's *Meditations*," *PQ* (April, 1971), 161-174.

Sayers, Dorothy L. "The Beatrician Vision in Dante and Other Poets." *Nottingham Mediaeval Studies*, 2 (1958), 3-23.

Schelling, Felix E. *The English Lyric*. Boston and New York: Houghton Mifflin, 1913.

Scherer, Gertrude Roberts. "More and Traherne." *MLN*, 34 (January 1919) 49-50.

Sherrington, Alison J. *Mystical Symbolism in the Poetry of Thomas Traherne*. 1970.

Spencer, Sidney. *Mysticism in World Religion*. Baltimore: Penguin, 1963.

Spencer, Theodore, and Mark Van Doren. *Studies in Metaphysical Poetry*: Two Essays and a Bibliography. New York: Columbia Univ. Press, 1939.

Spurgeon. Caroline F. E. *Mysticism in English Literature*. Cambridge: Univ. Press, 1913.

Staley. Thomas F. "The Theocentric Vision of Thomas Traherne." *Cithara*, 4 (November 1964), 43-47.

Starkman, Miriam D., ed. *Seventeenth-Century English Poetry*, vol. I. New York: Knopf, 1967.

Stewart, Stanley. *The Expanded Voice: the Art of Thomas Traherne.* San Marino, California: The Huntington Library, 1970.

Stranks, C. J. *Anglican Devotion.* Greenwich, Conn: The Seabury Press, 1961.

Anon. "A Student of Felicity," *The Living Age*, 251 (October 13, 1906) 116-118.

Suzuki, D. T. *The Essentials of Zen Buddhism*, ed. Bernard Phillips. New York: E. P. Dutton. 1962.

Tanner, Lawrence Melvin. "Thomas Traherne's *Centuries of Meditations*: A Critical Introduction with Annotations for the First and Second Centuries." *DA*, 20 (1960), 3310-3311 (NYU).

Anon. "Thomas Traherne," *Contemporary Review*, 142 (September, 1932), 386-388.

Thompson, Doris Stevens. "Thomas Traherne of Hereford: A Study of the Poet's Background." Doctoral dissertation. Radcliffe College, Harvard University, 1950.

Thompson, Elbert N. S. "Mysticism in Seventeenth Century Literature," *SP*, 18 (April 1921), 170-231.

_____. "The Philosophy of Thomas Traherne." *PQ*, 8 (April 1929), 97-112.

Towers. Frances. "Thomas Traherne: His Outlook on Life," *The Nineteenth Century*, 87 (June 1920), 1024-1030.

Underhill, Evelyn. *The Mystics of the Church.* London: Clarke, 1925.

Vaughan, Hilda. Introduction to *Centuries.* London: The Faith Press, 1960.

Wade, Gladys I. "The Manuscripts of the Poems of Thomas Traherne," *MLR*, 26 (October, 1931), X, 401-407.

_____. "Mrs. Susanna Hopton," *English Review*, 62 (January 1936), 41-47.

_____. "St. Thomas Aquinas and Thomas Traherne," *Blackfriars* 12 (1931). 666-673.

_____. *Thomas Traherne: A Critical Biography, with a Selected Bibliography of Criticism* by Robert Allerton Parker. Princeton: University Press, 1944.

_____. "Thomas Traherne as Divine Philosopher," *Hibbert Journal*, 32 (April 1934), 400-408.

_____. "Traherne and the Spiritual Value of Nature Study," *London Quarterly and Holborn Review*, 159 (April 1934), 243-245.

Wahl, Jean. "Thomas Traherne," *Études anglaises*, 14, 2 (1961), 117-123.

Wallace, John Malcolm. "Thomas Traherne and the Structure of Meditation," *ELH*, 25 (June 1958), 79-89.

Watkins, Alfred. "Thomas Traherne," *TLS* (October 20, 1927), 742.

Webb, William. "Thomas Traherne's Poem 'Silence,'" *N & Q*, 11 (1964), 96.

Webber, Joan. *The Eloquent 'I': Style and Self in Seventeenth Century Prose*. Madison: Univ. of Wisconsin Press, 1968.

White, Helen C. *The Metaphysical Poets: A Study in Religious Experience*. New York: Macmillan, 1936.

_____, Ruth C. Wallerstein and Richardo Quintana, eds. *Seventeenth Century Verse and Prose*. Vol. II: 1660-1700. New York: Macmillan, 1952.

Wilde, Hans-Oskar. *Beiträge zur Englischen Literaturgeschichte des 14. Jahrhunderts*. Breslau: Priebatsch, 1932.

Willcox, Louise Collier. "A Joyous Mystic," *The North American Review*, 193 (June 1911), 893-904.

Willett, Gladys E. *Traherne: An Essay*. Cambridge: Heffer, 1919.

Williams, Melvin G. "Thomas Traherne: Center of God's Wealth," *Cithara* 3 (1963), 32-40.

Willy, Margaret. *Life was Their Cry*. London: Evans Brothers, 1950.

_____. "Thomas Traherne: 'Felicity's Perfect Lover,'" *English*, 12 (Autumn 1959), 210-215.

_____. *Three Metaphysical Poets*. London: Longmans, Green, 1961.

Wilson, A. "A Neglected Mystic: Thomas Traherne," pt. 1, and "Thomas Traherne: Poet and Mystic," pts. 2 and 3, *The Poetry Review*, 16 (1925), 11-22, 97-104, 178-182.

Wilson, Cecil H. S. "Traherne and Wordsworth," *London Quarterly and Holborn Review*, 164 (July 1939), 355-358.

Winterbottom, Kenneth Marion. "Certain Affinities to Wordsworth in the Poetry of Vaughan and Traherne." Unpublished Master's thesis. University of Pittsburgh, 1933.

Wood, Anthony A. *Athenae Oxonienses*, ed. Philip Bliss, 4 vols. London: F. C. and J. Rivington, 1813-20. First published, 1691-92.

B. GENERAL (Other literature cited more than once)

Adams, Thomas. *Main Principles of Christian Religion in 107 Articles*. London, 1675.

Allestree, Richard. *The Whole Duty of Man*. London, 1731.

Alting, Henrici. *Methodus theologiae didacticae*. Groningen, 1645.

Ames, William. *Medulla SS. theologiae*. 4th ed. London, 1630.

_____. *The Substance of the Christian Religion*. London, 1657.

Anderson, F. H. *The Philosophy of Francis Bacon*. Chicago, 1948.

Andrewes, Lancelot. *Institutiones Piae, or Directions to Pray*. London, 1633.

_____. *Private Devotions*. London, 1630.

Apsley, Thomas. *Order and Disorder: Or, The World Made and Undone*. London, 1679.

Aquinas, Thomas. *Compendium of Theology*. Translated by Cyril Vollert. St. Louis: Herder, 1957.

_____. *Summa Contra Gentiles*. 5 vols. London: Burns, Oates, 1928-29.

_____. *Summa theologica*. 22 vols. London: Burns, Oates, 1912-36.

Aristotle. *Ethics*. Translated by J. A. K. Thomson. Harmondsworth, 1953.

Ashley, Maurice. *England in the Seventeenth Century*. Harmondsworth, 1968.

Augustine. *City of God*. Edited by Vernon J. Bourke. Garden City, New York: Doubleday, 1958.

_____. *Confessions*. Translated by John K. Ryan. Garden City, New York: Doubleday, 1957.

Austin, William. *Devotionis Augustinianae Flammae*. London, 1635.

Bacon, Francis. *The Works of Francis Bacon*. Edited by James Spedding. 15 vols. London, 1858.

Baker, Augustine. *The Confessions of Venerable Father Augustine Baker*. London, 1922.

_____. *Sancta Sophia*. Edited by Dom Sitwell. London, 1964.

Baker, Herschel. *The Dignity of Man*. Cambridge, Mass., 1947.

_____. *The Wars of Truth*. New York, 1952,

Barclay, Robert. *An Apology for the True Christian Divinity*. London, 1678.

Barrow, Isaac. *On the Duty and Reward of Bounty to the Poor*. London, 1671.

Baxter, Richard. *Methodus Theologiae Christianae*. London, 1669.

_____. *Christian Directory*. Vol. I. London, 1672.

Bayly, Lewis. *The Practice of Piety*. London, 1640.

Becon, Thomas. *Pomaunder of Prayers*. London, 1560.

Bettenson, Henry. *Documents of the Christian Church*. New York: Oxford University Press, 1943.

Beumleri, M. Marci. *Hypotyposis theologiae methodice et scholasticae exarata*. Zurich, 1607.

[Boehme] Behmen, Jacob. *A Compendious View of the Grounds of Teutonick Philosophy*. Translated by John Pordage. London, 1620.

Boethius. *The Consolation of Philosophy*. Translated by V. E. Watts. Harmondsworth, 1969.

Bona, John. *A Guide to Eternity*. Translated by Roger L'Estrange. 5th edition. London, 1709.

Boyle, Robert. *Excellency of Theology compar'd with Natural Philosophy (as both are Objects of Men's Study)*. London, 1665.

Braithwaite, William C. *The Beginnings of Quakerism*. London, 1912,

Brereton, Geoffrey. *A Short History of French Literature*. Harmondsworth, 1968.

Browne, Sir Thomas. *Religio Medici and Other Writings.* Introduction by Frank L. Huntley. New York, 1951.

Bullinger, Heinrich. *Gleanings and expositions of some of the more difficult places of scripture.* London, 1646.

Burgersdicius, Francis. *Institutionum Metaphysicarum.* 2 vols. 3rd. ed. London, 1653.

_____. *Idea Philosophiae Moralis ex Aristotle.* Luguni Batavorum, 1623.

Burton, Robert. *An Anatomy of Melancholy.* Edited by Holbrook Jackson. New York, 1932.

Burscough, John. *England's Great Happiness.* London, 1677.

Calvin, John. *Institutes of the Christian Religion.* Translated by Henry Beveridge. 2 vols. London: James Clarke, 1962.

Carré, Meyrick. *Phases of Thought in England.* Oxford, 1949.

Cary, Lucius [Lord Falkland]. *Of the Infallibility of the Church of Rome.* London, 1654.

Casaubon, Meric. *A Treatise concerning Enthusiasme, as it is an Effect of Nature.* London, 1655.

Cappellus, Ludovicus. *Theses theologicae.* Saumur, 1641-45.

Cassirer, Ernst. *The Platonic Renaissance in England.* Translated by James P. Pettigrove. Edinburgh, 1953.

_____. and Paul Kristeller, John Randall. *The Renaissance Philosophy of Man.* Chicago, 1961.

Charron, Pierre. *Of Wisdome. Three Bookes.* Translated by Samson Lennard. London, 1640.

Chillingworth, William. *The Religion of Protestants, A Safe Way to Salvation.* London, 1637.

Clark, George. *The Later Stuarts.* Oxford, 1955.

Collier, Thomas. *The Body of Divinity.* London, 1674.

_____. *The Marrow of Christianity.* London, 1646.

Comber, Dean. *Roman Forgeries in the Councils.* London, 1680.

Conant, James. See *Library.*

Cosin, John. *The Religion, Discipline and Rules of the Church of England.* London, 1707.

Costello, William T. *The Scholastic Curriculum in Early Seventeenth Century Cambridge.* Cambridge, Mass., 1958.

Cragg, Gerald R., ed. *Cambridge Platonists.* Oxford, 1968.

_____. *The Church and the Age of Reason.* Harmondsworth, 1966.

_____. *From Puritanism to the Age of Reason.* Cambridge, 1950.

Crocius, Ludovicus. *Syntagma sacrae theologiae.* 4 vols. Bremen, 1616.

Crofts, Robert. *Paradise Within us: or, The Happie Mind.* London, 1640.

_____. *The Terrestrial Paradise or, Happinesse on Earth.* London, 1639.

_____. *The Way to Blessednesse*. London, 1658.

_____. *The Way to Happinesse on Earth*. London, 1641.

Cross, F. L. *Anglicanism*. Milwaukee, 1935.

Cudworth, Ralph. *The True Intellectual System of the Universe*. London, 1678.

Culverwel, Nathaniel. *An Elegant Learned Discourse of the Light of Nature*. London, 1652.

Curtis, Mark H. *Oxford and Cambridge in Transition: 1558-1640*. Oxford, 1959.

Davies, Godfrey. *The Early Stuarts: 1603-1660*. Oxford, 1938.

Dent, Arthur. *The Plain Man's Pathway to Heaven*. London, 1625.

Durr, R. A. *On the Mystical Poetry of Henry Vaughan*. Cambridge, Mass., 1962.

Earle, John. *Microcosmographie*. London, 1628.

Eustache de Saint Paul. *Summa philosophiae quadripartite (de rebus dialecticis, moralibus, physicis, et metaphysicis)*. Cambridge, 1640.

_____. *Summa theologica tripartita*. Paris, 1613.

Featley, Daniel. *Ancilla Pietatis*. London, 1626.

Fenner, Dudley. *Sacra Theologia*. London, 1636.

Ficino, Marsilio. *Opera*. Paris, 1641.

Fisher, Edward. *The Marrow of Modern Divinity*. London, 1645.

Frankland, Thomas. *The Annals of King James and King Charles the First*. London, 1681.

Gale, Theophilus. *The Court of the Gentiles*. 2 vols. Oxford, 1671.

Gerard, John. *Meditations*. Cambridge, 1627.

Glanville, Joseph. *Plus Ultra*. London, 1668.

_____. *The Vanity of Dogmatizing*. London, 1661.

Good, Thomas. *Firmianus and Dubitantius*. Oxford, 1674.

Grabo, Norman. *Edward Taylor*. New York. 1961.

Griffiths, John., ed. *Statutes of the University of Oxford*. Oxford, 1888.

Grotius, Hugo. *The Truth of the Christian Religion*. Translated by Simon Patrick. London, 1694.

Gutch, John, ed. *The History and Antiquities of the University of Oxford*. 3 vols. Oxford, 1786-96

Hakewill, George. *Apology of the Power and Providence of God in the Government of the World*. London, 1627.

Hall, Joseph. *The Great Mysterie of Godliness*. London, 1652.

_____. *Select Thoughts. One Century*. London, 1648.

Hampshire, Stuart. *The Age of Reason*. New York, 1956.

Hanmer, Meredith. *The Auncient Ecclesiasticall Histories of the First Hundred Yeares after Christ*. London, 1577.

Harrison, A. W. *The Beginnings of Arminianism*. London, 1926.

Harrison, J. S. *Platonism in English Poetry*. New York, 1903.

Herbert of Cherbury [Lord]. *De Religione*. London, 1645.

Hermes Trismegistus. *His Divine Pymander*. Translated by John Everard. London, 1657.

Hobbes, Thomas. *Leviathan*. Introduction by A. D. Lindsay. New York, 1950.

Hooker, Richard. *The Laws of Ecclesiastical Polity*. 2 vols. London, 1907.

Hopton, Susanna. *Devotions in the Ancient Way of Offices*. 2nd. ed. London, 1701.

Inge, W. R. *Mysticism in Religion*. Chicago, 1948.

Jackson, Thomas. *The Works of the Reverend and Learned Divine, Thomas Jackson*. 3 vols. London, 1623.

Jagerd, William. *Catalogue*. London, 1619.

James, King (the First). *Basilikon Doron*. London, 1599.

James, Thomas. *A Treatise of the Corruption of the Fathers*. London, 1611.

Johnson, James William. *The Formation of English Neo-Classical Thought*. Princeton, 1967.

Jones, Rufus. *Spiritual Reformers in the Sixteenth and Seventeenth Centuries*. London, 1914.

_____. *Studies in Mystical Religion*. London, 1909.

Kearney, Hugh. *Scholars and Gentlemen*. London, 1970.

Library. A Library for Younger Schollers (Compiled by an English Scholar-Priest about 1655), ed. Alma De Jordy and Harris Francis Fletcher. (*Illinois Studies in Language and Literature*. Vol. XLVIII) Urbana, 1961.

Lichtenstein, Aharon. *Henry More*. Cambridge, Mass., 1962.

London, William. *Catalogue of the most Vendible Books in England*. London, 1657-58.

McNeill, John T. *The History and Character of Calvinism*. New York, 1967.

Malabranche, Nicolas. *Decalogues on Metaphysics and Religion*. Translated by Morris Ginsberg. London, 1923.

Milton, John. *Complete Poems and Major Prose*. Edited by Merritt Y. Hughes. New York: The Odyssey Press, 1957.

Moorman, John R. H. *A History of the Church of England*. London, 1963.

More, Henry. *An Account of Virtue*. Translated by Edward Southwell. London, 1690.

_____. *Enthusiasmus Triumphatus*. London, 1656.

_____. *Divine Dialogues*. London, 1668.

_____. *An Explanation of the Grand Mysterie of Godliness*. London, 1660.

_____. *Immortality of the Soul*. London, 1659.

More, Sir Thomas. *Utopia.* Translated by Paul Turner. Harmmondsworth, 1965.

Musculus. *Commonplaces of the Christian Religion.* Translated by John Man. London, 1578.

Overton, J. H. *Life in the English Church: 1660-1714.* London, 1885.

S. P. [Simon Parker]. *A Brief Account of the New Sect of Latitude-Men Together with some Reflections upon the New Philosophy.* London, 1662.

Patrides, C. A. *The Cambridge Platonists.* London, 1969.

Perkins, William. *A Bodie of Scripture and Theology.* London, 1621.

_____. *A Golden Chaine, or The Description of Theologie.* Translated by Robert Hill. London, 1621.

Pinto, Vivian de Sola. *Peter Sterry.* Cambridge, 1934.

[Plotinus]. *The Essential Plotinus.* Translated by Elmer O'Brien. New York, 1964.

_____. *The Enneads.* Translated by S. Mackenna. London, 1957.

Polanus, Amandus. *The Substance of Christian Religion.* London, 1608.

Pufendorf, Samuel. *The Whole Duty of Man According to the Law of Nature.* Translated by Andrew Tooke. 4th ed. 1716.

RGG Die Religion in Geschichte und Gegenwärt. Edited by Hans Freiherr von Campenhausen and Erich Dinkler. Tübingen, 1957.

Reynolds, Edward. *A Treatise of the Passions and Faculties of the Soule of Man.* London, 1640.

Rops, H. Daniel. *The Church in the Seventeenth Century.* Translated by J.J. Buckingham. London, 1963.

Ross, Alexander. *A Centurie of Divine Meditations.* London, 1646.

Scheibler, Christopher. *Philosophia compendiosa, Exhibens l. logicae, 2. metaphysicae, 3. physicae, 4. geometriae, 5. astronomiae, 6. opticae, 7. ethicae, 8. politicae, 9. oeconomicae, compendium methodicum.* 7th edition. Oxford, 1647.

Schmidt, Martin. *"Biblicizmus und Natürliche Theologie in der Gewissenslehre des englischen Puritanismus. Archiv für Reformations Geschichte"* 42 (1951), 198-219; 43 (1952), 70-87.

_____. *"Christentum und Kirche in Grossbritannien," Englandkunde* (Frankfurt, 1960). *Sonderausgabe.*

_____. *Eigenart und Bedeutung der Eschatologie im Englischen Puritanismus. Sonderausgabe, aus Theologia Viatorum.* Berlin, 1952.

_____. *"England und der deutsche Pietismus." Evangelische Theologie,* 13 (1953).

_____. *John Wesley.* Translated by Norman P. Goldhawk. 2 vols. London: Epworth Press, 1962.

_____. *Wiedergeburt und Neuer Mensch.* Witten, 1969.

Scrivener, Matthew. *A Course of Divinity*. London, 1624.

Sheldon, Richard. *Mans Last End*. London, 1634.

Smith, John. *Select Discourses*. Edited by John Worthington. London, 1660.

Sparke, Edward. *Scintillula Altaris*. London, 1652.

Sparrow, Anthony. *A Rationale upon the Book of Common-Prayer*. London, 1665.

Sterry, Peter. *A Discourse on the Freedom of the Will*. London, 1675.

_____. *The Rise, Race, and Royalty of the Kingdom of God in the Soul of Man*. London, 1683.

Stoudt, John. *Sunrise to Eternity*. Philadelphia, 1957.

Strankes, C. J. *Anglican Devotion*. London, 1961.

Taylor, Jeremy. *Holy Dying*. London, 1651.

_____. *Holy Living*. London, 1650.

_____. *Great Exemplar*. London, 1649.

Thorndike, William. *The Reformation of the Church of England better than that of the Council of Trent*. London, 1670.

Traherne, Philip. The *Soul's Communion with God her Saviour*. London, 1685.

Trelcatius, Lucas. *A Brief Institution of the Common places of Sacred Divinitie*. Translated by John Gawen. London, 1610.

Tulluch, John. *Rational Theology and Christian Philosophy in England in the Seventeenth Century*. 2 vols. London, 1872.

Underhill, Evelyn. *Mysticism*. London, 1911.

_____. *The Mystic Way*. London, 1913.

Usher, James. *A Body of Divinitie*. London, 1645.

Ursinus, Zacharaius. *Corpus doctrinae orthodoxae*. Heidelberg, 1616.

Wakeling, C. N. "The History of the College: 1603-1660." *Brasenose College Quatercenterary Monographs*. Vol. II, Part I.

Warnke, Frank J. *European Metaphysical Poetry*. New Haven, 1961.

Wendelinus, Marcus. *Christianae theologiae*. Hanover, 1634.

Whichcote, Benjamin. *Works*. 4 vols. Aberdeen, 1751.

Whiting, C. E. *Studies in English Puritanism from the Restoration to the Revolution*. London, 1931.

Whole Duty of Man. See Allestree.

Willey, Basil. *Seventeenth Century Background*. Garden City, New York, 1933.

Wollebius, John. *The Abridgement of Christian Divinitie*. Translated by Alex Ross. 3rd ed. London, 1660.

_____. *Compendium Theologiae Christianae*. Amsterdam, 1633; Oxford, 1645.

Wood, Anthony. *Athenae Oxoniensis*. Edited by Philip Bliss. 4 vols. London, 1813-1820.

Zöckler, Otto. *Die Tügendlehre des Christentums geschichtlich dargestellt in der Entwicklung ihrer Lehrformen, mit besonderer Rücksicht auf deren zahlensymbolische Einkleidung*. Gütersloh, 1904.

Appendix
(May 1, 2005)

Boydell & Brewer Ltd. (Woodbridge, UK, and Rochester, New York) are publishing an eight-volume definitive edition of the works of Thomas Traherne. The first volume, edited by Jan Ross, appeared in the Spring of 2005 (too late to be included in this study). It will contain manuscripts possibly by Traherne discovered in 1996 and following. Most of the works to be included in later volumes were already available and analyzed in my study. Future volumes are to be published in 2007, 2009, 2011, and 2013. The eighth and last volume will include commentary and an index. A study of these resources may alter some of the emphases and add some insights to this study. Those will need to be investigated and compared to the conclusions in this work.

The best introduction to current research on the theology of Thomas Traherne is that of Dr. Denise Inge. In a review article entitled, "A Poet Comes Home: Thomas Traherne, Theologian in a New Century," published in the *Anglican Theological Review* in the Spring of 2004, she describes the renewed interest in Traherne occasioned by a number of things, but especially by the discovery of previously unknown manuscripts and the planned critical edition of the works of Traherne by Boydell & Brewer Ltd.

In that article she surveys research in the field and refers to *The Commentaries of Heaven*, which I have not seen, as well as to the most recently discovered manuscripts of Traherne in 1996–97: one, an unfinished epic poem based on Genesis and Exodus of approximately 1,800 lines entitled *The Ceremonial Law*, found in the Folger Library in Washington, D.C., and the other, in the Lambeth Palace Library in London of some 952 pages, which contains five different prose works, including serious theological debate. These have been published only in part, but Denise Inge underscores how these discoveries "redefine Traherne as a serious theologian." She points out that Traherne "has seldom been discussed . . . as a real theologian." Instead, "interest in his work at this time seems to break roughly into two main veins—those whose interest is mainly in his poetic and the structure of this work, and those . . . placing him in the historical and intellectual milieu of the seventeenth century."

The Lambeth Manuscript contains five separate works of Traherne. The first is entitled *Inducements to Retiredness*, which Dr. Inge says focuses on the importance of prayerfulness as well as the demands of the ordained ministry.

The second work is entitled *A Sober View of Dr. Twisses*, which includes discussions of choice and free will and examines the theological position of William Twiss, a Calvinist, and Samuel Hoard, an Arminian. Denise Inge calls it the "most theologically detailed work of Traherne's known to date."

The third work is evidently a fragment, *Love*, which is only part of an intended longer work.

The fourth work entitled *Seeds of Eternity* shows the capacity of the human soul in part by surveying the views of a number of pagan philosophers and church fathers.

The fifth and last work in the Lambeth Manuscript, *The Kingdom of God*, is the longest and most complete according to Denise Inge. There are forty-two chapters in which Traherne uses Aristotelian categories to describe God's kingdom.

Denise Inge then concludes that when all of Traherne's existing works are considered "the greatest volume of his work is not 'mystical' or 'poetic' . . . but theological." In fact, she says many recent studies are done by theologians. She concludes her article by saying that "In this 100th anniversary year of the first publication of his poems, Traherne is a poet coming home to theology."

In reviewing other research published since I completed my own study, mention should be made of the following:

Allchin, A.M. *Profitable Wonders: Aspects of Traherne*. Oxford: The Amate Press, 1989.
_____. *Landscapes of Glory*. London: Darton Longman Todd, 1989.
Beal, Peter. *Index of English Literary Manuscripts*, vol. 2, 1625–1700, pt. 2 (London: Mansell), 1993, 477–485.
Belden, Lane. "Thomas Traherne and the Awakening of Want." *Anglican Theological Review*. 81/4 (Fall 1999): 656–658.
Cefalau, Paul. "Thomist Metaphysics and Ethics in the Poetry and Prose of Thomas Traherne." *Literature and Theology*. 16/3 (August 2002): 248–269.
Day, Malcolm M. *Thomas Traherne*. Boston: Twayne, 1982.
Dowell, Graham. *Enjoying the World*. Harrisburg, PA: Morehouse, 1993.
Inge, Denise. "A Poet Comes Home." *Anglican Theological Review*. 86/2 (Spring 2004): 335–348.
_____. *Thomas Traherne: Poetry and Prose*. London: SPCK, 2002, 64–66.
Inge, D. and Macfarlane. "Seeds of Eternity: A New Traherne Manuscript," *Times Literary Supplement*. June 2, 2000: 14.
Johnson, Carol. "Heavenly Perspectives." *Criticism* 43 (2001): 1–35.
Jordan, Richard D. "The New Traherne Manuscript 'Commentaries of Heaven.'" *Quadrant* 27 (1983): 73–76.
Kelliher, Hilton. "The Rediscovery of Thomas Traherne." *Times Literary Supplement*. September 14, 1984: 1038.
Matar, Nabil. "Prophetic Traherne: A Thanksgiving and Prayer for the Nation." *Journal of English and Germanic Philology*. 81 (1982):16–29.
Pritchard, Allan. "Traherne's 'Commentaries of Heaven.'" *University of Toronto Quarterly*. 53 (1983), 1–35.
Seelig, Sharon. *The Shadows of Eternity*. Louisville: University of Kentucky Press, 1982.
Smith, J. "The Ceremonial Law." *Poetry Nation Review*. 25/2 (Nov.–Dec. 1998): 22–28.
Smith, J. and L. Yeandle. "'Felicity Disguised in Fiery Words': Genesis and Exodus in a Newly Discovered Poem by Thomas Traherne." *Times Literary Supplement*, November 7, 1997: 17.
Suarez, Michael. "Against Satan, Sin, and Death: Thomas Traherne and the 'Inward Work' of Conversion," in *Reform and Counter Reform*. (Berlin: Mouton de Gruye, 1994).

Curriculum Vitae
of
Thomas Richard Sluberski

Born in Jersey City, reared in and around Cleveland, Ohio, was graduated from Independence High School in 1958 as a National Merit Scholar Finalist, attended the Cleveland Institute of Art (life drawing and water color); Western Reserve University; Concordia College, St. Paul, Minn.; Concordia Senior College, Ft. Wayne, Indiana (B.A., 1962); Concordia Seminary, St. Louis (Masters in Divinity, 1966); Washington University (Masters in English, 1970); the University of Vienna, Austria; the University of Erlangen-Nuremberg, Germany; awarded a Doctorate with Honors (rare for a foreigner) from Heidelberg University in Germany in 1972; and New York University.

Served as Mission Developer for Faith Lutheran Church, Mansfield, Ohio in 1963; a Vicar at Zion Lutheran Church, Wausau, Wisconsin (1964/65); Research Assistant and Literary Survey Editor for the Lutheran World Federation (1968/69); Assistant to the Dean of the Chapel and Instructor in Religion and ordained at Valparaiso University 1969/70.

From 1972 to 2004 a tenured professor of English, Religion and the Humanities at Concordia, Bronxville, New York; later simultaneously Pastor of St. Matthew's Lutheran Church, Hastings-on-Hudson, NY (1977–87); Executive Director of the American Lutheran Publicity Bureau and Managing Editor of *Lutheran Forum* (1987–89); the first LC–MS Missions Consultant to Russia (1992–94); taught at the University of St. Petersburg and the Alexander von Herzen University in St. Petersburg; the University of Omsk, Siberia; the Merchant Marine Academy and the University of Vladivostok in Vladivostok, Russia; and the University of Khabarovsk, Russia.

While in Russia was on the staff of the Russian/American Press Center; a Warden for the U.S. Consulate; Co-Coordinator of Volunteers for the Goodwill Games (1994); taught at the first (since the 1917 Revolution) Russian Lutheran Seminary as well as the Deacon's Training School (1992–94); on the Board of the Ben Weider College and the Peterschule; judged three Mr. Russia contests for the Russian Federation of Bodybuilders; advisor for the International Shaping Federation; produced films with Russkoi Film Video; co-directed the first four-continent live television broadcast from St. Petersburg, Ghana, Korea, and Minneapolis (1993).

My entire education was financed by scholarships and fellowships from the District and the Synod; the Kiwanus Club; the Institute of International Education; a William and Tona Shepherd Fund Travel Grant; an Austrian and later a Bavarian State Scholarship; the Lutheran World Federation; the World Council of Churches; the Martin Luther Bund Heim (Erlangen); the Aid Association for Lutherans; and the Deutsche Akademischer Austauschdienst.

Appointed a National Faculty Member of the United States Sports Academy (1995 to the present); taught Sports Marketing and Sports Journalism for them in Kuala Lumpur, Malasia; Hong Kong; and Singapore (1995); elected to the National Academy of Television Arts and Sciences and a Judge for the TV Emmy Awards (1995 to the present); served as a Judge for the USA National Physique Committee (1983-87); on the Board of Directors of the Lutheran Society for Worship, Music and the Arts (1971-73); as a Coordinator of the 9th and 10th Inter-Lutheran Forums (1988-90); on the Executive Board of the 15th Annual Workshop on Jewish/Christian Relations, Stamford, Conn.; a Juror for the American Film Festival (NYC 1976-87); a member of the American Film Institute; the Society for Religion, Arts, and Culture; elected to the Salmagundi Club; a member of the Polish Academy of Arts and Sciences (discovering that the spelling of the family name had been changed at Ellis Island from Suliborski in 1907); holder of the Duda endowed chair (Concordia, NY) since 2001.

In 2004 began work for the Lutheran University of Brazil (ULBRA) which has over twenty campuses with over 100,000 students. Served as a Judge for the 35th, 36th, and 37th national contests of the Brazilian Federation of Bodybuilding and Fitness; a major presenter for the 6th International Congress on Literature and Language in Mercosul/Mercosur Countries (2004) and the First International Congress for Executive Secretaries (2004) in Canoas (near Porto Alegre), Brazil; a presenter for the 2006 A.B.R.A.L.I.C (Brazilian Comparative Literature Association) in Rio de Janeiro; elected to the Board of Governors of the American Society of Rio de Janeiro (2006); and in 2006 granted a Brazilian government Visa to research and report on drugging and doping in athletics especially in connection with the Pan American Games held in Rio de Janeiro in July of 2007.

Cleveland, Ohio; Bronxville, New York; Porto Alegre and
Rio de Janeiro, Brazil.
January 2008

Index of Important People, Places, and Ideas